SYDNEY SMITH

SYDNEY SMITH

ALAN BELL

CLARENDON PRESS · OXFORD

1980

Oxford University Press, Walton Street, Oxford OX2 6DP

OXFORD LONDON GLASGOW
NEW YORK TORONTO MELBOURNE WELLINGTON
KUALA LUMPUR SINGAPORE JAKARTA HONG KONG TOKYO
DELHI BOMBAY CALCUTTA MADRAS KARACHI
NAIROBI DAR ES SALAAM CAPE TOWN

Published in the United States by
Oxford University Press, New York

British Library Cataloguing in Publication Data
Bell, Alan, *b. 1942*
 Sydney Smith.
  1. Smith, Sydney, b. 1771 – Biography
  2. Authors, English – Biography
  824'.7   PR 5458   80–40472

ISBN 0–19–812050–8

Printed in Great Britain by
Butler & Tanner Ltd,
Frome and London

To OLIVIA

PREFACE

❊

EARLY in 1969, with the encouragement of the Oxford University Press, and later with the generous assistance of the Leverhulme Trust, I started to search for letters of Sydney Smith not included in the thousand or so edited by Nowell Charles Smith, published in two volumes by the Clarendon Press in 1953. The results of these investigations are reported in the *Bulletin of the John Rylands Library* LIX (1976): briefly they are that I have found, instead of enough letters for the slim supplementary volume I hoped to produce, about double the number of those in print, and enough corrective information to make a complete revision of Nowell Smith's edition essential. Work on this four-volume edition is now, after several interruptions, proceeding apace, and I hope to have it ready for the printer by 1981 (until then—and indeed afterwards—information about additional letters will be gratefully received).

This biography, which precedes the new edition, has been written after the main search for new documentary and printed sources was completed. Because the revised corpus of Sydney Smith's correspondence will be available for consultation relatively soon, I have tried here to reduce the technicalities of presentation, without—I hope—imperilling its credentials as a work of scholarly endeavour. Quotations have been normalized throughout, discursive footnotes abandoned, and references (here systematically presented as end-notes) pared to a minimum. I can only ask for the patience of those seeking fuller information. I do not think the full range of epistolary material, old and new, which should soon be ready, will disappoint those who know Sydney Smith's writings, particularly his letters. Having lived with them for a decade, I can testify to the constant and enduring delight they provide. This is a pleasure which I have done my best to convey by basing this book as far as possible on the available correspondence.

Over so long a period I have built up an embarrassingly long string of debts, to owners of documents, to fellow library officials, and to scholars and friends who have been generous of their time and tolerant of my enthusiasms. Those who have kindly allowed me to use their manuscripts for this book are listed at the end; I am grateful to them all, but a glance at the References may show that it is not invidious to mention particularly Mr D. R. Bentham, Mr David Holland, Mr George Howard, Mr Gordon Ray and Lord St Aldwyn, along with the officials of the Henry E. Huntington Library, India Office Library, and New College, Oxford, all of whose holdings have been drawn on so extensively. I am particularly grateful to Dan Davin and Simon Nowell-Smith for their early encouragement, and to Martin Higham and William Thomas for reading parts of the typescript. An earlier and shorter version of the Yorkshire chapters was published in 1972 by the St. Anthony's Press, York, and I am grateful to the Borthwick Institute of Historical Research, University of York, for permission to reprint parts of this pamphlet. Mrs D. L. Mackay and Miss Christina Sharp have, as always, proved prompt and accurate typists; and I am especially grateful to the Oxford University Press for their patience while waiting for a book that for far too long has been—and this was entirely its author's fault—'forthcoming'.

Edinburgh   ALAN BELL

CONTENTS

※

LIST OF PLATES

❖

CHAPTER I

❧

SYDNEY Smith, who was born in 1771, was celebrated from his mid-thirties onwards as a periodical essayist and for some forty years until his death in 1845 became increasingly famous as one of the greatest wits of his day, whether in his political pamphlets, his excellent correspondence, or above all in his ordinary conversation and social intercourse. He came to enjoy a leading position in the circle which at his suggestion founded the *Edinburgh Review* as the principal critical journal of its day. His literary eminence and skilful support of the Whig cause secured him early in life, even when he was an unbeneficed clergyman, a privileged entrée to the great Whig political salon in which Lord and Lady Holland brought together the intellectual and social notabilities of their party in a coterie of outstanding brilliance throughout the early years of the nineteenth century. Yet for one so much sought after, and so well known even in his own time, Sydney Smith's origins and early years are unexpectedly obscure.

His correspondence survives plentifully from his mid-twenties onwards to show his multifarious activities. It covers his more mundane activities as a country parson and as a husband and father, as well as the glories of his greatest successes in the aristocratic world that soon took him up but never took him over. He lived an open, uncomplicated life, with nothing to hide, and it is easy from his published writings and correspondence—as well as from his many reported sayings—to build up a picture of a stout and jovial clergyman thoroughly enjoying himself, and almost to hear the chuckle that was rarely far from his lips. He had his occasional depressions, his tensions, and his minor irritabilities, but they were more than offset by his constitutional affability, and even these temporary departures from his normal joviality were discussed with an admirable candour. His letters form the principal source of his biography, and where they are lacking for his early years few other sources are available to fill the gap.

'The Smiths never had any arms,' he once told a Somerset genealogist, 'and have invariably sealed their letters with their thumbs.'* Sydney Smith's family origins—and he himself never showed much of a genealogical, or even of a retrospective, cast of mind—are difficult to unravel, but though they are obscure they are neither mean nor discreditable. His early years are ill-recorded, and one of the most elusive characters in the story of his life has been his own father. Saba Lady Holland, Sydney's daughter, described her grandfather as 'a man of singular natural gifts; very clever, odd by nature, but still more odd by design'.* She recalled him as 'a very handsome and picturesque old man when I knew him; his hair long, thin and perfectly white, and his figure slight and rather bent. To add to the effect of his appearance and manner, he used to affect the drab-coloured dress of a Quaker, with a large flap hat, rather like those of our coal-heavers.'* The family correspondence amply confirms this view of his contrived oddity. The Quaker garments may well have been donned for economy rather than piety, for Robert Smith, though fairly rich, was a person of miserly habits. He was an ill-tempered man, who treated all his children badly, and Sydney, his most famous son, worst of all.

Family tradition, Lady Holland wrote, told that he had parted from his wife at the church door, leaving her until he returned from prolonged wanderings in America, where he improved a small inherited fortune. His few surviving papers reveal a little of his transatlantic business interests, showing West Indian investments as early as 1774–5, followed by prolonged efforts to recover debts due to him from badly managed Granada properties. In 1781 he wrote to a business associate in Charlestown, South Carolina, that 'I am entirely out of business and thank God and the assistance of my family live independent with a fair prospect of seeing my five children provided for after me, yet I shall never be happy till I see some prospect of settling my old accounts.'* William Burrows had written from Charlestown advising Robert Smith that: 'This you may rely on, that as your affairs in this country were in an indifferent situation before the troubles commenced between England and America, they are now infinitely worse.... I hope God of his infinite Mercy will grant us peace, or we shall all be ruined!'* Vague indications like these are all that survive to show Robert Smith as a prosperous London businessman of wide interests, including sizable share-holdings in the New River Company, which supplied London with its drinking-water.

He was apparently excitable on the stock exchange. Sydney wrote to a friend when the royal madness was reported in 1801 that 'My poor father will, I am sure, lose several ounces of flesh *per diem*. He grows heavier and lighter with every post and rises and falls with the stocks.'* Robert Smith was a Bath friend of the Duke of Northumberland, he was closely associated with distinguished City families such as the Trowers and the Cazalets, and he had the ear of Directors of the East India Company— a connection which proved useful when placing three of his sons in life. By the time Sydney was born his father had settled down and occupied himself, as his granddaughter recorded, 'partly in diminishing his fortune by buying, altering, spoiling and then selling about nineteen different places in England; till, in his old age, he at last settled at Bishop's Lydeard, in Somersetshire, where he died', aged 88, in 1827.*

He married Maria Olier, the youngest daughter of a Huguenot refugee from Languedoc by his English wife (a collateral descendant of Newton); little is recorded of her, though her generally poor health is sometimes alluded to, and she died after a long illness late in 1801. Robert and Maria Smith had five children, two of whom were quite outstanding. The eldest Robert Percy (1770–1845) gained a reputation for superior talents (and the universally used nickname 'Bobus') early in life at Eton and at King's College, Cambridge; he prospered as a lawyer in India and as a politician in England, and enjoyed considerable social esteem for his witticisms, but he never achieved his next brother's permanent reputation as a wit. Sydney Smith, the second son, was born at Woodford, Essex, on 3 June 1771 (the connection with Woodford seems to have been a temporary one, as his family is more closely associated with the city of London, with Bath, and later with rural Somerset). His two younger brothers, Cecil (1772–1814) and Courtney (1773–1843), were less distinguished, but both occupied high and lucrative civilian positions in India.* Robert Smith's youngest child was a daughter, Maria, born in 1774, a pleasant woman of good sense and good temper, who lived with her father. Sydney's wife, an old friend of Maria's, described her as much deformed by 'some spinal weakness'; she died in 1816. As an intermediary during unpleasant passages of correspondence between her brothers and father, she was to prove herself invaluable to the family.

The gaiety of spirit which dominates in Sydney's life, and is apparent in Bobus's, manifests itself also in Cecil's later carefree financial and domestic escapades in India, which embarrassed his family at home, and in Maria's even-tempered reaction to family disputes. It is probably derived from their mother, whereas their father's morose and irritable disposition was inherited principally by Courtney. Even Sydney himself, at first sight blessed with a uniformly pleasing and equable temper, was not free from a stubborn and irritable strain in his character. As a young man, and sometimes during his maturity, there were occasions when an unpleasant sharpness was apparent under the surface of an increasingly genial temper. This querulousness is quite different from the thorough passion against injustice and intolerance which informs his published writings. It takes the form, as we shall see, of sustained personal outbursts against apparently insignificant slights. The harassing manner in which they were pursued may be due to inexperience of the world, but it may also be an inherited trait: Sydney's letters to his father provide several examples which show that he received many more of these prolonged and repeated attacks than he returned. There is nothing else in what little we know of his early life and education to explain them.

Sydney and his brothers seem to have been argumentative and competitive amongst themselves at home; 'the result', he told his daughter, 'was to make us the most intolerable and overbearing set of boys that can well be imagined, till later in life we found our level in the world'.* As early as six years of age, Sydney was sent to a school in Southampton kept by a clergyman called Mant, whom he remembered with pleasure; his father was then living at South Stonham.* Robert and Cecil were sent to Eton, Sydney and Courtney went to Winchester. The school (then under the headmastership of Joseph Warton) was a rough and cruel place. The boys were ill-fed, and Sydney was once praised by the master for his ingenuity in making a catapult which was in reality intended for a plump turkey to provide extra rations. Courtney, also a clever boy, whose linguistic ability later displayed itself in the study of Eastern languages, was so miserable that he twice ran away.* Although no contemporary records survive of Sydney's unhappy sojourn at Winchester, a few later references exist, and he used to 'speak with horror of the wretchedness of the years he spent there: the whole system was then, [he] used to say, one of abuse, neglect and vice'.* William Howley, a few years Sydney's senior, was at the school; after he became Archbishop of Canterbury and legislation threatened the patronage of St. Paul's, Sydney was able to introduce a reference to his schooldays in to his defence of his Cathedral's endowments, the *Letters to Archdeacon Singleton* (1837):

I was at school and college with the Archbishop of Canterbury; fifty-three years ago he knocked me down with the chess-board for check-mating him—and now he is attempting to take away my patronage. I believe these are the only two acts of violence he ever committed in his life.*

Remarks made by Sydney in an *Edinburgh Review* article on public schools, published in 1810, were obviously coloured by his personal experiences:

At a public school ... every boy is alternately tyrant and slave. The power which the elder part of these communities exercises over the younger, is exceedingly great—very difficult to be controlled—and accompanied, not unfrequently, with cruelty and caprice. It is the common law of the place, that the young should be implicitly obedient to the elder boys; and his obedience resembles more the submission of a slave to his master, or of a sailor to his captain, than the common and natural deference which would always be shown by one boy to another a few years older than himself.

Sydney held that 'to give to a boy the habit of enduring privations to which he will never again be called upon to submit ... is surely not a very useful and valuable severity in education'.*

The exclusively classical basis of public-school education was several times referred to in his writings. Ideally, Sydney felt that 'in a place of education, we would give to all knowledge an equal chance for distinction', and pointed out that 'The prodigious honour in which Latin verses are held at public schools is surely the most absurd of all absurd distinctions. You rest all reputation upon doing that which is a natural gift, and which no labour can attain.' He argued against compulsory versifying, stressing its wastefulness and irrelevance. 'The English clergy, in whose hands education entirely rests bring up the first young men of the country as if they were all to keep grammar schools in little country towns; and a nobleman, upon whose knowledge and liberality the honour and welfare of the country may depend, is

5

diligently worried, for half his life, with the small pedantry of longs and shorts.'*

Another passage has some personal relevance. Continuing his argument against the tyranny of boy over boy, Sydney wrote:

The system also gives to the elder boys an absurd and pernicious opinion of their own importance, which is often with difficulty effaced by a considerable commerce with the world. The *head* of a public school is generally a very conceited young man, utterly ignorant of his own dimensions, and losing all that habit of conciliation towards others, and that anxiety for self-improvement, which result from the natural modesty of youth. Nor is this conceit very easily and speedily gotten rid of;—we have seen (if we mistake not) public school importance lasting through the half of after life, strutting in lawn, swelling in ermine, and displaying itself, both ridiculously and offensively, in the haunts and business of bearded men.*

Sydney was Prefect of Hall in his final year at Winchester, so it was with the authority of actual experience that he wrote of the headship of a public school. In spite of his successes there, he always hated his schooldays. The attacks on the system which he was to bring out in the *Edinburgh Review* of 1810, though they naturally gain in colour from the traditional aggressions of the journal and from his skill as an advocate, were caused by a personal memory of his deeply loathed days there; they gradually attracted much support and formed the basis of a movement for reform of the public schools which by the 1830s had become 'an irresistible force'.*

Between leaving Winchester and obtaining his New College fellowship, Sydney spent half a year in Normandy, improving his knowledge of French at Montvilliers. For safety during the early stages of the Revolution, he prudently had himself enrolled as a member of one of the local Jacobin clubs—'Le Citoyen Smit, Membre Affilié au Club des Jacobins de Mont Villiers'. Lady Holland's *Memoir* is unfortunately the only authority for this interesting episode which apparently extricated him from trouble with the police when sketching the harbour at Cherbourg and suspected of spying on the fortifications.*

Sydney had proceeded from Winchester as a scholar to New College, Oxford, early in 1789, and at the end of his second year of residence exchanged his scholarship for a fellowship worth £100 a year. He was to remain on the foundations of William of Wykeham for nine more years, relinquishing his fellowship on marriage in 1800. One of the privileges of his college was exemption from the public examinations of the University; his intellectual performance at Oxford is therefore not a matter of record. No mention survives, either, of his social life in the jovial but indolent fellowship of the time. His father refused to support him and Sydney had to provide for himself out of the college's limited stipend; he apparently contrived, however, to settle a debt of £30 which Courtney had contracted at Winchester.* As with his school-days we can only discern his feelings for Oxford from the occasional references in his later writings. And as with his public school, the main protest was against the undue predominance of classical studies:

Classical literature is the great object at Oxford. Many minds so employed have produced many works, and much fame in that department: but if all liberal arts and sciences useful to human life had been taught there,—if some had dedicated themselves to chemistry, some to mathematics, some to experimental philosophy,—and if every attainment had been honoured in the mixt ratio of its difficulty and utility,—the system of such an University would have been much more valuable, but the splendour of its name something less.

His plea for a broader course at the university argued that

A genuine Oxford tutor would shudder to hear his young men disputing upon moral and political truth, forming and pulling down theories, and indulging in all the boldness of youthful discussion. He would augur nothing from it, but impiety to God, and treason to kings.*

Limited and restrictive though he may have found Oxford during his residence, Sydney was able to rejoice at the beginnings of university reform later in his life. Thus in 1810, on the introduction of Honours examinations:

If Oxford is become at last sensible of the miserable state to which it was reduced, as everybody else was out of Oxford, and if it is making serious efforts to recover from the degradation into which it was plunged a few years past, the good wishes of every respectable man must go with it.*

Sydney took his bachelor's degree in 1792, proceeding MA in 1796. He had to choose a profession. His daughter writes that 'His own inclinations would have led him to the Bar, in which profession he felt that his talents promised him success and distinction, and where a career was open to him that might gratify his ambition.'* As it was, however, his father reputedly objected to a legal career and urged Sydney to go into the Church. This

7

is not improbable, knowing Robert Smith's habitual wish to interfere, his notorious meanness which would limit his support of a second barrister son, and above all his probable reckoning of the eventual profits of a College office and a lucrative living in due course. It was without apparent enthusiasm that Sydney was ordained Deacon in 1794 (he took Priest's orders at Oxford two years later). He belonged to an age which took Vocation less seriously than did Victorian biographers, and no insincerity can be imputed to him for a seemingly casual response to the call of the Church of England, based on the admittedly imperfect evidence of a few sentences of early biography. He was to become a vigorous and conscientious parson, making up for a want of obvious zeal at the opening of his career by a modest and energetic ministry during the rest of his life. His practical abilities were immediately put to the test. Following his ordination he left Oxford to be curate of the parish of Netheravon on Salisbury Plain. After a year of its bucolic fastness, he wrote that 'Nothing can equal the profound, the unmeasurable, the awful dulness of this place, in the which I lie dead and buried, in hopes of a joyful resurrection in the year 1796'.*

The Netheravon curacy was a depressing start to Sydney's professional career. 'I have no news to send you from this dull, and melancholy country,' Sydney wrote to his father in 1798 when he had a definite prospect of release, '—in which there is nothing good but two or three families, and some fresh air.'* The gentle families of the locality were to provide him with some much-needed civilized diversion, but fresh air was a doubtful advantage where his accommodation was in such poor shape: one of his earliest letters to Michael Hicks Beach, the squire of Netheravon, includes the phrase 'You may assure yourself, Sir, that the parsonage house, owing to the uncommon heat of the Summer, is perfectly dry.'* Painting had made it tolerable, and the vicarage was to be Sydney's main residence for nearly four years.

He intended to devote himself to his books and to his parishioners. 'My stock of theological doctrine which at present is most alarmingly small will necessarily occupy a great deal of my time,' Sydney told Hicks Beach; 'and I mean to try if I cannot persuade the poor people to come to church, for really at present ... my preaching is like the voice of one crying in the wilderness.'* Something of the backwardness of the Wiltshire parish is conveyed by a list of the local poor, prepared by the Beach family's steward in March 1793. The list was later sent to Sydney for comment, so that he could direct Mrs Hicks Beach's charity to the most deserving recipients. There are some worthy cases, but the list generally shows a depressing record of ignorance, brutality, and disease. 'John Head has a wife and four children (one born before marriage)—a wretched family, neither sheet or blanket, and only a miserable straw bed for the children. Only straw to burn and very little of that; no linen to wear and very badly clothed. Children four years to four months.' 'Weak, witless people, totally wretched without sense to extricate themselves from their wretchedness' was Sydney's stern comment on this family in the steward's report; 'a ragged, wretched, savage, stubborn race' he wrote of another. He was fair in his judgements, directing his patroness's charity where it would best be used and appreciated—'very neat, industrious and deserving' is a comment characteristic of the better cases. But Netheravon was a wilderness indeed.*

Sydney managed to keep up his own cheerfulness even amidst such rural squalor. A letter written to a neighbouring clergyman at the end of 1794 shows his high spirits: 'You was so obliging as to say that you would put on the linen ephod, and minister in the temple for one Sunday ...' he wrote, asking his colleague to do his duty in two parishes. 'Tell me fairly whether this exertion will be too much for you, and how far your vocal, theological, equitating, and all other powers which such an undertaking would call into action are sufficiently strong to carry you through.'*

He applied himself to his duties energetically, reporting to Mrs Hicks Beach on the ill-clad children she wished to help:

On Sunday last there were three or four children with their feet upon the cold stones without any shoes, and one came a perfect *sans culottes*—or at least only with some grinning remnants of that useful garment, just sufficient to show that he was so clad from necessity, and not from any ingenious theory he had taken up against such a useful invention. If the Sunday School had begun, I should have imagined that the poor boy thought it his duty to come ready for whipping, as a fowl is sent from the poulterers, trussed and ready for roasting.*

The Sunday School was established shortly afterwards. Sydney found a teacher, recommended books to be bought, acknowledging them 'in the name of my *sans culottes*' in a letter of May 1795, reporting a good attendance and a diligent master.* Some time afterwards a School of Industry for poor girls was set up with Mrs Beach's assistance—darning, sewing, and knitting, with spinning in prospect—and it made good progress. Sydney urgently requested a supply of prayer books for the Sunday scholars—'of which from the *really surprising* manner in which the children come on under Bendall [the master], there will soon be great need'.*

Satisfying though such small improvements must have been, Sydney obviously doubted the wisdom of remaining in so remote a spot. It was, however, by no means easy to resign his charge, as he reported to Mrs Hicks Beach in January 1795—'a Gentleman Curate called today to survey the place, and premises, and galloped away in two minutes with every mark of astonishment and antipathy'.*

His first surviving letter to his father, in June 1796, is written from Oxford, where he appears to have returned briefly to resume a resident fellowship. He gives a detailed account of his precarious financial position, begging an extra ten pounds from his father to cover the expenses of moving, the loss on the sale of his furniture, and the repairs necessary to make his Oxford chambers habitable.

I hope my dear Father you will not look upon it in a bad light, if I apply to you to make good these small sums, but really they are serious sums to me, and in spite of all my oeconomy—and the assistance you are so good as to afford me—I am sometimes without a shilling in my pocket ... A College Tutorship is exactly £50 per annum. If I could get one I should in that case exonerate you—but I will be entirely guided by you in this respect. Were I to consult inclination alone, I do assure you, I had rather after some time return again to a curacy— but I think you will be very much burthened with Robert, and will be glad of such an alleviation of expense.

The outlook seemed as bleak at Oxford as it had been at Netheravon; bleak, too, between father and son, as Sydney's letter begged a reply, 'as it will be a proof that you begin to feel a returning regard for me'.*

There was clearly much dissension in the air between the two of them. In July 1796 Sydney had acknowledged a letter from his father as 'a proof of returning affection', and although he apologized for previous offences he protested that 'I never did directly or indirectly make use of the expressions you impute to me— to this assertion I must adhere. You are under a great mistake if you suppose that I do not love my Father and reverence his talents ..."* Sydney was on his guard against his father's querulousness; his own mood was sometimes sombre, and in November 1797 he addressed his father in distressing terms:

I hope the conversation upon suicide which passed between us had produced no other unpleasant sensation in your mind than the want of respect to you, of which I am sorry to say you have a right to accuse me. You know the world too well to believe that a bookish man like myself governs his conduct by the metaphysical nonsense which he petulantly or pedantically advances in company.... To these new sentiments of the fair and rational obedience which a Son owes to his Father, I will not insult your understanding by adding anything of real or apparent servility. You want a respectful manner, and where acquiescence is not possible, a silence upon certain subjects. To be sulky is the pitiful resource of a man who dares not be imperious, and overbearing, and who is too ill tempered, and indolent, to be respectful, and polite.*

It was from such sad and painful reflections that he was soon to be removed by the kindness of his Netheravon friends.

The close relationship which Sydney had established with Mr and Mrs Hicks Beach at Netheravon developed in a warm friendship. He visited them at their other house, Williamstrip Park in Gloucestershire, and spent a lot of time in 1797 finding an accomplished governess for their younger children; in 1798 he bought in Bath a large quantity of material for Mrs Hicks Beach, and made himself generally useful to the family. The eldest Hicks Beach boy, Michael, was about to leave Eton, and it was natural for his father to invite his personable young clerical friend to act as the young man's tutor on a tour of the Continent. The changing political scene made Mr Beach hestitate, as Sydney reported to his father in April 1797:

I began with saying that times were so much changed since he first took up the idea of placing his son under my care, that I thought him wholly justified in abandoning the idea if he wished to do so; that if he still did me the honour of wishing the connexion to subsist, but was alarmed at the state of the continent, I was extremely willing to attend his son to Edinburgh.... Mr B. assured me in the warmest manner, that his first wish was that his son should be under my care; he confessed that he had a considerable degree of alarm at the state of the continent, but that his mind was not yet made up—he was balancing between Germany and Scotland, and wished for a fortnight to see the progress of political events and to consult people in Town well informed upon the subject.... Nothing was said of salary, nor can be I suppose with propriety till our plan is definitely arranged.*

Towards the end of Summer 1797 Sydney and Mr Hicks Beach decided that they should go to Germany. Sydney made enquiries and found that Saxe-Weimar would be the most enlightened place for them, with the University of Jena as a goal: 'The Duke (who is himself an extremely well informed, sensible man) has drawn to this town some of the most sensible men in Germany, who have by their example diffused there a very strong spirit of Improvement.'* By November Sydney was preparing himself for the Continent with a tutor in Oxford. 'I have open'd my German campaign,' he wrote to his father; 'I hope it will not turn out so difficult and tedious as I am told. I have engaged a French and German master three times a week each.'* By the end of the year, however, Switzerland seems to have been preferred. Sydney wrote to his father that they were definitely to set off in May 1798, 'for the university of Neufchâtel in Switzerland, if that country is not revolutionized before—if it is, for Saxe Weimar'.* He asked his father's advice on travelling arrangements and was able to tell Mr Hicks Beach about how travelling credits could be negotiated.*

Sydney visited his parents at Beauchamp (near Tiverton) and at Bath, in the autumn and winter of 1797-8, residing at New College between his excursions. There was also a trip to Bowood early in December to marry his brother Bobus to Miss Caroline Vernon. Sydney was pleased with his future sister-in-law (a connection of Lord Lansdowne's)—'her figure and appearance are commanding, her manners very affable, her temper sweet, her understanding very superior, all solid, effective, fit for sterling practice, in short just the woman to win Bobus's heart, and to govern him with the greatest possible advantage'.* The wedding took place on 9 December, Sydney having spent the previous week at the great Lansdowne country house; he enjoyed himself immensely, breaking off a letter to Mr Beach—'I would write to you more at large, but it is dinner time and this aristocrat or rather democrat gives such good dinners, that they are by no means to be neglected, and especially not by such an epicure as me.'*

The chronology of Sydney's movements at this time is not clear enough to establish really firm dates for his movements to and from Bath, which he visited in October and January. The details (unusually for Sydney's biography) are significant, as a young woman was also visiting Bath with her family in November 1797, and wrote down her impressions in the first half of the following year. Henry Tilney, the vivacious and attractive young clergyman of *Northanger Abbey*, notable for the 'fluency and spirit' of his talk and the 'archness and pleasantry in his manner', bears (as Mr John Sparrow has carefully argued) some striking resemblances to Sydney Smith.* The parallels are perhaps less in appearance than in manner. Sydney, who in later life was to become notorious for his stoutness, was almost certainly not remarkable for slim elegance in his twenties, however agreeable his facial expression must have been; Henry Tilney was 'rather tall, had a pleasing countenance, a very intelligent and lively eye, and, if not quite handsome, was near it'); the witty conversation is similar, and Henry Tilney's prattle about muslins is dangerously close to Sydney's letters discussing stuffs with Mrs Beach. Sydney Smith and Jane Austen moved in similar social circles in Bath; there are other minor connections between the Austens and Hicks Beaches: the inference is tempting, but the evidence for the movements of both parties is, tantalizingly, too weak to prove a meeting at this time. The fictional parallels should not be ignored because the clinching biographical detail is lacking, and the equation of Henry Tilney with Sydney Smith remains an under-documented but intriguing possibility.

In the event, the worsening political situation on the Continent made it possible for tutor and pupil to go either to Switzerland or Weimar, and Edinburgh was decided on instead.

Late in spring 1798 Mr Hicks Beach finally approved such a plan, and Sydney set off with young Michael on 1 June.* Robert Smith, with characteristic financial meddlesomeness, had been pressing Sydney about the salary he should ask. Sydney was unwilling to urge the matter with his patron, feeling he had received too much kindness from the Beach family to make an ordinary commercial agreement suitable. Nor was he willing to allow his father the pleasure of negotiating for him. 'I thank you very sincerely for your offer of interference in my favour; I am sure you consulted my interest in making it, and I am as sure you will respect those feelings which induce me on this occasion to decline it.' In any case, Sydney could not help feeling that a travelling tutorship was 'a service extremely overpaid'.* He finally overcame his embarrassment, broached the question of payment, and the day before leaving for Edinburgh was able to tell his father that Hicks Beach had given him £500 in 8% Imperial Funds and a promissory note for £500 maturing in June 1800; travelling and other charges would be paid by the father, but the tutor's pocket expenses would have to be covered by the interest on the government stock and from his fellowship. He dutifully offered his father the consolation that 'Nothing has given me a greater pleasure in this transaction, than the probability it affords me of not being any longer hereafter the burthen I have always reluctantly been to you.'*

Sydney and his pupil had left for Scotland well provided with letters of introduction which saw to their comfort on the journey via Birmingham, Liverpool, and the Lake District. Their ascent of Skiddaw provided one anecdote to amuse Michael's worried mother:

Off we set, Michael, the guide and myself, at one in the morning to gain the summit of Skiddaw. I, who find it rather difficult to stick upon my horse on the plainest roads, did not find that facility increased by the darkness of the morning, or the precipitous paths we had to ascend. I made no manner of doubt but that I should roll down into the town of Keswick the next morning and be picked up by the Town Beadle dead in a gutter. Moreover I was moved a little for my reputation, for as I had a bottle of brandy in my pocket, placed there by the special exhortations of the guide and landlord, the Keswick Coroner and jury would infallibly have brought me in 'a parson as died of drinking'.

However, fortified by biscuit and brandy, they were eventually rewarded with some fine views before resuming their journey through 'dust and desolation' to the city with whose literary history Sydney was to be so closely connected. 'With this town I am delighted and surprised,' he wrote in his first letter from Edinburgh, 'though it is as offensive to the nose as it is delightful to the eye.'*

Sydney's early impressions of Edinburgh were summed up in a letter to his friend John Clarke, of Swakeleys, early in December 1798, written after he had been living there for some five months. His comments combine an appreciation of the bracing atmosphere and architectural grandeur which still first strike the visitor, with a sense of the intellectual cultivation of the place that takes somewhat longer to discern. They also reveal a keen awareness of the contrast between the foetid wynds and alleys of the crowded old city, and the spacious and formal architecture of the (Georgian) New Town: the change was by 1798 well under way, and Sydney was quick to nose it out:

I like this place extremely and cannot help thinking that for a literary man, by which term I mean a man who is fond of letters, it is the most eligible situation in the island. It unites good libraries liberally managed, learned men without any other system than that of pursuing truth; very good general society; large healthy virgins, with mild pleasing countenances, and white swelling breasts; shores washed by the sea; the romantic grandeur of ancient, and the beautiful regularity of modern buildings, and boundless floods of oxygen. Some little defects it has to be sure, but they are frivolous and ludicrous; one is, as you must have observed, a total want of all fæcal propriety and excremental delicacy ...*

The slop-pails of old Edinburgh became a frequent subject of jest. As Sydney explained to Mr Hicks Beach:

No smells were ever equal to Scotch smells. It is the school of physic; walk the streets, and you would imagine that every medical man had been administering cathartics to every man, woman and child in the town. Yet the place is uncommonly beautiful, and I am in a constant balance between admiration and trepidation—
    Taste guides my eye, where'er new beauties spread
    While prudence whispers, 'Look before you tread'.*

    Soon after their arrival in Scotland Sydney and his pupil set off on a brief Highland tour. He reported the journey to Michael's mother in the conventional language of picturesque appreciation ('He knows not the Earth ... who has never trod on the margin of the fearful precipice', etc.), but tempered his rapture with practicalities—'Yet we have mortified the body in gratifying the mind, we have been forced to associate Oat Cakes and Whisky with Rocks and Waterfalls, and humble in a dirty room the conceptions we indulged in a romantic Glen.'
    The most striking feature of the whole excursion had been a visit to the cotton-spinning factory which Dale had established in New Lanark in 1786:

Near Lanark is settled a Mr David Dale—a man so largely concerned in the cotton works that he alone without any partner employs 1700 souls. He is a very religious and benevolent man, and is remarkably attentive to the morals, as well as the comforts and happiness of the manufacturing children—they are admirably instructed, and brought up with an attention to cleanliness that is truly delightful. He very often gives them a dance—the evening we were there, after the hours of work there was a general country dance, of above 200 couples. We knew nothing of it till the following morning, or of course we should not have missed so pleasing a spectacle. I love to see the beauties of nature, but I love better to see the hand of active piety stretch forth to such young orphans as these the innocent pleasures of life, the benefits of instruction, and the blessings of religion. It is dreadful to observe in Manchester and Birmingham how manufactures brutalise mankind, how small the interval is between a weaver and a beast. What does his country not owe to a man who has promoted industry without propagating vice, who has enlarged the boundaries of commerce and strengthened the ties of moral obligation?*

Sydney's prose style was gradually to lose some of these fineries of conventional appreciativeness, but his early impressions and feelings on the social reponsibilities of employers were later to find an outlet in his *Edinburgh* reviews.

Sydney's other early descriptions of the social condition of Scotland were partly aimed at helping Mrs Hicks Beach in her plans for improving the lot of the peasants on her husband's estates. The state of the Scottish urban poor was reckoned satisfactory—'no country can afford an example of so much order, morality, œconomy, and knowledge amongst the lower classes of society. Every nation has its peculiarities—the very improved state of the common people appears to me at present to be the phenomenon of this country, and I intend to give it a good deal of my attention.'* Rumford's *Essays* were recommended to Mrs Beach for information on feeding the poor, and Sydney gave them a practical test by assisting a schoolmaster whom he found starving in the throes of genteel poverty. He devoted much attention to different breads for the lower classes, hoping that one day he might 'become master cook, as well as master parson, of my village'.* He later enrolled for elementary medical classes, telling Clarke that 'I attend the hospitals where I learn the elements of a puke and the rudiments of purging—the viscera rustica will pay for this when I am settled in my parish.'* It was to be twelve years before he could use his alimentary learning in parochial practice.

There was a lighter side to his observation—'We are just going to Church,' he wrote to Mrs Beach in September 1798: 'The wind is outrageous, to the infinite joy of those ladies who can boast of good ankles, who will not fail this day to be punctually attentive to the public duties of religion, while those of more clumsy fabric will no doubt discover that prayers read at home are quite as efficacious.'* A letter sent to John Clarke the following February contains an early experiment in the cumulative burlesque which was to become one of the most successful devices of his literary style:

The Turbot fishery has begun, and every man is laying in his stock of Soy, Cayenne Pepper and Chili Vinegar. I never witnessed anything equal to the voracity with which this savoury monster of the deep is devoured. A serious silence prevails at table—the passage of the voice is entirely shut up—people are hermetically choked. No sooner is one mouthful reduced to atoms of Turbot than another, that has been resting impatiently against the lips and panting for maceration, is admitted dripping with liquid lobster, and rushes down the common sewer of culinary filth—a profuse perspiration breaks out—the eyes stare—the garments are loosened—the labour is intense—it would seem as if the end of all things were expected, and as no turbot was looked for elsewhere men all had joined in the common sentiment of Let us eat and drink, for tomorrow we die.*

The first lodgings they took in Edinburgh were in the New Town, at 38 South Hanover Street, where they were well placed in rooms with a servant. As boarding tables were so bad, Sydney undertook the housekeeping with the help of Mithoffer, the excellent courier-valet who had travelled north with them.* After about six weeks, Sydney reported that 'Mithoffer continues to behave extremely well. As he is not a very good judge of meat, I have been forced to go to market myself two or three times, but now the courier is very much improved. We all tried to make a pie by our joint efforts ... [but] the crust was as hard as biscuit and we could not eat it. There is always some beef in the salt tub, and I look into the family affairs like a fat old lady of forty.'*

At the end of 1798, Sydney had to start thinking of the following summer's arrangements, to square things with his landlady:

I have been a terrible quandary about lodgings. The woman of the house where I live was extremely civil all the summer when lodgings are of no value, but at the approach of winter, when the town was so full that no lodging was to be got, because I would not give her twelve guineas a month instead of nine, she called me a Levite, a scourge of human nature and an extortioner, and gave me notice to go out instantly bag and baggage, without beat of drum, or colours flying. I refused to stir and after a very severe battle, in which I threatened to carry it through all the Courts of Justice in England, and from thence to Russia, she began to make the amiable and to confess that she was apt to be a little warm, that she had the most perfect confidence in my generosity, and the old story. I made her sign an agreement with the subscription of two witnesses, and am now lord of the castle for the time I tell you.*

Although they had travelled north well provided with letters of introduction, society was out of town at the time they arrived and their acquaintance was at first quite limited. Lord Webb Seymour, a son of the Duke of Somerset and a man of developed scientific taste and enlightened conversation, was one of the first people Sydney met in Edinburgh—a bridge between the *beau monde* of his patrons and the Whig cronies amongst whom he was to establish himself. Dugald Stewart and Dalzel the Professor of Greek were Sydney's earliest academic acquaintance; Baron North (of the Exchequer court) and Charles Hope, later Lord President of the Court of Session, were among the eminent legal personalities to whom he carried letters of introduction. An invitation to Dalkeith in August must also have arisen from the Hicks Beach testimonials: 'We have dined at the Duke of Buccleuch's, and met the French King's brother there and his suite— we were not much pleased with our day. Her Grace is a most excellent woman, but a very stately piece of ancient life as I ever saw—the Duke seems to be one of those kind of men who baffle all attempts to hate, praise or blame them.'*

Formal dining in ducal palaces was much less to Sydney's taste at that time than the company of the younger advocates and literateurs to whom his social gifts, obvious sense of humour, and already clearly apparent Whig point of view naturally led him to gravitate. Sydney himself remarked on the contrast when writing late in life of his early friendship with Francis Horner, the brilliant young Whig politician who died early in a promising parliamentary career:

I first made the acquaintance of Francis Horner at Edinburgh, where he was among the most conspicuous young men in that energetic and infragrant city. My desire to know him proceeded first of all from being cautioned against him by some excellent and feeble people to whom I had brought letters of introduction, and who represented him to me as a person of violent political opinions; I interpreted this to mean a person who thought for himself—who had firmness enough to take his own line in life, and who loved truth better than he loved Dundas, at that time the tyrant of Scotland. I found my interpretation to be just, and from thence till the period of his death [in 1817] we lived in constant society and friendship with each other.*

Edinburgh was then a particular home of small debating societies and dining clubs of young professional men; it remains perhaps their last refuge. At the turn of the century the oppressively Tory atmosphere of the town gave them a pungency and an air of conscious daring which must have been exciting to a newcomer. Furtive, dedicated, and witty the societies may have been, but the familiarity of the members with each other, and the repetitiveness of their disputations, must have made them somewhat sterile; a new arrival of unquestionable originality would have provided a fresh ingredient promoting renewed vivacity. Thus Francis Horner wrote in his journal in October 1799 of Sydney Smith and Lord Webb Seymour, 'I promise myself much pleasure and much instruction from their conversation. I shall perhaps improve my powers of argumentative dexterity, which are still very low; and, at any rate, I cannot but learn candour, liberality, and a thirst for accurate opinions and general information, from men who possess in so remarkable a degree these valuable dispositions.'* Two years later, Horner paid further tribute to the leavening powers of the visitors: 'To one resident in the stagnation or poverty of Edinburgh conversation, the *beaux-esprits* of London are entertaining and instructive novelties.'* Sydney, for his part, was able to appreciate his new friends the more, and men such as Francis Jeffrey (at the time an impoverished and disconsolate advocate) were stimulated by his approval.*

Something of Sydney's feelings for his Edinburgh friends is conveyed in a letter he wrote to Jeffrey while away on a visit to London in June 1801, just after he had met James Mackintosh, whose conversation he much admired:

He has lived much among various men with great observation, and has always tried his profound moral speculations by the experience of life. He has not contracted in the world a lazy contempt for theorists, nor in the closet a peevish impatience of that grossness and corruptibility of mankind, which are ever marring the schemes of secluded benevolence. He does not wish for the best in politics or morals, but for the best which can be attained; and what that is, he seems to know well. Now what I object to Scotch philosophers in general is that they reason upon man as they reason upon X — they pursue truth, without caring if it be useful truth ... in short a Scotchman is apt to be a practical rogue upon sale, or a visionary philosopher.*

Clearly Sydney had undergone a baptism by dialectic into the solemn and pedantic metaphysics of the north. Scotch philosophers, like Scotch smells and Scotch itches, were to become a perpetual object of amusement for him:

It requires a surgical operation to get a joke well into the Scotch understanding. Their only idea of wit, or rather of that inferior variety of this electric talent which prevails occasionally in the North, and which, under the name of WUT, is so infinitely distressing to people of good taste, is laughing immoderately at stated intervals. They are so imbued with metaphysics that they even make love metaphysically. I overheard a young lady of my acquaintance, at a dance in Edinburgh, exclaim, in a sudden pause of the music, 'What you say, my Lord, is true of love in the *aibstract*, but—' here the fiddlers began fiddling furiously, and the rest was lost.*

Sydney's nocturnal gatherings in Edinburgh were never as serious. 'We will pass many evenings together,' he wrote to Jeffrey from England, 'arguing and joking amidst eating and drinking; above all being stupid when we feel inclined, a rare privilege of friendship, of which I am frequently glad to avail myself.'*

The tutorial plan for Michael Hicks Beach was stated simply to the boy's mother: 'If I can (in spite of the reluctance to study) carry him on in a course of improvement, tell him his faults, and retain his esteem, I shall succeed almost beyond my hopes, and entirely to my satisfaction.'* A little earlier, Sydney had discovered how to deal with his rather unwilling pupil, whom he had criticized for spending too much time about his toilet: 'This Michael took in high anger, and was extremely sulky.... Without the smallest appearance of anger or vexation on my part, I turned his sulkiness into ridicule, and completely laughed him into good humour.' The lad was indolent, with no affection for his books, because he had been so badly taught at Eton. By carefully regulating his work and play, Sydney gradually persuaded him to study: 'In adjusting the time of study, my object was to occupy him fairly, without exciting his disgust; I think I have succeeded.'* After six months, however, Sydney realized that he could not instil in his pupil a genuine love of learning suited to his eventual position in life:

Whatever share of knowledge Michael may gain by reading with me, it is quite out of my power to give him a taste for books ... I cannot give him new habits in this respect; I can only obviate in some degree the bad effects of his old ones.... Do not be disheartened by this opinion. Michael will, as I have often told you, be a very worthy, prudent man, with a sufficient share of sound understanding leading to conduct, an excellent heart, and manners by time and his father's assistance soft, and gentlemanlike; and though literature is an excellent addition to all these it is hardly worth the least of them.*

Sydney and Michael became good friends, and the tutor gradually allowed his pupil to study more of the 'accomplishments', such as writing and drawing, than of more straightforward academic subjects. Nor did they live an enclosed life; Michael developed a great passion for dancing which Sydney was, within limits, prepared to indulge, and he was allowed to mix with some of his contemporaries. His mother had been alarmed at the thought of the boy's getting into vicious company. Sydney sensibly reassured her that 'If you attempt to preserve him from danger by keeping him out of the way of it, you render him quite unfit for any state of life in which he may be placed. The great point is not to turn him out too soon, and to give him a pilot at first.'* The report which Sydney sent Hicks Beach in June 1789, when they had returned to England for a few weeks, seems to confirm the wisdom of this latitude, and an affectionate letter survives from Sydney to his pupil ('My dear Comrade ...').*

It was perhaps a few weeks' separation from his tutor and the prospect of continuous supervision during the winter which changed Michael's behaviour for the worse on their return journey. While they were travelling northwards through Wales, Sydney was obliged to complain of his pupil's conduct.

You have no conception of his frivolous minuteness and particularity in every thing which concerns his dress and person; it is more than feminine and upon my venturing the other morning to make some observation about the inutility of his travelling with his own boot-jack his behaviour was so extremely improper and disrespectful that I did not open my lips to him for two days. In all this time no sort of apology ...*

The insult must have been a powerful one to cause this first and only major complaint to the boy's father, who was asked to write and remonstrate with his son on such unpleasant conduct. The result is seen in a heartfelt apology which young Michael sent his father soon afterwards:

You little think how much I am obliged to you for your letter, so justly severe (though I hope I may never deserve such another), for as I foolishly thought I was forgiven, I am afraid that without so positive a command from you, I should not even by this time have apologized for being so impertinent to one whom at least I ought to have esteemed too much to have offended in that manner. I have at last attempted to make a proper apology: but Mr Smith was so good he would not suffer me; he said 'My dear friend one word by way of apology is enough'. I can never forget those words, and only hope that I may then prove what he then called me.*

'I dare say we shall be only better friends for what has passed', Sydney wrote to the father, closing the incident.* Having learnt his lesson, Michael seems to have enjoyed his tutor's company the more until he left his charge in 1800. They dined out in society a good deal, and Michael's letters home are much more mature and relaxed—'I am become *a great politician*, and read the newspaper every day', he wrote to his father; or, 'It is astonishing how much more easily I can write a letter or read a book in an evening since I have taken to tea.'* The young man, though he had confessed to Sydney an early infatuation, seems to have been without any romantic attachments, rather to his tutor's amazement: 'I am rather surprised that no lassie has set her cap at him, as he is known to be a man of fortune in this place, and these needy Northern nymphs are upon the look out particularly for anything coming from the South.'*

The vacation in England in 1799 had been arranged not only for Michael to see his parents but for Sydney to see his fiancée at the same time. Towards the end of 1798 he had privately engaged himself to marry Catharine Amelia Pybus, who was an old friend of his sister Maria and lived in Cheam with a widowed mother (her father had been a banker in a Bond Street partnership). Sydney's father was the first to be told, in a long letter unusually enough phrased to match the situation (and indeed the addressee):

My dearest Father—When a man has been reflecting a long while upon a mode of doing an important thing, he generally finds the simplest way is the best. I do not see the necessary connexions between subjects of consequence and words of many syllables, or phrases of studied arrangement, and therefore shall tell you my story plainly and shortly—taking care not to sacrifice to brevity that respect and regard which I feel for you, and owe to you.

I have long wished to marry and think that state of life to be almost the only happiness that is worth looking forward to. I know but one woman who unites fortune, understanding and good disposition in a degree that makes an alliance desirable with her, and who at the same time is not in a situation of life that puts her out of my reach. Under this impression I engaged myself to Miss Pybus while I was in Town, and just at the time I was leaving it. Some letters have passed between us since to settle more fully a subject which we had settled very imperfectly before. We have nothing more to settle and, in consequence, I communicate to you our intentions.

The first sensation that will arise in your mind upon reading this (and it is the first which has suggested itself to me) is, why my intentions were not carried into execution. But you my dear Father must know how these things are carried on. Nobody sets out with a systematic intention of making himself fond of any woman—but he thinks himself quite safe and free at first, but assiduity is added to assiduity and kindness heaped upon kindness on both sides, till affection which has gathered by slow and unperceived degrees is at last so great that the option is taken away, and all consultation and advice is a mockery. At the proper time of asking it, nobody means to marry—at the usual time of asking it, nobody means to follow advice, unless it agrees with his previous determination. I hope therefore you will attribute my conduct in this respect to the ordinary tenor and impulse of men's actions and thoughts, and not to any want of respect and affection. It would be more pleasing and flattering to you and my mother, if I had united myself as my brother has done to a family of distinction, but when I look to my pretensions I really think I had done as well as I had any fair reason to expect—and when I look to my heart, I am quite content.

I know you think Miss Pybus's person very disagreeable, but this consideration is so entirely confined to opinion, and the evil (if it exists) is so exclusively my own, that I am sure you will not give me unprovoked pain by commenting on the subject. Her fortune is I believe £8000 Sterling—so I have understood her account. I think that if we can make up £500 a year clear between us that we shall be able to marry.... Will it be in your power to afford me any assistance? Till fortune or my own exertion renders it unnecessary, any will be of service to me—but of none will I accept, upon any account whatsoever, which goes to deprive you of what you may deem an important comfort. You have done enough for me. I am more obliged to you for the education you have given me, than if you had put me in a way to get rich—and so I will say if my poverty keeps me single all [my life].*

Sydney swore his father to secrecy. No letters survive from him to his family for the whole of 1799, probably because of an unsympathetic reply to Sydney's letter announcing his betrothal. It had ended 'I entertain a hope that this news will not be wholly unacceptable to you'; but that hope was a distant one, as the letter anticipated an unfavourable reaction in its closing humilities, from a child 'who though he cannot boast of having curbed a bad and unruly nature, from a sense of filial respect and obedience has always loved you from the bottom of his heart'.* All that we know of Robert Smith's reaction is recorded tersely in a 'Narrative' written by his daughter-in-law for her family after Sydney's death: 'Not one penny. If you had remained unmarried your fellowship would have been your provision by giving you a living.'*

Sydney was less dismissive about his fiancée when writing to his friend Clarke late in October 1799: 'As for the lady, she is three years younger than me, a very old friend of mine—a good figure, and *to me* an interesting countenance, of excellent disposition, extremely good sense, very fond of music, and me—a wise, amiable woman such as without imposing, specious qualities will quietly for years and years make the happiness of her husband's life.'* So it turned out. Writing to Robert Smith in jocular anticipation as 'Father' in December 1798, Catharine had politely acknowledged his good opinion, and in her gossipy way sought to increase herself in his regard, at least by an 'œconomical distribution of letter paper'—one of his perpetual meannesses.* Mrs Pybus had rather wished that the match could have been postponed until Sydney was assured of preferment; she added with splendid impercipience that 'as to his principles, whether *Whig* or *Tory*, he has the good sense I make no doubt never to make them unnecessarily conspicuous'.* True to form, Sydney's father took umbrage at the tone of Mrs Pybus's letter, which he felt to be insulting to his own family by its lack of enthusiasm. He had to be pacified by long explanations from Catharine: 'I doubt not but that she might have felt a desire to see me what she would call *well* married provided it *had been compatible with my happiness*. . . . [but] from the moment she felt convinced that my comfort could only be ensured by my marriage with Sydney (and the short space of one day was sufficient to persuade her of this), every other consideration instantly vanished from her mind, and she became as warm an advocate for it, as we could be ourselves.'*

Sydney's contribution to the capital of his household was necessarily a small one, but quite characteristic. His daughter recorded that 'my father's only contribution to their future *ménage* (save his own talents and character) were six small silver teaspoons. . . . One day, in the madness of his joy, he came running into the room and flung them into her lap, saying, "There, Kate, you lucky girl, I give you all my fortune!" '* The sale of some of Catharine's family pearls provided plate and linen for the household in Edinburgh, but their financial problems were made worse by the unwillingness of the Pybus executors to transfer Catharine's portion. Catharine's brother Charles proved particularly obstructive, and a Chancery suit had to be threatened to stir the Pybus family. It was not until June 1800 that Sydney could tell his father that 'all my difficulties are over after a battle of two years'.* But new troubles with his father were beginning. Robert Smith was angry at not being a trustee of Sydney's marriage settlement; Catharine later recalled that her father-in-law's opposition was based on his wish to buy a farm and invest the money under his own management.* The settlement was decidedly in the bride's favour, and Robert Smith accused her and her mother of conspiring against Sydney's interests. Sydney replied moderately early in 1801: 'As I am convinced by long experience of that latitude of interpretation with which your warm expressions are to be understood, I feel less hurt at your severity, than I otherwise should do.'* He pointed out that for her part Catharine had not wished for *any* settlement, which he had himself suggested to secure her money and protect himself against accusations of mercenary motives from the Pybus family. The matter rankled for years, and became one of the main weapons in the armoury of parental reproof. In March 1803 Sydney wrote firmly to his father:

you consider the settlement of her fortune to have been made in great part at the suggestion of my wife. Whether that settlement be right or wrong I do not intend to discuss—but let it be what it may the fact is she had no sort of share in its construction. There is nothing whatever upon this point that she would not have consented to at my request. The mother and daughter were both so ignorant of the subject that with them I could have done anything. The settlement as it now stands was entirely my own act and deed, dictated by the strongest sense of honest duty. So help me God.*

It had been Sydney's intention at the time of his engagement to stay out his two years with Michael Hicks Beach; after that, he wrote to his father, 'it is my wish at present to push myself as a preacher either in Bath or London. I have been flattered that I have some talents for this kind of exertion—but there is time enough to think over this.'* He explained a similar plan to Clarke a year later, adding in an unusual mood of self-analysis: 'I shall do very well in the world I dare say—but if I had as much apparent and exterior, as I have of real and intrinsic prudence, I should do much better. This is very vain—but if you will not admit it to be true—you will I am sure have the politeness to allow I am deficient in both. Happy is the man who possesses the appearances of good qualities rather than their essences—

by old women shall he be praised, and muffins and hyson shall be his lot.'*

Sydney was able to tell Clarke that he would be taking charge of William Hicks Beach, Michael's younger brother. After family discussions it had been decided that he too should go to Edinburgh. Sydney pointed out that there would be little extra expense involved in sending William there rather than to Bath. The choice was to be Mr and Mrs Beach's, but he added: 'There cannot possibly be any spot in England where a young man can be so advantageously educated as here, and he will have the advantage of mixing with other young men, which he is not sure of in the other case. *Mrs Smith in future* has no objection to the plan.... Let Mr Beach consult entirely his own inclination, and convenience. I wish to have no other guide.' Sydney then frankly broached the question of payment, mentioning that he would have about £600 a year clear—'sufficient to live here with œconomy', but not large enough to bear the £80 or so of the annual travelling expenses of the tutorship.* Towards the end of June, when the Pybus executors had released Catharine's portion and enabled them to marry, Sydney came to a financial arrangement with Mr Hicks Beach too. He was able to assure his patron of careful management of his funds: 'I have no sort of turn to expense, nor has Mrs Smith, for I look upon her to be full as great an œconomist as myself.'* Sydney Smith was married on 2 July 1800. His bride (who was generally referred to by her husband as 'Mrs Sydney', the name their friends also adopted) was an outstandingly cheerful, good-natured woman, with a vein of quiet humour that shows itself in her few surviving letters. She soon proved herself a capable domestic manager in the narrow circumstances of their early life together, and she was fully capable, socially and intellectually, of accompanying her husband as he rose in life. Their partnership was recognized, and his friends came to value her company for her own sake as well as a mere appendage to his more striking social presence. Catharine Pybus provided Sydney with the happiest possible domestic background, and in due course became a devoted mother to their children. Whatever his father may have feared—or hoped—Sydney's marriage was the greatest possible success, and all was set for another happy and productive period in Edinburgh.

Shortly after his marriage, however, Sydney was involved in an ugly dispute with Mrs Hicks Beach which shows something both of the sensitive pride of a newly married husband, and that unfortunate tenacity in trifles which Sydney probably inherited from his father. Although the Hicks Beach family always considered that it was Mrs Smith who had irritated Sydney into writing the letters,* other examples show that it was probably her husband who was at fault. The Hicks Beaches travelled north with the Smiths when taking William back to Edinburgh with them in the autumn of 1800. They were puzzled, however, by Sydney's 'exceeding ill-temper' ('indeed for one day he never spoke at all') but an explanation of his moodiness only came later. 'When people of good breeding and education travel together they share equally the pleasures and the inconveniences of the journey, amongst the rest in the article of sleeping rooms', Sydney wrote to Mrs Hicks Beach in a very long letter alleging that Mrs Smith had always been given the worst room throughout the tour and that she had not been given the choice which courtesy demanded. Although Catharine reckoned herself to be of an uncomplaining nature, Sydney felt that remonstrance was necessary. 'All this seems much to write about a bed—but negligence and contempt may be shewn in a thousand different ways.'* The language Sydney used was strong but not immoderate; however, considering their relative positions, the tone was disrespectful. Mrs Hicks Beach replied with a moderation the tutor's letter scarcely deserved: 'Your letter has not offended me, on the contrary I think you have done well in accounting for your very extraordinary behaviour.'* She denied Sydney's charges politely but firmly, writing that Mrs Smith had often been given better rooms than the Beaches. Sydney retorted that a *choice* should have been given, and although he professed to have forgotten the matter, it clearly rankled and provoked a needlessly querulous reply.* Mrs Hicks Beach remained remarkably even-tempered and understanding, and despite a further piece of querulousness from Sydney—arguing like a (Scotch) moral philosopher upon the simple letter of a gentlewoman—the matter appears to have blown over. Another protest from Sydney might have permanently impaired their relationship; as it was, Sydney returned to a footing with his pupil's mother where gentle teasing, advice on reading, and a kindly interest in the whole family were more normal than this isolated explosion.

'I continue to preach every now and then and see the faithful yawning at my feet', Sydney had written to John Clarke in 1799.* He frequently remarked the somnolence of his Edinburgh congregation—usually at the Charlotte (Episcopal) Chapel—writing to Mrs Beach on the Queen's Birthday the following year that 'everybody dances to show their loyalty, except me; and I show it by preaching, and have the pleasure of seeing my audience nod approbation as they sleep'.* Occasionally his theme kept the congregation awake—a few weeks earlier he had proudly written to Mrs Beach: 'I preached a sermon here upon adultery last Sunday, a very singular subject, and such as every parson would not have ventured upon. If you will excuse my vanity for telling you so, I got some little credit for it.'* Sydney's early pulpit style was vividly remembered by Henry Cockburn, who wrote in his *Journal* in 1849, when meditating on extempore delivery:

The best calm sermon I have heard was one preached in Edinburgh by Sydney Smith. It was a defence, upon grounds of mere reason and expediency, of the institution of death; the particular object being to show that the present brevity of life was best suited to the other circumstances of our condition. He held the manuscript in his hand, and read it exactly as an ordinary reader holds and reads from a printed book; but the thoughts had been so well considered, the composition was so proper, and the reading so quiet and impressive, that I doubt if there were a dozen dry eyes or unpalpitating hearts in the church; and every sentiment, and many of the expressions, and the whole scope and pathos of the discourse, are still fresh upon my mind at the distance of many years.*

In the spring of 1800 he gathered six of his discourses into a small volume dedicated to Lord Webb Seymour—'I shall print about 100 copies—of which I expect to sell at least half' he told his father.* John Leyden met Sydney shortly after their publication, and wrote to their common friend Richard Heber that 'he was expressing his design of sending you a copy to make you sleep at nights when disturbed with insomnia. Hereby shall all men know, says your friend the divine, that we are His disciples, since we wake that others may sleep as we compose sermons in the night watches to lull others to sleep even in the broad day.'* The sermons—three unexceptional political discourses and three plain moral essays—seem to have been well received by the *Monthly Review* and the *British Critic*.

Emboldened perhaps by the favourable reviews, in 1801 he added six more sermons, publishing them in two volumes with the previous six, as 'the second edition, with considerable additions'. He inserted a long preface lamenting the decline in church attendances, citing long and dreary services, clerical indifference, and 'the low state of pulpit eloquence' as causes.* Sermons had become disagreeable because of their content—stale scriptural allusion, or ill-considered profundity—as well as because of the restrained manner of the preachers: Sydney held that the Church of England could learn much about effective delivery from the dissenters.

A clergyman clings to his velvet cushion with either hand, keeps his eye riveted upon his book, speaks of the ecstasies of joy, and fear, with a voice and a face which indicate neither, and pinions his body and soul into the same attitude of limb, and thought, for fear of being called theatrical and affected.... Is it wonder, then, that every semi-delirious sectary who pours forth his animated nonsense, with the genuine look, and voice of passion, should gesticulate away the congregation of the most profound and learned divine of the established church, and in two Sundays preach him bare to the very sexton? Why are we natural everywhere but in the pulpit?...

We have cherished contempt for sectaries, and persevered in dignified tameness so long, that while we are freezing common sense, for large salaries, in stately churches, amidst whole acres and furlongs of empty pews, the crowd are feasting on ungrammatical fervour, and illiterate animation in the crumbling hovels of Methodists.*

Sydney ended his preface, as he often ended letters to his father, with a barbed note of apology. 'I hope I shall not give offence; I am sure I do not mean to do it. Some allowance should be made for the severity of censure, when the provident satirist furnishes the raw material for his own art, and commits every fault which he blames.'*

The *Anti Jacobin* did not take so kindly to such remarks and the second volume of sermons was severely handled. Dismissing the sermons themselves as 'light, airy and fashionable', it gave most of its space to the preface (the work of 'this Hortensius, this very Dionysius of the pulpit'), defending a moderate preaching manner and the tradition of scriptural quotation.* Archdeacon Nares, editor of the *British Critic*, who had praised the first volume, also turned against its successor: the presumptuous preface was considered revolutionary and was roundly criticized. Sydney defended himself in a letter published in the *Anti Jacobin* of August 1801 against some of the reviewer's misrepresentations of his view of biblical quotation. The letter ended cryptically: 'On the personalties against *me* which you have mingled with your review of *my writings*, I will make no remarks at present; but shall choose another mode of addressing you upon the subject'.* There, perhaps, is the first available allusion to the meditated establishment of the *Edinburgh Review*, in which, significantly, Nares himself and several *Anti Jacobin* personalities were to be attacked.

Towards the end of 1800 Sydney had revived with the Hicks Beaches the discussion of his salary which had been broached in the summer. His first letter (in November) pointing out that they were 'all so much agreed that this kind of explicit conduct is so much the most agreeable for all parties' asked, clearly but politely, whether, if he dedicated himself to William for a further two or three years, 'have I any further remuneration of any kind to expect from Mr Beach than the £200 per annum I now receive?'* A month later he asked more specifically for a note of hand of £300 in addition to the £200 salary, for each of the one or two further years he stayed with the family. If he were to stay until June 1803, he calculated: 'I shall have given up five of the best years of my life to the education of your children, and shall be a richer man by about £1330. This Sum, if sunk in an income of 9 per cent, would bring me in an income of £125, which in recollecting the various instances of emolument derived either from money or preferment by gentlemen of my profession does not appear to me exorbitant.'* Even though Sydney's request was couched in affectionate terms, Mrs Beach rightly decided that it required a firm reply. She wrote on her husband's behalf that they had decided that *some* extra remuneration was necessary after the end of Sydney's first year with William; they felt that £300 was too large a sum, and proposed an addition of £200. Mrs Beach added that they felt Sydney's tutorship ('five of the best years' as he had put it) had been a voluntary connection; it was scarcely a bargaining point.*

On 28 December 1800 Sydney wrote that he felt obliged to resign his charge during the spring, 'with that reluctance for his loss, which his charming understanding, and amiable disposition will most unfeignedly inspire'.* Sydney showed himself quite set on resigning by giving notice at his lodgings, and tried to place William with Dugald Stewart, Archibald Alison, or Daniel Sandford. The first two of these had their full quota of pupils for the coming year, and Daniel Sandford (later Bishop of Edinburgh) could not be wholeheartedly recommended. The lack of a suitable place for his pupil weakened Sydney's resolution. 'If you feel uneasy at leaving your son [at Mr Sandford's],' he wrote to Mrs Beach, 'I will return here with pleasure and resume his education upon your own terms—or upon any others whatever you choose to dictate.'* At this stage Robert Smith intervened.

Sydney's father sent a long and agitated letter on his son's behalf to Mrs Hicks Beach, whom he knew socially and visited from time to time. Writing from Bath on 1 February (following another letter to Mr Beach in London which has not survived), he told his son's patroness that

> I am sure you will have the goodness to allow my freedom on a subject so very near my heart, and I will flatter myself not quite indifferent to you—the happiness and honour of my *misguided boy*....
>
> I had not the most distant information of the business from Sydney, till last week ... and it is with grief I confess myself very much hurt from this pointed neglect, so recent after his marriage of which and all its arrangements I am equally an utter stranger.
>
> Yet I am convinced he is a good man, holding you and Mr Beach in the highest esteem and attached to your son William warmly.... He has mistaken the point of honour, of which he thinks improperly, and fearful of sinking in your opinion, had not courage to recede from a point to which he never should have committed himself.

Robert Smith had clearly been alarmed by Sydney's suggestion that he should set up speculatively as a tutor in England (and perhaps alluded to the possibility that he might become a charge on his father): 'I am convinced his coming either to London or Bath will be followed with the consequence I dread of all others.' This unusual intervention was justified by a proper parental concern, 'the leading passion and object of my life having been to establish my boys, whose exertions and conduct have hitherto justified my most sanguine hopes'.*

Robert Smith's letter may well have been effective in reconciling the Beaches to retaining his son. Early in February Sydney reported the continuing arrangement to his father:

> I think Mr B. is offering me too little for his son—I think I am injuring myself by staying here—but I think after his friendship to us both, it would not have been proper in me to have quitted his son unless I could have settled him advantageously in this place. I have therefore obeyed my sense of duty and am here for two years longer. Mr B. is a man of warm feelings, but I confess I have no implicit confidence in the permanence of his attachments or intentions.*

On the 21st Sydney was able to write to Mrs Hicks Beach that he would take a house in Edinburgh until spring 1803—'I am flattered with the confidence in me which Mr B. and you both express, and which I hope you will not find misplaced. . . . I hope now when we meet, we shall be as good friends as we used to be.'* Sydney soon restored himself to his old footing with his patrons, but the episode of the salary negotiations had taken its place with the marriage settlement in the growing repertory of paternal acrimony.

As some compensation for the restricted salary he received for William Hicks Beach, Sydney was allowed to take other pupils. The first to arrive was a young Powlett, son of Lord Bolton, who entrusted him to Sydney on satisfactory terms (£400 a year) in October 1801—'young Powlett is about 19, awkward, and reserved, and not of interesting appearance,'* Sydney told his father, 'but he appears to be mild and ductile. With his father I have had some correspondence, he writes like a gentleman and man of sense.' Sydney realized that his father would be stimulated by the thought of noble patronage, so added the observation that:

Every parson and every relation of the said parson imagine that the moment he is connected with a Lord, that he has nothing to do but to study tithe law, to amuse himself in planning barns of different constructions, and to order a buggy of the very best sacerdotal shape. As for me, I confess my ideas are rather lower and more practical— a few dinners, my salary well paid, the power of applying for a frank, a bow in the public streets, and a good deal of commendation behind my back—these are the limits of my expectation, and the probable limits of my good fortune.*

Powlett was not a good catch ecclesiastically, Sydney writing a fortnight later that 'I have already discovered three clergymen his relations who are hanging upon him—so that you see my chances of any advantage beyond my salary is not very brilliant.'* And although he had assured Mrs Hicks Beach 'that William cannot possibly be injured by his society', Sydney clearly found something odd about the young man—'a very eccentric being' (as he had told his father) 'but I am in hopes I shall make something of him'.* Sydney's efforts were unsuccessful, however, and early in the new year he had to report to Mrs Beach that 'Mr Powlett ran away, and behaved in so extraordinary a manner, that I was forced to desire Lord Bolton to remove him immediately—the melancholy particulars you will learn from William. I pity the father extremely, who appears from his letters to be a very amiable feeling man.'*

The second additional pupil was much more satisfactory. He was 'a Mr Gordon natural son of the late Lord Aberdeen, aged

18', who arrived in December 1801.* 'A very mild amiable young man' was Sydney's considered judgement on young Mr Gordon (later of Ellon) who proved to be an excellent companion for William Hicks Beach and remained a friend of Sydney's for the rest of his tutor's life.* William himself was a much more apt pupil than his brother—trustworthy, moderate, and studious. Sydney's reports to his parents are therefore rather dull reading: 'He evinces ... above all, a steady, unshaken good conduct in the midst of the liberty I have purposely indulged him—I have always said that the greatest object in education is to accustom a young man to be his own master.'* Not even the freedom Sydney allowed his pupil could bring him out to paternal satisfaction. Sydney wrote to William's father in May 1802, when sending his annual account and reporting the progress of his studies:

You hinted to me that his disposition was more reserved than you wished—the remark is certainly just, but the habit of mind is I am afraid too strong for correction. He will probably remain a cautious, deliberate man as long as he lives—a character not certainly exactly the very model we should select, but which contains many advantages if it has some unpleasant traits—but on the whole, my dear Sir, you must allow me to say, you have not only no cause to complain, but much to be proud.*

Any resentment Robert Smith may have felt at not being allowed to solicit Lord Bolton's interest on Sydney's behalf was dispelled by the illness and death of his invalid wife. She had long been in poor health, as Sydney's letter of condolence pointed out: 'the only rational topic of consolation to all of us is that a life harassed by constant sickness of body, and threatened with a total imbecility of mind, is better closed—after the feelings of nature are subsided there can be no doubt of such an opinion. I will not, however, renew a set of feelings in your mind calculated only to inflict pain ...'* Sydney invited his bereaved father and sister to Scotland by way of diversion, in a letter which should have had a soothing effect. Not at all. Robert Smith's reaction can be judged from Sydney's next letter:

I have received an answer to my invitation in which you call me Rascal, Villain, Fool, Scoundrel, Pedant, etc. All these opprobrious epithets, as well as your animadversions upon my wife, I *do* now as I have often *done* before very sincerely forgive. Any condemnation of my conduct by you founded upon facts, and expressed with moderation and dignity I should very seriously regret. But after an experience of fifteen years, this very energetic language produces no other effect upon me than to make me regret the unhappy state of mind which must have given birth to it.*

The marriage settlement problem and a slanderous accusation of his being a mercenary adventurer passed on by Robert Smith from a London gossip are again explained, but to no avail. Sydney's Christmas letter of 1801 puts an end to the correspondence, ending with a forgiveness (which his father must have found most unwelcome) 'for the numberless and most injurious invectives that my well meant invitation to the family has drawn down on myself and my poor wife'.*

The settlement of the tutorial problem for the time being allowed Sydney to plan ahead for his next few years of residence in Edinburgh, and this stability may have helped a promising literary scheme to germinate. Towards the end of 1801 Sydney's acquaintance in Edinburgh had grown amongst the younger and brighter Whig advocates and others about the University, in the Academy of Physics, and on the fringes of the Speculative Society, the even then well-established debating club. Such contacts led to the projecting of an unusual venture which is the foundation of his main claim to literary fame. Sydney's best-known account of the foundation of the *Edinburgh Review* is given in the preface to his *Collected Works* in 1839. Recalling his time in Edinburgh, he wrote that

Among the first persons with whom I became acquainted were Lord Jeffrey, Lord Murray (late Lord Advocate for Scotland), and Lord Brougham; all of them maintaining opinions upon political subjects a little too liberal for the dynasty of Dundas, then exercising supreme power over the northern division of the island.

One day we happened to meet in the eighth or ninth story or flat in Buccleuch-place, the elevated residence of the then Mr Jeffrey. I proposed that we should set up a Review; this was acceded to with acclamation. I was appointed Editor, and remained long enough in Edinburgh to edit the first number of the Edinburgh Review. The motto I proposed for the Review was
    'Tenui musam meditamur avena'
    ('We cultivate literature upon a little oatmeal')
But this was too near the truth to be admitted, and so we took our present grave motto ['Judex damnatur cum nocens absolvitur'—'The judge stands condemned when the guilty is acquitted'] from Publius Syrus, of whom none of us had, I am sure, ever read a single line;

and so began what has since turned out to be a very important and able journal.*

This account written late in life contains a number of inaccuracies—Brougham's early involvement cannot be proved, for example—and several other biased or jocular reminiscences by the contributors fail to clarify the history of the foundation. Professor John Clive has analysed the conflicting evidence carefully in his *Scotch Reviewers* (1957). His findings are strikingly confirmed and expanded by a letter of 13 January 1802 from Sydney to James Mackintosh, which provides the earliest detailed evidence of the planning of the *Review*:

Allen, Thomson, Horner, Murray, Jeffrey, Hamilton and myself intend to undertake a review. The two first confine themselves to chemical and medical subjects. Hamilton is extremely strong in oriental languages and has already reviewed a good deal in the Asiatic Register. Jeffrey is an extremely clever little man who will write *de omni scibili*. Brown will assist. I mean if possible to persuade Maltby to give us some classical articles, and we shall have aid from many other literary men more obscure than they deserve to be. It is our intention to comprehend foreign as well as domestic publications, to put out a 5s. volume every quarter day, selecting works of some merit and passing over all the refuse of the press.

The rocks and shoals to be avoided are religion, politics, excessive severity, and irritable Scotchmen. If nothing else, the common sense of every man concerned will of course teach him the necessity of the utmost decency upon the two first points, in the third point I do not think we shall offend over much, and in the last the danger of a broken head will make us wise.

You will do me and my associates a very great favour if you will point out to us what bookseller in London is mostly likely to be active in pushing forward the publication. We wish to derive no pecuniary emolument from it for the first year, and have chosen Constable for our Edinburgh bookseller.

What do you think of the form of the publication, and of the probability of sale? We wish to weigh the matter well, and if your literary experience can suggest anything for the improvement of the plan, we shall be extremely thankful to you for your counsel.

I have less scruple in troubling you, because I have observed that you are very demotic to poor authors, and that you often make use of your eminence to give others a helping hand. If any of the members of the King of Clubs have a mind to barbecue a poet or two, or strangle a metaphysician, or do any other act of cruelty to the dull men of the earth, we are in hopes they will make our journal the receptacle of their exploits. We shall make it a point of honour neither to mutilate contributions, nor to reveal the names of contributors.

We are rather sanguine as to the success of the scheme—indeed so much so that we talk of hiring a critics' room in the old town at fifty shillings per annum, though to this the more prudent part of the confederates object as a rash anticipation of ideal funds and imaginary prosperity.

Whatever good may result from the scheme, or whatever evil, it will at least have the effect of imparting some degree of animation to this metaphysical monastery....

We do not intend to publish our first volume before Midsummer....
We shall certainly have Dugald Stewart, Parr, and Rennel in the first Number, and I hope you will give us an opportunity of adding another celebrated name.*

There, at some length (a little gossip has been omitted), is Sydney's own account of the origins of the *Review*, which first appeared in October 1802. Except for the vague threat of retaliation against the *Anti Jacobin* for its partial treatment of his *Sermons*, this is the earliest available evidence, and it confirms the patient reconstructions of modern scholarship. Sydney had first met Mackintosh in London the previous summer, when he had reported to Jeffrey 'I never saw so theoretical a head which contained so much practical understanding'—not his usual opinion of Edinburgh metaphysicians.* Mackintosh, then making his reputation as a lawyer and as a man of letters, was one of the founders of the King of Clubs, a small Whig dining club, several of whose members became contributors to the *Edinburgh Review*. Despite Sydney's pressing invitation, he did not write for the *Review* until 1812, after he had returned from India.

From this letter and other evidence, it can be seen that it was Sydney Smith who proposed the idea of a review to Jeffrey and Horner late in 1801; others joined them, such as the scientific and oriental specialists mentioned, but Brougham (who later claimed an early involvement, but is significantly absent from Sydney's list) was apparently not fully admitted until the following April, by which time his early enthusiasm for the scheme had waned. Sydney may not have been appointed editor quite so formally as he later described, but along with Jeffrey and Horner he supervised the production of at least the first issue. The administrative particulars of the early numbers are less important, however, than the actual suggestion of the scheme. It was clearly Sydney Smith who proposed the foundation of the *Edinburgh*

Review. As an independent and original Whig quarterly it was to set a standard and a pattern for much of the serious periodical journalism of the nineteenth century. The debt which Edinburgh owed to its *Review* was enormous, and Sydney's role in the foundation was not forgotten. In 1823 Sir Walter Scott (an occasional contributor to the early numbers, though no sympathizer with its politics) remarked in a letter: 'Constable who was here on a visit the other day was very scholarly tracing an animated change which took place in Scottish letters some thirty years ago to the various associations formed round a certain Soph of Oxford, who set all our latent energies a-stirring; and truly when I recollect some passages of that time I cannot help being much of his opinion.'*

Sydney Smith's contribution to the *Edinburgh Review* was not merely that of general activator and editor of the first issue or issues. He was a contributor from the beginning, writing with a surprising maturity from the very first, in a plain style that remains remarkably consistent. Although the reviews and essays he wrote while still in Edinburgh had not had engrafted on to them the campaigning style of his later *Edinburgh Review* articles, his earliest contributions did help to set the tone of the journal, in aggressiveness as well as in pertness and humour. As with the development of the periodical itself, where a project undertaken with commendable lightness of heart soon began to find that it carried real literary and political weight, Sydney was to find that his own contributions, started lightheartedly enough, possessed a considerable force. Absurdity was originally reckoned part of the game. 'You may very possibly consider some passages in my reviews as a little injudicious and extravagant,' he had written to Jeffrey while the first number (to which Sydney contributed no less than seven of the twenty-nine essays) was being prepared: 'Never mind, let them go away with their absurdity unadulterated and pure. If I please, the object with which I write is attained; if I do not, the laughter which follows my error is the only thing which can make me cautious and tremble.'*

Many of the books he undertook while in Edinburgh were volumes of sermons, and he had not yet turned his attention to the major public issues where his impact was really felt. Occasionally he reviewed literature—Madame de Staël's *Delphine* was dismissed with bland insularity as 'dismal trash, which has nearly dislocated the jaws of every critic among us with gaping'—but he was sensibly to keep away from purely literary matters in which Jeffrey and others were to give the journal a formidable reputation. His opening contribution, a review of a sermon by Samuel Parr, with an overlong appendix, was typical:

Whoever has had the good fortune to see Dr Parr's wig, must have observed, that while it trespasses a little on the orthodox magnitude of perukes, in the anterior parts, it scorns even Episcopal limits behind, and swells out into boundless convexity of frizz, the μεγα σωμα of barbers, and the terror of the literary world. After the manner of his wig, the Doctor has constructed his sermon, giving us a discourse of no common length, and subjoining an immeasurable mass of notes, which appear to concern every learned thing, every learned man, and almost every unlearned man since the beginning of the world.*

The reviewer was, however, prepared to allow some merit to the Doctor, in spite of an excessive weight of learning—and an excessive ponderousness of style. Sydney's very first *Review* paragraph contains many of the features of apposite simile, and of judiciously mixed light and heavy vocabulary ('convexity of frizz') which were to make his contributions so memorable.

Another characteristic note is discernible in a review of a sermon (dealing incidentally with the Corn Laws) by Archdeacon Nares (he of the *British Critic*) which was also published in the first volume of the *Review*:

A clergyman cannot be always considered as reprehensible for preaching an indifferent sermon; because, to the active piety, and correct life, which the profession requires, many an excellent man may not unite talents for that species of composition: but every man who prints, imagines he gives to the world something which they had not before, either in matter or style; that he has brought forth new truths, or adorned old ones; and when, in lieu of novelty and ornament, we can discover nothing but trite imbecility, the law must take its course, and the delinquent suffer that mortification from which vanity can rarely be expected to escape, when it chooses dullness for the minister of its gratification.*

There is Sydney in his judicial mode, employing a tone which was also to be developed in his writings. It was concluded of Nares that 'He may be a very hospitable archdeacon, but nothing short of a *positive miracle* can make him an acute reasoner.' Even Jeffrey, himself no stranger to severity, was rather alarmed by these strictures when he saw them in proof. Sydney, in reply, begged him to recollect the facts.

That Nares is in point of talents a very stupid and a very contemptible fellow nobody pretends to deny. He has been hangman for these ten years to all the poor authors in England, is generally considered to be hired by government, and has talked about social order till he has talked himself into £6 or 700 per annum. That there can be a fairer object for critical severity I cannot conceive. . . . I confess I cannot see why the cumulation of public and private vengeance should not fall upon his head. If you think that the violent attack may induce the generality of readers to sympathize with the sufferer rather than the executioner . . . then your objections to my criticism are good for the very opposite reason to that which you have alleged—not because they are too severe, but because by diminishing the malice of the reader they do not attain the greatest possible maximum of severity.

And as for the *ad hominem* nature of the attack, on which Jeffrey must have registered a protest:

As for personalities grant that the man is a proper object of punishment, and in these literary executions I do not care for justice or injustice a fig. My business is to make the archdeacon as ridiculous as possible. The readers to whom I write will allow me some personalities and refuse me others. I could not, and would not, say that the man was a bad husband or a cruel father, but nobody (but the very correct few) will be offended with my laughing at his dignities in the church.*

We have already come a long way from Sydney's prospectus to Mackintosh, that 'excessive severity' would be avoided by the common sense of the projectors.

The *Review* caught on and soon acquired a following well beyond the expectations of the conspirators, and of the publisher who in the spring of 1803 sought Sydney's opinion on whether it should be continued after the preliminary experimental period. Naturally enough, the reply was enthusiastic:

I have no manner of doubt that an *able, intrepid* and *independent* review would be as useful to the public as it would be profitable to those who are engaged in it. If you will give £200 per annum to your editor, and ten guineas a sheet, you will soon have the best review in Europe. This town, I am convinced, is preferable to all others for such an undertaking, from the abundance of literary men it contains, and from the freedom which at this distance they can exercise towards the wits of the south. The gentlemen who first engaged in this review will find it too laborious for pleasure; as labour, I am sure they will not meddle with it for a less valuable offer.*

Thus the *Edinburgh Review* was firmly founded, a major gift by Sydney to the city in which his all too brief sojourn was coming to an end.

The Smiths' domestic routine had been disturbed in February 1802 by the birth of their first child—a daughter, as they had hoped. She was called Saba ('merely because she must have some name, and I thought that a pretty one') in humorous biblical reference.* The baby did well, but the mother was left very weak after her lying in. 'Mrs Smith is compelled to give up her nursing', Sydney wrote to Mrs Beach late in March, 'a great mortification to her, but a sacrifice to absolute necessity. With a set of strange servants, and in a foreign land, I have been forced to be head nurse, and head everything, and my variety of occupations have left me but little leisure for correspondence.'* In spite of her husband's busy nursing, Catharine Smith only recovered slowly, and two months later they set off for Burntisland on the other side of the Forth. As Sydney wrote to Caroline Fox (Lord Holland's sister) in June, 'The little town hitherto only celebrated for the cure of herrings will I hope in future be equally so for the cure of wives.'* Sea bathing and a quiet summer mended the ailing mother, with the help of Sydney's cheerful expedients:

Nothing can be more delightful than the situation in which we are placed, and you would laugh to see the various contrivances to which we have had recourse to make our cabin comfortable. Our meat larder is a hamper and is slung to a beam, Mrs Smith's dressing table a herring barrel—her bell a pair of tongs passed through the door—the books are kept in the corner cupboard with the yellow pickles—and all sorts of articles for the brains and the stomach, hard and soft, sweet and sour, corruptible and incorruptible, are huddled together.*

As for the baby, Sydney found her a charming child—'the only defect I have yet found in her character is that when I take her in *my* arms, she is apt to express her gratitude in a manner that makes it necessary she should be restored to the arms of her nurse; this little imperfection I am assured will disappear as she comes to years of discretion.'*

A short tour to Loch Lomond and the West seems to have finally restored the mother's health. 'Nothing amused me so much on the tour,' Sydney wrote to Mrs Beach, 'as the severe censure Mrs Smith received from the landlady at Luss for asking for a clean towel in preference to a dirty one—a preference the good hostess seemed to attribute entirely to caprice.'*

In January 1803 he received an invitation to stay on for yet another year with William Hicks Beach, but wisely declined the offer, as he now had pressing personal considerations:

I have one child, and I expect another: it is absolutely my duty that I should make some exertion for their future support. The salary you give is liberal; I live here in abundance; but a situation in this country leads to nothing. I have to begin the world at the end of three years, at the very same point where I set out from; it would be the same at the end of ten. I should return to London, my friends and connexions mouldered away, my relations gone and dispersed; and myself about to begin to do at the age of forty, what I ought to have begun to do at the age of twenty-five.*

It was not just his own career and his family's prospects which Sydney had in mind. He felt that William ought to go to university, in spite of his mother's anxiety that he might fall into bad company. Sydney gently set aside these maternal apprehensions—'I said that there could be *no good education* without danger, and that the age and disposition of the party were such as to reduce that danger within bounds in which it would be timidity rather than prudence to fear it.'* Given William's studious mind and his bent for mathematics, Sydney recommended that he should be sent as a commoner to Trinity College, Cambridge. 'You know what a lottery Education is,' he told the boy's mother, 'but as far as wisdom has any influence upon it, I think this scheme the best.'* He acquiesced quite willingly, however, when the parents decided to send William to Oxford, and made arrangements for his journey south and reception at the university. His final letter from Edinburgh to Mrs Hicks Beach contains a pleasing tribute to a relationship which, although it had not been without its awkward patches, had also been of enormous personal importance to Sydney:

I cannot take leave of you in silence without thanking you individually for the distinguishing kindness that you have ever shown to me. If ever I can be of any service to you and yours, you will find me sincerely desirous of showing my respect and regard. I would say more on this point if I were not aware of your incredulity.*

So ended the delicate but beneficial tutorial relationship with the Hicks Beach family. The breaking off from Edinburgh friends was no less difficult. Two years previously Sydney had written to Jeffrey: 'It will cost me much to tear myself away from Scotland, which, however, I must do when the fulness of time is come. I shall be like a full-grown tree transplanted—deadly sick at first, with bare and ragged sinews, shorn of many a root.'* Jeffrey himself, with whom Sydney had made the closest of his Edinburgh friendships, was as distressed at the uprooting as Sydney. He wrote to Francis Horner just after the Smiths had left:

I am quite inconsolable at the departure of the Smiths. They leave Edinburgh, I believe, this day, and they leave nobody in it whom I could have spared more easily. There has been a sad breaking up of the society in which we used to live so pleasantly; Hamilton, and Horner, and Allen, and now the Smiths. I hope we shall meet somewhere again, though I despair of seeing those careless and cordial hours that we have formerly spent together. In Heaven it will be quite another thing, I am told. However, let us write to each other, and keep away the approaches of strangeness as long as possible.*

Jeffrey had obviously just written to the Smiths in a similarly affectionate tone. Sydney acknowledged it with his farewell to Edinburgh, written from the inn at Tuxford on the London road:

I left Edinburgh with great heaviness of heart. I knew what I was leaving, and was ignorant to what I was going. My good fortune will be very great if I should ever again fall into the society of so many liberal, correct, and instructed men, and live with them on such terms of friendship as I have done with you, and you know whom, at Edinburgh.*

CHAPTER II

�֎

LONDON was to bring the Smith family a greater but more precarious prosperity, a much increased social circle, and the opportunity for Sydney to develop his literary range as lecturer and pamphleteer. Even though he was only thirty-two when he first settled in London, he was of course far from unknown in the metropolis, where he had already many friends—most of them lawyers—and where his entrée at Holland House had previously been established. While they looked for a house of their own they were lent a house in Cavendish Square by Sir Gerard Noel, who also had Sydney made auditor of the New River Company, a small job producing a useful £70 of extra annual income. Within a few weeks they had moved to 8 Doughty Street, near Gray's Inn, which was to be their home for some three years until, with improved finances, they moved to 18 Orchard Street, Portman Square. They were able to establish themselves decently in Doughty Street because Catharine's mother had died soon before they left Edinburgh, bequeathing her some valuable jewellery. Feeling that such jewels would be out of place on an impoverished clergyman's wife, Mrs Sydney raised £500 for them from Rundell and Bridge, which conveniently covered all their modest requirements on setting up house in town.*

The small house in Doughty Street, convenient for their legal friends, was their first independent home and the focus of Sydney's social and domestic life. A second child, Noel, was born shortly before they left Edinburgh. He fell ill there, with alarming symptoms of convulsive fits and whooping cough. 'I sat up with him for two nights, expecting every moment to be his last', Sydney wrote to Jeffrey (who had lost an only child the previous year): 'My great effort was to keep up Mrs Smith's spirits, in which I succeeded *tolerably* well.'* The little boy's recovery was only temporary, and he died in December. 'Children are horribly insecure: the life of a parent is the life of a gambler', Sydney wrote.* The following year Catharine became pregnant again, occasioning her husband further anxiety. 'I have been expecting she would be brought to bed every night for the last eight days', Jeffrey was informed in February 1805, 'but to the amazement of the obstetric world she is still as pregnant as the Trojan horse. I will advertise you of her delivery.'* Sydney was too harassed at the time of the birth to send news to Edinburgh, as his wife and the baby son—Douglas—were extremely ill for several weeks; but they rallied and all was well by April. A second daughter, Emily, was born in 1807—apparently quite safely, as her arrival elicited scarcely any comment; a fifth child, Wyndham, came six years later when they were living in Yorkshire.

Doughty Street soon became a meeting place for an ever-increasing circle of acquaintance. Neighbouring lawyers such as Romilly, Scarlett, and Mackintosh were amongst Sydney's earliest friends in London. Edinburgh friends who had left for London gathered in a small group at Mackintosh's for one night a week and at Sydney's another; Samuel Rogers and Richard ('Conversation') Sharp also joined in.* The pattern of intimate and informal sociability established in Edinburgh was continued into Sydney's London life with regular weekly suppers providing the atmosphere in which his humorous and mental gifts developed so rapidly. He often reported to Jeffrey on the progress of their common friends. Francis Horner (who 'lives very high up in Gordon Court, and thinks a good deal about mankind') they both regarded with affection, but his busy public life prevented Sydney from seeing much of him. 'He has four distinct occupations,' Sydney wrote to Jeffrey, 'each of which may very fairly occupy the life of a man not deficient in activity: the Carnatic Commission, the Chancery Bar, Parliament, and a very numerous and select acquaintance.' Some time earlier, Sydney had sent another favourable report: 'Horner is a very happy man; his worth and his talents are acknowledged by the world at a more early period than those of any independent and upright man I ever remember. He verifies an observation I have often made, that the world do not dislike originality, liberality, and independence so much as the insulting arrogance with which they are almost always accompanied. Now Horner pleases the best judges, and does not offend the worst. He will entirely excel Brougham.'* Henry Brougham, a later starter, was still jealously waiting for his parliamentary career to begin. After he had been sent as secretary to a foreign mission in 1806, Sydney wrote to the diminutive Jeffrey that 'Brougham is just returned from Portugal. It is rumoured that he was laid hold of by the Inquisition, and his buttocks singed with wax-tapers, on account of the Edinburgh Review. They were at first about to use flambeaux, conceiving him to be you; but upon recurring to the notes they have made of your height, an error was discovered of two feet, and the lesser fires only administered.'*

Occasionally Sydney was able to write cheerfully of being briefly neglected by an old Edinburgh friend, as of Dr 'Tim' Thomson in 1806: 'I met Timothy at a Club but he has not yet found his way here, at which I very much rejoice as it is a proof he is rising in the world—nothing affords me such genuine satisfaction as to be deserted by old friends because I love their prosperity much better than I love their company.'* Other Scottish friends aroused equally affectionate comment. 'Archy Alison is a charming fellow, his courtesy and affability like the loaves and fishes might easily be divided among 5,000 of his countrymen and many fragments left; he is an excellent man and improves by drink.'* Charles Bell, beginning his distinguished medical career in London, was 'modest, amiable, and full of zeal and enterprise in his profession. I could not have conceived that anything could be so perfect and beautiful as his wax models. I saw one today, which was quite the Apollo Belvedere of morbid anatomy.'*

Pen-portraits such as these show something of the range and the verve of Sydney's intimate social life during his early period in London; they also owe much to his having a regular and appreciative correspondent in Edinburgh. Sydney's friendship with Francis Jeffrey, which had been founded and fed on convivial intercourse, developed steadily by correspondence during the years Sydney spent in London. *Review* business kept them in touch, and Sydney's letters to his Edinburgh friend contain a remarkable mixture of editorial advice, private counsel, and general praise. He rejoiced in Jeffrey's growing personal reputation, coupled with that of the *Review* itself. He wrote late in October 1803 that 'you have raised up to yourself here, *individually*, a very *high and solid* reputation by your writings in the E.R. You are said to be the ablest man in Scotland, and other dainty phrases are used about you, which show the effect you have produced. Mackintosh ever anxious to bring men of merit into notice is the loudest of your panegyrists, and the warmest of your admirers.'* Such praise was not passed on uncritically; Sydney often comments adversely on the editor's own contributions, as in February 1807:

I must be candid with you, my dear Jeffrey, and tell you that I do not like your article on the Scotch Courts; and with me think many persons whose opinions I am sure you would respect.... You have made too some egregious mistakes about English law, pointed out to me by one of the first lawyers in the King's Bench. I like to tell you these things, because you never do so well as when you are humbled and frightened, and if you could be alarmed into the semblance of modesty, you would charm everybody; but remember my joke against you about the moon and the solar system;—'Damn the solar system! bad light—planets too distant—pestered with comets—feeble contrivance;—could make a better with great ease.'*

Three years earlier, he had sent Jeffrey a similar rebuke:

I ... protest against your increasing and unprofitable scepticism. I exhort you to restrain the violent tendency of your nature for analysis, and to cultivate synthetical propensities. What's the use of virtue? What's the use of wealth? What's the use of honour? What's a guinea but a damned yellow circle? What's a chamber-pot but an infernal hollow sphere? The whole effort of your mind is to destroy. Because others build slightly and eagerly, you employ yourself in kicking down their houses, and contract a sort of aversion for the more honourable, useful and difficult task of building well yourself.*

But well-developed suggestions of this sort are less frequent than occasional comments on individual articles and issues of the *Review*. Their letters show genuine regret of Jeffrey's distance from London: 'When are we to drink copiously of warm rum and water to a late hour of the morning?' Sydney asked him; 'When am I to see you again, and John Murray and everybody in the North whom I love and respect?'* Jeffrey had visited London in 1804, partly (as he wrote to his brother) 'on the pretext of recruiting for reviews, and of attending an appeal cause or two, but *entre-nous*, my chief motive has been to enjoy the society of some of my best friends, that are now settled in this place ...'.* His visits however were more infrequent, and Sydney looked forward to them with pleasure: 'You have earned a very high reputation here,' he told his friend in 1808, 'and you may eat it out in turbot at good people's houses if you please; tho' I well know you would prefer the quiet society of your old friends.'*

As in Edinburgh, Sydney relished the intimate conviviality of small dining clubs, and almost as soon as he arrived in London he was elected to the King of Clubs, the Whig group from which he had tried to recruit reviewers before the foundation of the *Edinburgh*. He was nominated by John Wishaw and James Mackintosh (who was soon to set sail for a recordership in India) in December 1803. The King of Clubs became one of the centres of Sydney's life and he played an important part in its activities, writing to Bombay about its members from time to time. A year after his election he reported to Mackintosh:

Nothing has occurred in the club. We have been Lemonade ever since you left us—we were punch before, and stronger in old Bobus's time whom God preserve and restore to his affectionate subjects at the Crown and Anchor.... The austere and decorous Romilly sometimes appears among us, but confines himself to his usual allowance of eight words, of which half are yes or no—I wish to God the prophet's mantle had fallen upon him, and that we could hear from him some of those interesting discussions ... which we all heard, and enjoyed in the society of the great Oriental Recorder.*

A similar jovial regret infused his letter to Mackintosh a few weeks later: 'We go on vigorously at the King of Clubs—and tho' we have lost two such vigorous limbs as Bobus the Priapist, and yourself, we are a very merry *torso* and are resolved to live it out to the last.'* Lady Holland, whose husband was a member, occasionally received information about their activities. Even Romilly's conversation improved, as early in 1809 Sydney wrote to Lady Holland that 'We have admitted a Mr. Baring, importer and writer, into the King of Clubs, upon the express promise that he lends £50 to any member of the Club when applied to. I proposed this amendment to his introduction, which was agreed to without a dissenting voice. I wish you would speak to Romilly about the levity and impropriety of his conversation—he is become an absolute rake, and Ward and I talk of leaving the Club if a more chaste line of dialogue is not adhered to.'*

The main innovation in Sydney's social life in London, and indeed one of the principal formative influences on his intellect and character, was his close association with Lord and Lady Holland and their circle at Holland House. His family connections (Bobus's wife was related to Lord Holland) and his other friendships had already secured him a first entry; what is remarkable is the speed with which he established himself as a habitué of the famous Whig *salon*. By 1805 he could write to Mackintosh in India:

With Lady Holland I believe you are acquainted; I am lately become so. She is very handsome, very clever, and I think very agreeable. She has taken hugely to the Edinburgh Reviewers, particularly to little John Horner—whose reputation as well as Brougham's are so high for political œconomy that they are fêted everywhere; and as in addition to their knowledge they are young and muscular, I have no doubt they will be called in to the personal assistance of the vicious part of the female nobility. Lord Holland is quite delightful; I hardly know a talent, or a virtue, that he has not little or big. The Devil could not put him out of temper; I really never saw such a man. In addition to this think of his possessing Holland House and that he reposes every evening on that beautiful structure of flesh and blood Lady H.*

Thirty years later, when Mackintosh's son returned Sydney's letters to his father, Sydney was able to allude to the 'magnificent [sic] structure of flesh and blood' reference, much to Lady Holland's amusement.* By then their intimate relationship had long settled into a pattern of sympathetic badinage: even in its early stages the friendship of Lord and Lady Holland was to be invaluable to a young man establishing his social and intellectual position.

Holland House—in still rural Kensington, just sufficiently out-of-town—provided the grand hospitality to which Sydney always responded so well, and a freedom of atmosphere in which his public personality could develop. His hosts were quick to discern his gifts, and he to appreciate their very different but complementary qualities. Lady Holland, rich and imperious, a vivacious and temperamental intriguer, but undeniably attractive mentally and socially; Lord Holland, benign almost to the point of blandness, disabled by a certain political naïvety and a too general liberality of thought from an effective political career, modest, tolerant, and lovable. They matched each other well and the mixture made their house the obvious and exciting gathering-place of the literary and political eminences of Whig society throughout the early nineteenth century. Their intimate companion, John Allen, contributed a great deal to the reputation of the house, more as a resident intellectual stimulus than as its librarian, physician, and familiar: and the Hollands owed their acquisition of this essential component of their *ménage* to Sydney. In 1802 he had written from Edinburgh recommending Allen as a travelling doctor: 'That he is a very sensible man you cannot long be ignorant, tho' I sincerely hope you may that he is a very skilful physician. You will speedily perceive that my friend Mr Allen (who has passed his life in this monastery of infidels) has not acquired that species of politeness which consists in attitudes and flexibilities—but he is civil, unaffected and good-natured. What to compare his French to, I know not: I never heard a sound so dreadful.'* By 1805 Sydney was able to report to Jeffrey that 'John Allen is come home in very high favour with Lord and Lady Holland. They say he is without exception the best-tempered man that ever lived, very honourable, and of an understanding superior to most people; in short, they do him complete justice. He is very little altered, except that he appears to have some faint notions that all the world are not quite so honourable and excellent as himself.'*

Sydney got on so well with Lady Holland partly because he was prepared to stand up to her notorious imperiousness, and determined not to be overawed. His response to her 'Sydney ring the bell!' was 'Oh Yes! and shall I sweep the room?', a neat rebuke and a warning which was well heeded.* And to Lord Holland he provided severe but pleasant criticism of his *Lope de Vega* (1806): 'You are naturally such an enemy to all kinds of affectation and foppery in style that you write in an untidy slovenly manner, and come in with your knees unbuttoned, coat and cravat untied, that nobody may call you a coxcomb.'* Such frankness was a good foundation for their friendship.

Sydney's name appears in the Holland House dinner books on innumerable occasions during his London years, and he was to be a frequent and discriminating guest there for the rest of his life. Most of the surviving anecdotes relate to his later years, but a letter from Lady Bessborough to Lord Granville Leveson Gower in December 1807 catches Sydney's conversational style during this earlier period:

At the Hollands' there were a motley company of lawyers, statesmen, critics and divines—Sydney Smith the only one of the latter class, in high glee attacking Mr Ward and Allen, telling them the best way to keep a merry Christmas was to roast a Scotch atheist, as the most intolerant and arrogant of all two legged animals. Allen did not look pleased, but kept clasping his hands together till his fingers cracked (a great trick of his). S.S. called out, 'See! there's one beginning to crackle already.'*

There were occasions, however, when others had the advantage of him in conversation. A few months earlier, the Prince of Wales (who did not know Sydney properly by name at the time) was present at dinner. The talk turned to wicked men: Sydney froze the table by announcing too challengingly that 'the wickedest man that ever lived was the Regent Duke of Orleans, and he was a *Prince*'. But the Prince of Wales was fully equal to such a remark. 'No,' he replied, 'the wickedest man that ever lived was Cardinal Dubois, the Regent's Prime Minister, and he was a *Priest*, Mr Sydney.'*

Later in life, he spoke to his daughter of his first introduction to Holland House—'the most formidable ordeal', as she put it, 'that a young and obscure man could well go through'. 'He was shy then', she added; but by the time he left London he had gained enormously in poise and confidence.* Acknowledging Lady Holland's New Year's gift of 1809, he wrote: 'Many thanks for two fine Gallicia hams; but as for boiling them in wine, I am not as yet high enough in the Church for that; so that they must do the best they can in water.'*

When announcing his betrothal to his father, Sydney had told him that 'It is my wish ... to push myself as a preacher either in Bath or London'.* This was easier said than done. Soon after his arrival in town, he reported to Mrs Hicks Beach: 'I have as yet found no place to preach in; it is more difficult than I had imagined. Two or three random sermons I have discharged, and thought I perceived the greater part of the audience conceived me to be mad. The clerk was as pale as death in helping me off with my gown, for fear I should bite him.'* The best he managed to acquire for himself, through the good offices of Sir Thomas Bernard, the philanthropist, was an evening preachership at the Foundling Hospital between March 1805 and October 1808; to this he later added another preachership at the Berkeley Chapel at the invitation of the owner Mr Bowerbank; these appointments and a similar one at the Fitzroy (proprietary) Chapel were to adorn the title-page of his second collection of sermons in 1809.

There was strong competition for these minor but lucrative appointments amongst the unbeneficed clergy of London. The bibliographical writer Thomas Frognall Dibdin reminisced about the 'combat-trials for preacherships', and wrote of the scores of candidates who proposed themselves for a newly erected Philanthropic Chapel. 'There was talk, too, of the Rev. Sydney Smith coming forward, the admitted pulpit-giant of the day,' Dibdin wrote with exaggerated hindsight thirty years later. He described Sydney's pulpit style as being like Caravaggio to the Guido of Moore (later of St. Pancras), who alternated with him at the Foundling Hospital. Sydney, Dibdin wrote, 'came down upon you as an overwhelming hailstorm of reasoning and invective, not unmingled with that occasional thunder and lightning of moral power, which drives the erring wretch into his lurking place and strongholds—if vice can be said to have *strength* anywhere!'* In spite of such florid testimony, Sydney was never successful in obtaining a chapel of his own in London.

A few comments have survived about his preaching at this time, which show that he could not have been reckoned an altogether safe candidate for a permanent appointment to a comfortable pulpit in one of the fashionable chapels. Haydon and Wilkie both approved—'I never heard a more eloquent man',* Haydon wrote after hearing a sermon of Sydney's in 1808. But his friend Ward (Lord Dudley) wrote to Mrs Dugald Stewart four years earlier that 'I am afraid his style is not likely to please London congregations. Its defects are obvious, and its merits, which are certainly not inconsiderable, quite beyond their comprehension.'* Lady Shelley, who attended the finishing school kept by Sydney's Aunt Olier in Gloucester Place, recalled late in life that 'He often preached at the Chapel we attended, his sermons being excellent moral essays. He would afterwards enliven our Sunday evenings with his fun, and not very clerical conversation.'* Augustus Hare's *The Story of My Life* gives a reminiscence of an old lady about Sydney's preaching in London:

He described the end of man—the 'portals of mortality'. 'Over those portals', he said, 'are written Death! Plague! Famine! Pestilence!' etc., and he was most violent. I am sure the poor man that had read the service and was sitting underneath would rather have been at the portals of mortality than where he was just then, for Sydney Smith thumped the cushion till it almost touched his head, and he must have thought the whole thing was coming down upon him. The lady [next to me] in the pew was quite frightened, and she whispered ... 'This is Sir Sydney Smith, who has been so long in the wars, and that is what makes him so violent.'*

Yet another reminiscence of Sydney in the pulpit is provided by Sylvester Douglas, Lord Glenbervie, who wrote disapprovingly of Sydney Smith in his *Diaries*, regretting the familiarity of his preaching and the lack of scriptural content in his sermons. As for the delivery, Sydney was reported by Glenbervie as having 'the neck of a little bull and two hands like thick raw beef steaks. He uses much action for an English clergyman and particularly has an awkward habit of clenching his right fist. Miss Berry thinks no man with such a hand should pretend to action, grace, or even taste. He certainly wants both the last, and it would be better for him if he would leave off the first.'*

There was some risk in his opinions as well as in their delivery. When his wife asked him to moderate an outspoken Foundling Hospital sermon which might offend some of their friends, his answer was 'I fear it will, and am sorry for it; but, Kate, do you think, if I feel it my duty to preach such a sermon at all, that I can refrain from doing so from the fear of giving offence?'* In 1807, when the Catholic question was again being agitated, Sydney preached controversially on Toleration, in the Temple Church. In the published version of the sermon (which was to become something of a favourite with his congregations), Sydney admitted in the preface that the subject was disagreeable, but he justified the publication thus:

Charity towards those who dissent from us on religious opinions is always a proper subject for the pulpit. If such discussions militate against the views of any particular party, the fault is not in him who is thus erroneously said to introduce politics into the Church, but in those who have really brought the Church into politics. It does not cease to be our duty to guard men against religious animosities, because it suits the purpose of others to inflame them; nor are we to consider the great question of religious toleration as a theme fit only for the factions of Parliament, because intolerance has lately been made the road to power. It is no part of the duty of a clergyman to preach upon subjects purely political, but it is not therefore his duty to avoid religious subjects which have been distorted into political subjects, especially when the consequence of that disortion is a general state of error and of passion.*

A wholesome argument, but a dangerous one for a newly bene-ficed clergyman in search of preferment to set his name to.

Sydney's difficulty in obtaining a regular pulpit is well illustrated by his attempt to take over a chapel in the parish of St. James's, Piccadilly, in 1805. The Wedgwood company's London warehouse had attached to it the York Street Chapel, formerly Catholic but later occupied by Dissenters called Christians of the New Jerusalem. Sydney asked his friend Josiah Wedgwood for first refusal when the lease was up: 'I shall not be quite as enthusiastic a tenant as its present occupiers are, but I hope as good a one to you.'* Wedgwood agreed, but Sydney had to reckon with the rector of the parish, whose permission was essential. Dr Gerrard Andrewes (later to be Dean of Canterbury) was approached with a long and courteous request, urging that the applicant was not a merely fashionable preacher (one who would 'rather ... tell such truths as are pleasant than such as are useful') and that he would welcome the extra 'two or three hundred a year' which the York Street Chapel would give him. The tact of the first letter, which referred judiciously to Andrewes's own impecunious early career, was followed by one claiming that 'the question ... is a choice between fanaticism and the worship of the Church of England in your parish'.* Had Sydney been a Dissenter he could have set up shop without àny reference to the Rector, and with his keen eye for an embarrassing anomaly he reminded Andrewes of this. The reply was suave but discouraging; the Rector feared that it 'may not seem to indicate such a wish to promote your comfort as I in reality possess', and founded his refusal on his unwillingness to bind his successors by licensing an alternative place of Anglican worship in competition with his own church and its subsidiary chapels. Perhaps Andrewes's reference to 'your superior talents and abilities, with the happy gift you so eminently possess of rendering them useful', indicated also a feeling that the applicant was too clever by half.* The tone of the rectorial refusal provoked a reply from Sydney in which he argued against 'the absurd and disgraceful devotion going on there at present' and asked to be given precedence over 'a low and contemptible fanatic'.* Sydney also paraphrased his correspondent's argument between quotation marks (a sure sign of his indignation or mockery), but the letter cut no ice; Andrewes merely confirmed his unwillingness to admit the proposal, but added that 'at the same time I am sorry to be an obstacle in the way of your interest'.*

Although the Church provided obstacles to his working in London, Sydney received further encouragement from Sir Thomas Bernard, who had earlier obtained for him the Foundling Hospital preachership. The lay appointment which he owed to this benefactor brought him much popular renown. Bernard was an early supporter of the Royal Institution, where Davy's popular lectures on chemistry had caught the attention of a fashionable audience. Sydney was invited to give a series of Saturday lectures on moral philosophy, and eventually delivered three courses between November 1804 and the spring of 1806. 'I am reading lectures on moral philosophy at the Institution,' Sydney wrote to Mackintosh a month after he began, 'which I think is without any exception the most perfect example of impudence recorded in history.'* The effort of preparing the series was considerable, and at one time Sydney wrote to Jeffrey that he felt that he had overloaded himself with lectures as well as sermons: 'I wish I had your sanity and fertility at my elbow,' he added, 'to resort to in cases of dullness and difficulty.'*

Francis Horner wrote to Murray soon after Sydney's lectures started:

You would be amused to hear the account he gives of his own qualifications for the task, and his mode of manufacturing philosophy; he will do the thing very cleverly, I have little doubt, as to general manner, and he is sufficiently aware of all the forbearances to be observed. Profound lectures on metaphysics would be unsuitable to the place; he may do some good, if he makes the subject amusing. He will contribute, like his other associates of the institution, to make the real blue-stockings a little more disagreeable than ever, and sensible women a little more sensible.*

Horner's judgement is fair. Sydney did not intend his lectures to be anything more than elementary sketches, assembled largely from the works of major writers, but he did himself less than justice in referring to them years later as 'the most successful swindle of the season'.* The lectures were excellently adapted to their audience both in contents and in mood. Mrs Marcet recalled years later that 'I was a perfect enthusiast during the delivery of those lectures ... He who at one moment inspired his hearers with such awe and reverence by the solemn piety of his manner, that his discourse seemed converted into a sermon, at others, by the brilliancy of his wit, made us die laughing.'* Dibdin wrote in his gushing *Reminiscences* that although the subject of moral philosophy 'should seem to compose the muscles into unbending rigidity, and to forbid the exuberance of mirth, the humours, caprices, and follies of mankind were touched and treated with infinite power and effect; and now and then the lecturer would come down with a magnificently eloquent passage, or period, which showed the vigour of his conception and the felicity of his style, and which could not fail to electrify the audience.'* There are several examples of Sydney's hearers retaining throughout life a detailed memory of particular passages or illustrations, and many more must have recognized the portions which found their way into the *Edinburgh Review* a few years later in the essays on 'Professional Education', 'Female Education', and 'Public Schools'.

Sydney was agreeably surprised by the popularity of his lectures. There is ample testimony to his success. Miss Catherine

Fanshawe, a forgotten writer of decent light verse, sent an ode in the style of Gray to her friend Miss Berry, 'On buying a new bonnet to go to one of Mr Sydney Smith's lectures—"On the Sublime"':

> Lo! where the gaily-vestured throng,
>   Fair Learning's train, are seen,
> Wedged in close ranks her walls along,
>   And up her benches green!
> Unfolded to their mental eye
> Thy awful form, Sublimity,
> The moral teacher shows....
> Methinks we thus, in accents low
>   Might Sydney Smith address,
> 'Poor moralist! and what art thou,
>   Who never spoke of dress?
> Thy mental hero never hung
> Suspended on a tailor's tongue,
>   In agonizing doubt!
> Thy tale no flutt'ring female show'd,
> Who languished for the newest mode,
>   Yet dares to live without.'*

Sydney had an audience of up to six or eight hundred, and in April 1805 wrote to Jeffrey that 'My lectures are just now at such an absurd pitch of celebrity, that I must lose a good deal of reputation before the judgement of the public settles into a just equilibrium respecting them. I am most heartily ashamed of my own fame, because I am conscious I do not deserve it, and that the moment men of sense are provoked by the clamour to look into my claims, it will be at an end'.* While the clamour lasted, however, it was terrific. Mrs Spencer-Stanhope wrote to her husband in January that she had gone with 'five or six hundred others to hear Mr Sydney Smith lecture upon the "Conduct of the Human Understanding". His voice is fine and he is well satisfied with himself. I cannot say we came away much wiser, but we were well amused. I hear that Mr Smith protests that all women of talent are plain."* The tide of popular favour began to turn during 1805, and Sydney's notions and his levity were ridiculed in a prologue to a Westminster School play. According to the rather malicious Joseph Farington, 'this has caused him to adopt a *different manner*, and he cultivated the good opinion of the fair sex by warmly complimenting them on their natural talents and by urging them to devote themselves to substantial literary studies ..."* Attendances began to fall. In January 1806, Mrs Spencer-Stanhope wrote: 'What think you of Sydney Smith lecturing to small audiences? Such is popular favour. He may thank Westminster for the neglect he now meets with.'*

There was obviously a good deal of credit to be gained from such an appointment. Sydney himself remarked to Henry Reeve, for whom he tried to secure a medical lectureship from the organizing committee: 'I would advise you not to fling away this occasion, which is no despicable one for a physician; because he must be a devilish clumsy gentleman if in lecturing upon the moral and physical nature of man he cannot take an opportunity of saying that he lives at No 6 Chancery Lane, and that few people are equal to him in the cure of fevers.'* Sydney could not expect such direct benefits for himself, although there was a suggestion that he should become a professor at the London Institution, founded in 1805 to do for the City what the Royal Institution set out to do for Westminster; this proposal apparently came to nothing.* The three Royal Institution courses did much to establish his metropolitan reputation; they were adequately paid (though the fee does not seem to have increased with the attendance), but the receipts did nothing permanently to secure his precarious financial position.

Forty years later, William Whewell, Master of Trinity College, Cambridge, wrote to Sydney asking what had become of the lectures, and received a rather dismissive reply:

My lectures are gone to the dogs, and are utterly forgotten. I knew nothing of philosophy, but I was thoroughly aware that I wanted £200 to furnish my house. The success, however, was prodigious; all Albemarle Street blocked up with carriages, and such an uproar as I never remember to have been excited by any other literary imposture. Every week I had a new theory about conception and perception; and supported by a natural manner, a torrent of words, and an impudence scarcely credible in this prudent age. Still, in justice to myself, I must say there were some good things in them. But good and bad are all gone.*

The manuscript of some of the early lectures had indeed been destroyed, but his widow was able to salvage enough to make up a consecutive series of *Elementary Sketches of Moral Philosophy*, which was first privately printed for friends in an edition of 100 and then published in 1850. Jeffrey, who had at first doubted the wisdom of publication, was surprised by their quality, and urged Mrs Sydney to try a general issue.

The lectures contain no original or deep philosophical thought, but they are distinguished (as Horner had anticipated) by Sydney's wit and humour, and by the powers of arrangement and argument which his Edinburgh friends recognized as amongst his greatest accomplishments. In this they reflect the habits of mind he had acquired in Edinburgh as much as the debt which he owed to Dugald Stewart and the other Scottish philosophers he had met there. Perhaps the most important historical contribution of the lectures is their communication of contemporary Scottish thought to a general London audience. The lectures are packed with quotations, direct and indirect, from Reid, Brown, Stewart, and others. They open, indeed, with the definition of Moral Philosophy in the Scottish sense, as taught only at the Scottish universities—that is, not narrowly considered as ethics, but in the wider sense, contrasted with natural philosophy.*

Throughout the course, Sydney was careful to defend the philosophical speculations which he reports from the charge of scepticism. Even in 1804 he was bothered by the accusations— varying from those of mere heterodoxy to charges of out-and-out Holland House atheism—which were to be levelled at him by the ignorant or the prejudiced throughout his life. There are many phrases similar to the conclusion of his Introductory Lecture, 'All these things Moral Philosophy observes, and, observing, adores the Being from whence they proceed.'* They are not added to give a religious gloss to a secular text, but form an essential part of it. The lectures sometimes savour a little too much of the sermon. Occasionally there are ponderous cadences more suited to the pulpit than to the dais, and some of the tricks of style (such as long words used amusingly, or protracted assonances) which are found in the *Edinburgh Review* essays are missing from the lectures. But the general effect is far from drably parsonic.

Sydney gauged his audience well, sidestepping difficulties on their behalf: 'Professor Kant, the explanation of whose philosophy I really cannot attempt: first, from some very faint doubts whether it is explicable; next, from a pretty strong conviction that this good company would not be much pleased to sit for another half-hour and hear me commenting on his twelve categories ...'*

The lecturer's greatest expository skill was in analogy, and he makes many simple or topical allusions suited to his fashionable audience. Thus in the lecture 'On Taste':

So with a hiss: a hiss is either foolish, or tremendous, or sublime. The hissing of a pancake is absurd; the first faint hiss that arises from the extremity of the pit on the evening of a new play, sinks the soul of the author within him, and makes him curse himself and his Thalia; the hissing of a cobra di capello is sublime—it is the whisper of death!*

The confusion of beauty and utility is exposed in 'On the Beautiful' by the depiction of an extreme case, in the manner characteristic of much of his writings:

Go to the Duke of Bedford's piggery at Woburn, and you will see a breed of pigs with legs so short, that their stomachs trail upon the ground; a breed of animals entombed in their own fat, overwhelmed with prosperity, success, and farina. No animal could possibly be so disgusting if it were not useful; but a breeder, who has accurately attended to the small quantity of food it requires to swell this pig out to such extraordinary dimensions,—the astonishing genius it displays for obesity,—and the laudable propensity of the flesh to desert the cheap regions of the body, and to agglomerate on those parts which are worth ninepence a pound,—such an observer of its utility does not scruple to call these otherwise hideous quadrupeds, a beautiful race of pigs.*

The most famous of all Sydney's analogies comes in his lecture 'On the Conduct of the Understanding'.

It is a very wise rule in the conduct of the understanding, to acquire early a correct notion of your own peculiar constitution of mind.... It is a prodigious point gained if any man can find out where his powers lie, and what are his deficiencies—if he can contrive to ascertain what Nature intended him for: ... If you choose to represent the various parts in life by holes upon a table, of different shapes,—some circular, some triangular, some square, some oblong,—and the persons acting these parts by bits of wood of similar shapes, we shall generally find that the triangular person has got into the square hole, the oblong into the triangular, and a square person has squeezed himself into the round hole. The officer and the office, the doer and the thing done, seldom fit so exactly, that we can say they were almost made for each other.*

The example gained literary currency—Scott, in chapter IV of *The Pirate*, refers to this comparison made by 'a laughing philosopher, the Democritus of our day'—and it has long passed, with some variation of shapes, into general usage.

Two of the lectures deal with 'Wit and Humour'. The attempted definition reads heavily—Sydney's own practice is infinitely more amusing—but the lectures do contain a few points which are relevant to Sydney's own wit. One passage, for example, well describes his own effect in company and illustrates the reputation he was gaining in London society during his early years in the south:

the tranquil smile with which wit is received, is soon disturbed and roused into something more disorderly, when there is much reduplication of wit; when it comes out, as it does in some men, flash after flash, with a brisk multiplication of surprises, a continued irritability,—where one nerve no sooner ceases to vibrate than another is struck, and the mind is kept in a constant agitation of pleasure. In cases like this, I have very often seen wit produce loud and convulsive laughter.*

That description was certainly true of Sydney Smith's manner and effect in society, and British memoirs of over half a century contain frequent and unanimous references to it. The 'electric' nature of wit, which he sometimes refers to, means that it is essentially an ephemeral gift; conversations are writ in air. The autobiographers tend to recount the more elaborate jokes, and the then so fashionable puns which are not leavened by their exposition. Sydney's style was not merely one of *mots*; there was a high level of genial humour and banter which can never be recalled. His reference in his Royal Institution lectures to 'a constant agitation of pleasure' conveys something of the effect that he rarely failed to produce.

Not all Sydney's life in London was so happy or relatively successful. His relationship with his father deteriorated beyond redemption in these years, mainly (as one might expect) for financial reasons. At least Sydney was not the only brother to suffer at the time. During 1802 Bobus had been after a senior legal appointment in India, and he and his wife Caroline had urged Robert Smith to muster whatever interest he could manage with the Company. Bobus was appointed Advocate General of Bengal, but his father somehow contrived to find grounds for displeasure at the time of the appointment. Dissatisfaction was expressed and placated in a way which is familiar enough in Sydney's letters. Bobus was reasonable, his wife more passionate. 'Forgive one, forgive both your sons', she wrote to her father-in-law in the spring of 1803: 'if we are doomed to cross the sea with your curses receive at least the son that is left behind.'* Although communications between Robert Smith and his eldest son were resumed after Bobus had established himself in his lucrative Indian position, the breach was a serious one. It also helped to separate Sydney and his father the more. Thus Sydney had written in April 1803 to his father: 'my only dependance was upon the influence of my brother and Mrs Robert Smith—the moment I learnt what has happened with respect to them, I lost all thought of reconciliation'. 'I beg you will not take the language of despair for the language of indifference,' he continued; 'If writing like a suppliant would bring back days of peace to us all I would write like one—but I have no manner of doubt that your decision is taken, and I think it more manly and more respectful not to be your persecutor if I cannot be your son.' The marriage settlement and rejected invitation to Edinburgh were again rehearsed, and Sydney ended his letter humbly and benedictively:

I have always endeavoured to conduct myself like an honest and respectable man and not to disgrace the education you have given me. I am hurt I confess to find myself an outcast—but it will be a great consolation to me if you will notice my children as they grow up, and if anything happens to me, show some countenance to my wife—who has never meant harm to any human creature, and who has lost all her friends on my account. Accept my dear father my fervent thanks for all the kindness I have ever experienced from you, and may God Almighty bless and protect you.*

Thus by April 1803 the scene was set for the further animosities of the London years. Meanwhile Bobus had embarked for India, third of the brothers to seek and find his fortune there. Sydney reported sadly to Michael Hicks Beach that 'I have heard of my brother a day's sail from the Land's End, and hardly expect to hear from him again before he arrives in India. I feel quite an exile in England, and am almost tempted to consider India as my native country from the number of relations I have there.'*

Trouble was brewing in the East. Sydney's brother Cecil was a successful financial administrator in India, but had been concerned in several dubious ventures with Company money and with his wife. Sydney and his father had to act (usually at variance) as Cecil's agents in England. This scapegrace brother had been extravagant as a young man, and had married Eliza Topping, a spendthrift and flighty woman of discreditable parentage. Her habits had incurred Robert Smith's outspoken disapproval after she came home to England following the birth of an only child in 1798. Cecil was vigorous in his wife's defence, but he had to retract his praise soon after she returned to India early in 1802. Rumours of Eliza Smith's misconduct with a ship's officer on the journey out compelled him to send her straight back home again. Striking evidence of the liaison, including a ship-board abortion procured by massive doses of vinegar, and reports of the coarse jesting of the observant lascars, left no room for doubt. Cecil sent apologies to his father for his recent letters erroneously defending his wife; to her he indited a long and ring-ing rebuke. Her allowance was reduced (despite lachrymose and insincere protestations), and their child removed into the keeping of his grandfather and aunt. Robert Smith was urged to press for a divorce.* Sydney wrote to Caroline Fox that Mrs Cecil was to be reshipped: 'Government I suppose allow a bounty upon such re-exportations; her imprudence however is not a subject to joke about.'* A few months later, he added: 'Poor Mrs Cecil, her career is soon finished. She may still do her husband's fortune great injury, and I hope my father may consent to bring on a divorce.'*

Cecil had determined to sue for divorce up to the House of Lords itself, whatever the expense or the notoriety. He busied himself collecting evidence in India, urging his father in letter after letter to take steps in London to 'complete the first wish of my heart, viz. an eternal separation from all legal connection with that woman'.* Robert Smith delayed, eventually writing to say that he felt the evidence was insufficient and that he was unwilling to press the matter.* Cecil then turned to his brother for help, thus reviving the correspondence between Sydney and his father. Using Maria as an intermediary he wrote in November 1804, venturing to disagree that evidence was not obtainable: 'Sufficient evidence can only be procured by constant and un-remitting efforts of a person living in London, by free expenditure of money, and even by bribery—in short by all the arts well known to an active lawyer, and without the employment of which guilt would escape much more frequently than it does.'* Sydney therefore suggested that the money Cecil had sent should be put into trust, so that he could handle the business in London on his father's behalf, attempting to establish Eliza's guilt before the scheming and extravagance ruined her husband: 'I will pledge myself before six months are over my head to carry the divorce through the ecclesiastical courts and in a twelvemonth from that date to get it through the House, or ... to convince Cecil it is impossible. Even if the first divorce *a mensa et thoro* is obtained, he is protected from her debts though he cannot marry again.'*

Sydney had been greatly moved by an affecting letter he had received from India, part of which he quoted to his father: 'I do

not know whether my father has shown you the papers but I con-
jure you by all the ties which have ever united us to exert yourself
in this business and to see my father upon it. Do not let any little
quarrel which may exist between you and him deter you upon
this occasion. Consider that the happiness and salvation of the
brother who tenderly loves you is at stake.... my beloved
brother, try all means to relieve me from my misery.' 'I think
after this,' Sydney added, 'you will hardly call my interference
impertinent.'* He had already anticipated that difficulties would
arise from the 'little quarrel' and adopted an unusually concilia-
tory tone when first approaching his father through Maria. The
passage has been heavily deleted, but seems to read thus: 'I hope
my father will not imagine that any disagreement which exists
between us has induced me to stir in this business. He has treated
me and mine with concerted cruelty and injustice but I heartily
forgive him and wish him all happiness. I impute to him no
blame.'*

As usual, Robert Smith did not respond well to forgiveness.
He felt slighted by Sydney's activity, and the quarrel continued
in half a dozen letters in which Sydney attempted to maintain
as moderate a tone as his father's replies permitted:

It is not true (though I am sure you think it so) that I have arraigned
your *zeal*, your integrity, your abilities or your honour: I arraign only
your distance [from London] ... if I find that this correspondence cannot be carried on with more temper and good manners, I must also
beg leave to avoid that as well as our meeting. I have no longer anything to hope from you or anything to fear. You have long treated
me as an outcast, and a stranger, merely because I am poor, and therefore I must at least request that civility to which every stranger is
entitled.*

These sentences and others in the correspondence about Cecil's
divorce have the true ring of Sydney's most effective polemical
style. Beneath the firm tone there is a genuine desire for reconciliation throughout all the repetitive details of the divorce
negotiations. Their fruitless conclusion is explained in a letter
from Cecil to his father received in June 1806:

Your animadversions upon Sydney's conduct by no means accord
with the tenor of his letter to me—I never appointed him with any
power to interfere with your conduct, nor does it appear he ever
dreamt of such a thing. His letters express a serious regret at the unhappy cause of difference which divides you—and what he further

laments, his having enquired, for the sake of information to satisfy me, how the concern which he knew I had so much at heart was going on.... These are his own ... words from his letter now before me—'and as the matter stands at present, I do not see that a divorce could possibly be obtained. If any thing else comes out and there is any reason to believe that a more copious evidence is to come out, that may alter the nature of my father's proceedings, but at present I don't think he could do anything.' This my dear father is not like the arrogance of a fancied superiority or the impertinence of arranging your conduct—ideas as far, I am in my soul convinced, from Sydney's mind in writing, as they were from mine in writing to him, which was simply for information.*

Meanwhile a temporary reconciliation had taken place, and in spring 1805 Sydney had felt able to write to his sister Maria that 'I sincerely hope all difference of opinion is at an end between my father and me, and that I shall not give him cause to repent of this reconciliation for which I now sincerely thank him.... It is very probable I may have been misled by the very energetic, affecting letter of Cecil into a conduct disrespectful to my father—if so, I request him to include this in my apology also and he will add to the obligation he has already conferred upon me.'*
The simple background to this rapprochement is found in a letter Sydney wrote to Francis Jeffrey in April—'I am at last reconciled to my father. He was very ill, very much out of spirits, and tired to death with the quarrel the moment he discovered I ceased to care a halfpenny about it. I made him a slight apology—just sufficient to save his pride—and have as in duty bound exposed myself for these seven or eight years to all that tyranny, trouble and folly with which I have no manner of doubt at the same age I shall harass my children.'* Some sort of settlement was reached with Mrs Cecil. Her young son was brought up by his grandfather and his aunt Maria Smith. Sydney remained suspicious of his sister-in-law, later finding evidence of her continuing deceitfulness. For the moment, however, there was a lull in the storm between him and his father.
Such family problems, far removed though they are from the gayer round of dinners and sociabilities which are more characteristic of his life in London, have a particular place in his biography. Late in life, when he was settled in the opulence of private fortune and professional dignity, Sydney could afford to look back to his early years as a time of extreme poverty. His family

correspondence shows that in a far from uncommon manner he was inclined to exaggerate his sufferings. He seems to have been not too badly off as an unbeneficed clergyman; it was a lack of security rather than a lack of money which was so worrying, and his father's harassing attitude must have added to the difficulties. The incident of Cecil Smith's proposed divorce was to be followed by others equally provoking.

The uneasy peace which Sydney had reached with his father in 1805 was soon to be broken by another financial dispute, this time caused indirectly by the generosity of the Indian sons to their family at home. Sydney was selected as paymaster because Bobus was making him an allowance of £100 a year, of which nothing is known beyond Saba's record.* Sydney wrote to his father on 31 December 1805: 'I am happy to inform you that my brother Robert has sent over £500 to pay to you which I shall do to your banker tomorrow, and the same every first of January. All the observation he makes upon it is, "Say to my father that it will give Caroline and me much pleasure if out of this sum he can contrive to let Maria see London once a year". I am sorry he had made me the instrument of his offer to you, because I am afraid it will be unpleasant to you; but remember I only do so as I am instructed and that if any thing displeases you, the fault is not mine.'*

Cecil later made an addition of £100 yearly exclusively for Maria, and Courtney also joined them in sending regular remittances to their father. Bobus's payment for 1806 seems to have been received without further comment, but in 1807 Sydney's misgivings about acting as agent were shown to have been well founded. He paid £499 7s. 6d. into his father's credit on 6 January 1807; Robert Smith's reply may be pieced together from his endorsement on Sydney's letter written to his sister on 9 January informing her of the transaction. First, he calculated the cost of an excise stamp on £500 to be only five shillings, and insisted on a full payment. He criticized Sydney's handling of the arrangement, and then (perhaps referring to a missing letter) launched into a tremendous outburst: 'How in common sense could you send so serious an attack on my father's peace? [He was writing his daughter's reply for her.] ... My father looking ever to the motive than the fact acquits you of intention to hurt his peace, but insists upon it that you are the most [illegible] and dunderhead [illegible] priest that ever unjustly gluttoned and gorged on the labours of man.'*

Rarely can a few shillings have produced such energy of language. Sydney's reply (to Maria) was moderate: 'I am sorry, not surprised, that I have offended my father respecting the transmission of this money; because previous experience has shown me how difficult it is, either from my want of skill or from the nature of the arrangements, to avoid giving offence.'* His letters contain much detailed discussion of procedures for stamping bills; he wrote, not unreasonably, that 'The message my father has sent about the stamps ... would be ungracious enough if I was an attorney changing a bill; he must surely forget that I am a mere uninterested agent fulfilling a very unpleasant task.'* Nearly a month afterwards he alluded to his father's fulminations, as transmitted by Maria: 'I am very glad you were in joke, but your letter had as little the air of it as anything I ever saw.'* A note of more genuine humour is found in a postscript added by Sydney's wife to a letter written when the row was at its height: 'My dearest Maria, I have only time to repeat my request that you would have the goodness to send a pattern of the cotton and needles to Mrs Olier as soon as you can ...', with a page of amiable domestic chatter which nicely offsets Sydney's restrained anger.*

The brothers continued to send their remittances, with Sydney acting as agent for several years, always against a background of petty financial wrangling. Sydney kept in touch with his father, who seems to have stood as godfather to Emily in 1807. In December of that year Sydney wrote to Lady Holland (with a by now familiar parody of Scotch philosophers) that he had visited 'the preceding phœnomenon' and had found him and the 'co-effect' well, but the tone of the letters remained strained.* Robert Smith continued to acknowledge the tributes of the east with almost as little grace as he showed their intermediary: but the Indian sons could scarcely have expected any politeness. As agent for his brothers, Sydney was treated with uncommon ill-temper and coarseness.

While Robert Smith disputed with Sydney the minute particulars of the Indian remittances, news reached England of further misdemeanours by Cecil. 'I am afraid Cecil has been playing the fool in India most egregiously,' Sydney reported to his sister in January 1807, 'a whole host of accusations is come over against him upon the subject of accounts, and he is certainly suspended.'* Cecil was found at fault for having received the notes of a private bank not approved by the Company, instead of dollar bullion,

in defiance of official instructions. There was no charge of pecula-
tion, but party feeling was running high at Madras. Cecil was
first removed from his Chief Accountantship, with another senior
officer, but he was held competent to fill an equivalent post in
the future. Sydney busied himself in London throughout 1807
on behalf of the family, doing as much in his brother's favour
as propriety would allow. 'You need not make apologies to me
about trouble,' he wrote to his sister. 'I am always willing to take
any trouble whatever for my father or you—when the object is
reasonable, and the manner civil.'* Robert Smith remained in the
country, apparently accepting Sydney's news and advice.
'Lamentations are in vain,' Sydney wrote on receiving news of
the committee's decision; 'I am most heartily vexed and chag-
rined at this business—but we must make the best of it we can,
and contrive if possible that he be appointed to as good a situation as he held before.'* On appeal and after local investigation,
Cecil was eventually acquitted. Sydney kept discreetly in touch
with influential administrators in London and wrote to his sister
at the end of 1807: 'As I have *no doubt* of his honourable acquittal
he will be restored therefore with arrears about August 1808, and
the whole business will amount to a year's suspension—which
though unpleasant will teach him to confine himself to the letter
of his instructions and not to attempt to benefit the honourable
Company.'* Cecil worked in India for several more years, returning on leave (following a further dispute with the authorities) in
1809,* and again in 1813 after ill health had struck him; he died
at the Cape on the journey home. His son Cecil remained his
grandfather's ward and was sent to Eton and Balliol (Bobus's
contribution to the boy's expenses was long a cause of dispute
with his grandfather), and eventually became a clergyman. The
elder Cecil left a string of debts which were to trouble the family
until after Robert Smith's death. But no correspondence has survived between Sydney and his father about Cecil's later years.
The acrimonious communications about Cecil's scrape with the
Company, and about the tributes sent home by the other
brothers, virtually bring to an end Sydney's distressing exchanges
with his father, a prolonged and wretched series in his usually
cheerful correspondence. It forms an unexpected background to
a period in which Sydney Smith was becoming firmly established
as a social figure and, despite a formal anonymity, making his
reputation as a reviewer and pamphleteer of immediate and continuing renown.

Sydney had conveyed to Jeffrey the high regard in which he was held in London, but made it clear that it was the *Review* as well as its editor whose reputation stood so high. Soon after arriving from Edinburgh Sydney wrote that it had 'acquired a most brilliant and extensive reputation' and was 'uncommonly well done ... perhaps the first in Europe'. He and Horner promised to look out both for English and foreign books and for contributors: 'If any book enjoys a greater reputation here than you can conjecture it would from its title, we may send you information of it; and for a monthly search for foreign books you may depend upon us. I will stop such books as I want myself, but you had better give Horner a caution against stopping more books than he wants, as he is a sort of literary tiger, whose den is strewed with ten times more victims than he can devour.'*

From time to time Sydney had to complain of not receiving copies: 'That sebacic quadrupede Constable has omitted to send quarterly tributes of reviews to Horner and to me—to me, the original proposer of the Review, and to Horner, the frumentarious philosopher. If he is ever guilty of a similar omission, he shall be pulled down from his present exalted eminence to such distress that he shall be compelled to sell indecent prints in the open air in order to gain a livelihood.'* As soon as the *Review* arrived, it was eagerly read and subjected to close scrutiny and comment, which was not merely directed at the editor. For example, the review by Jeffrey which led Sydney to urge him 'to cultivate synthetical propensities' was discussed in a letter to Caroline Fox: 'I am almost certain at the time he wrote that review he had never heard of Dumont.... I would differ with you about the petulance of the review if by differing I could persuade you to adopt a contrary opinion, but as you have a very awkward knack of judging for yourself I make a merit of necessity and acknowledge you are right.'*

Praise was given where praise was due, severity was commended when it was justified. Sydney was always keen to notice lapses into the northern vernacular: of an 'exceeding good' number in 1804, 'were I to criticize it at all, I should say it was rather Doric.... There are several Scotticisms in Playfair's review.'* He was also obliged to warn the editor against a trend more potentially dangerous than linguistic provincialisms. 'I hear with great sorrow from Elmsley that a very antichristian article has crept into the last number of the E.R., inaccurate in point of history, and dull in point of execution', Sydney had written of a relatively inoffensive article in 1805: 'you must be thoroughly aware that the rumour of infidelity decides not only the reputation but the existence of the Review. I am extremely sorry too on my own account because those who wish it to have been written by me, will say it was so.'* Although Sydney did not contribute between January 1804 and October 1806, he remained necessarily cautious about his association with the *Review* while he was in search of preferment. But even after his ecclesiastical position was made more secure, he remained sensitive on the subject and in January 1808 wrote to Jeffrey regretting some 'levities' which he maintained Thomas Campbell had made in dealing with Hoyle's monstrously dull Miltonian epic, *Exodus*. Considering them 'ponderous and vulgar as well as indiscreet,' he held that 'Such sort of things destroy all the good effect which the liberality and knowledge of the Edinburgh Review is calculated to produce, and give to fools as great a power over you as you have over them. Besides the general regret which I feel from errors of this nature, I cannot help feeling that they press harder upon me than upon anybody—by giving to the Review a character which makes it perilous to a clergyman in particular to be concerned in it.'* Campbell's amusing strictures on a dreary religious poem seem quite mild and legitimate teasing: it is interesting to see that Sydney considered them objectionable, when the same issue of the *Review* contained his own notorious attack on the Methodists.

In the issue of October 1808, Brougham and Jeffrey collaborated in an essay on 'Don Pedro Cevallos and the French Usurpation of Spain', in which they praised the Spaniards who had risen against Napoleon, and condemned the upper classes generally, and demanding 'reform—change—revolution—salutary, just and necessary revolution' in the constitution of Britain as of other states. The Tories were deeply shocked, and many Whigs too. Sydney tried to reassure Jeffrey, when 'subscribers' were believed (in Scott's phrase) to be 'falling off like withered leaves', that 'Brougham's review is imprudent in its expressions—more than wrong in its doctrines; but you will not die of it this time, and are, I believe, more frightened than hurt.'* To Lady Holland he later reported on 'the consternation which the Sieur Brougham's attack upon the titled orders has produced: the Review not only discontinued by many people but returned to the Bookseller from the very first volume: the library shelves fumigated, etc.'*

The Tory reaction precipitated the foundation of the *Quarterly Review* as a strong right-wing rival to the *Edinburgh*: flattery by imitation, perhaps, but seen to be urgently necessary by Scott and the other founders when Jeffrey's journal appeared to be becoming more stridently radical. The radical swing was less obvious to the editor himself, who was distinctly frightened by the reaction the 'Don Cevallos' article had stirred up. Indeed he led Sydney to believe that there would be no more politics in the *Review*, but it turned out to have been *party* politics that he meant. The whole turmoil of the 'Don Cevallos' crisis made Sydney hesitate (but not for long) about continuing his contributions. 'I have not deserted you, nor had I the smallest intention of doing so,' he wrote to Jeffrey about an article he had been unable to write. 'Still, however, I am hesitating very much in my own mind about my future conduct with respect to the Review.... You will I am sure do me the justice to suppose that I am not making myself of consequence, but really reflecting upon a subject of importance to my future plans and future reputation.'* His rather hesitant letter enclosed a further review and his doubts were soon overcome, either in his own mind or at Jeffrey's persuasion.

The review which Sydney then had in mind was one on the Society for the Suppression of Vice, a sustained attack, as we shall see, on vigilante busybodies. It is typical of his *Edinburgh Review* output during his London years, before the Catholic question had come to dominate his political writings and before residence in the country turned his pen to rural causes such as Game Law reform. He was only an occasional contributor in his London years, not publishing anything in the *Review* between January 1804 and October 1806, when the pressure of lecturing work— and perhaps a certain prudence while actively in search of an ecclesiastical appointment—interrupted his flow of articles. Circumspection was essential. 'If I were to write on in the Review,' he had written to Jeffrey in February 1804, 'I would certainly not conceal myself, but I am much afraid it may not be in my power.'* He declared then that he was determined to write a book, but his resolution was wearing rather thin nearly two years later when he wrote to Jeffrey asking for titles of possible books for review: 'I am resolved to write some book, but I do not know what book. If I fail, I shall soon forget the ridicule; if I succeed, I shall never forget the praise. The pleasure of occupation I am sure of, and I hardly think my failure can be very complete.'* Even if his reviewing, intermittent throughout his London years, had dried up completely when he left town, his contribution to the *Edinburgh* up to 1808 would have been a very important one.

Some of his reviewing work is obviously related to his Royal Institution lecturing. Thus a short piece about Richard Lovell and Maria Edgeworth's *Essay on Irish Bulls* contains a definition similar to those he was delivering in Albemarle Street:

> Though the question [of the nature of bulls] is not a very easy one, we shall venture to say, that a bull is an apparent congruity, and real incongruity, of ideas, suddenly discovered. And if this account of bulls be just, they are (as might have been supposed) the very reverse of wit; for as wit discovers real relations, that are not apparent, bulls admit apparent relations that are not real. The pleasure arising from wit proceeds from our surprise at suddenly discovering two things to be similar, in which we suspected no similarity.... Practical wit discovers connection between actions, in which duller understandings discover none.*

It would, however, have been inappropriate to take such subjects too solemnly, especially in the context of such a 'rambling, scrambling book', written *con brio* by a 'nimble and digressive' Irishman whose literary energy Sydney describes with just a hint of pseudo-clinical vulgarity: 'He is fuddled with animal spirits, giddy with constitutional joy; in such a state he must have written on, or burst. A discharge of ink was an evacuation absolutely necessary, to avoid fatal and plethoric congestion.'*

A different reviewing technique was used in his article on the Methodists, published in 1808, and drawing on a jumbled string of quotations from enthusiastic testimonials to buttress a skilled and mocking attack on Dissenters, coupled with a warning to the established Church to beware the threat that was growing beneath them. The Methodist article, and a similar one on Protestant Missions in India, gave much offence to the Evangelicals and to late Victorian readers, when Wesleyan respectability was firmly established. Even in 1808 the levity of Sydney's descriptions of sectarian practices made Jeffrey (to whom the religious attitude of the *Review* was always a sensitive point) rather wary. Sydney wrote that he was glad the editor liked the Methodist article:

> Of the Scotch market you are a better judge than I am, but you may depend upon it it will give great satisfaction here [in London]; I mean, of course, the nature of the attack, not the manner in which it is executed. All attacks upon the Methodists are very popular with steady

men of very moderate understandings, the description of men among whom the bitterest enemies of the E.R. are to be found. I do not understand what you can mean by levity of quotation. I attack these men because they have foolish notions of religion. The more absurd the passage, the more necessary it should be displayed—the more urgent the reason for making the attack at all.*

It is, indeed, largly through the quotations that the review gains its comic force: the commentary is reasonable and not disrespectful of the religious decencies necessary to the writer's calling. Sydney's antipathy to the enthusiasm displayed in the absurd extracts from the *Methodist Magazine* was profound, an old-fashioned eighteenth-century low-church rationality. He felt that such ranting was a danger to true faith and to the establishment, and that he had a plain duty to attack it. Naturally enough, there were protests when his review was published, but in 1809 he returned to the offensive against 'the growing evil of fanaticism'. Indeed he began by congratulating himself on the first round: 'In routing out a nest of consecrated cobblers, and in bringing to light such a perilous heap of trash as we were obliged to work through, in our articles upon the Methodists and Missionaries, we are generally conceived to have rendered a useful service to the cause of rational religion.'*

Some of Sydney's best pages in the *Review* were not reserved exclusively for chastening the evangelical fervour of enthusiastic artisans. The proceedings of a body with the all-embracing title of Society for the Suppression of Vice were analysed in 1809 (some five years after the reports nominally under review), and were found wanting. The aims of the Society were felt to be misguided, and their attempts to enforce and strengthen laws against Sabbath-breaking and other immoralities offensive: 'We have no great opinion of the possibility of indicting men into piety, or of calling in the Quarter Sessions to the aid of religion. You may produce outward conformity by these means; but you are so far from producing (the only thing worth producing) the inward feeling, that you incur a great risk of giving birth to a totally opposite sentiment.' Nor were the Society's means commendable; the use of informers was discussed and ridiculed, and the pretensions of the organizers might give contrary results. 'There is something in the self-erection of a voluntary magistracy,' Sydney remarked, 'which creates so much disgust that it almost renders vice popular, and puts the offence at a premium.' He saw clearly the risk that a society like this, however well-meaning its founders, would 'degenerate into a receptacle for every species of tittle-tattle, impertinence and malice'.*

Sydney's main objection was to the social attitude of a Society largely made up of the prosperous classes, and entirely of members of the Church of England; its membership was by no means so all-embracing as its title. Their 'prevention of cruelty to animals' was in effect prevention of cruelty by the poor only; angling, fishing, hunting, boiling lobsters (all described in gruesome terms) were 'all high-life cruelties, with which a justice of the peace has no business to meddle. The real thing which calls forth the sympathies, and harrows up the soul, is to see a number of boisterous artisans baiting a bull, or a bear.... Heaven-born pity, now-a-days, calls for the income tax, and the court guide; and ascertains the rank and fortune of the tormentor before she weeps for the pain of the sufferer.' 'At present they should denominate themselves a society for suppressing the vices of persons whose income does not exceed £500 *per annum*' was the reviewer's conclusion.*

The Vice Society essay, with its apposite quotations, arguments turned upside-down, points thoroughly pressed home, with a fearless humour and clear, straightforward style, is typical of Sydney's approach as a periodical journalist. His contributions to the *Edinburgh Review* were of course anonymous, but they were often recognized as his—often enough to make his known association with that eagerly followed but discreditable journal a brave one for a man in his humble position. The risk was stated by none more clearly than George III himself. Sydney's daughter reports from about this time (the specific occasion is not known) that 'one of the earliest recollections I have, is that of being stopped at our door, when returning from a walk, by Mr.——, who desired me to tell my father that the King had been reading his reviews, and had said, "He was a very clever fellow, but that he would never be a bishop." '*

This regal prognostication was scarcely relevant at a time when Sydney was anxious to find an ecclesiastical position of any kind, however humble, but it indicates the attention, and opposition, he was beginning to receive. Nevertheless, a living was found for him. Unsuitably placed though it was, it was at least a living, providing a regular income; it carried too the privilege of non-residence and the possibility of exchange with somewhere more accessible. Foston-le-Clay, the Chancery living which his friends procured for him, lay off the road between York and Malton—

'twelve miles', as Sydney was to put it, 'from a lemon'.* He owed the nomination to a dinner-table conversation which had taken place at Holland House between Lady Holland and Thomas Erskine, a colleague of Lord Holland's and Lord Chancellor in the Ministry of All the Talents. Lady Holland had extracted from Erskine the promise that he would give the next vacant Chancery living to her nominee, and the Chancellor honoured his undertaking by presenting Sydney to Foston. Erskine acknowledged Sydney's thanks in an elegant letter on 6 October 1806: 'I should be guilty of insincerity, and be taking a merit with you which I have no claim to, if I were not to say that I should have given the living to the nominee of Lord and Lady Holland without any personal consideration; at the same time I can add very truly that I thought myself most fortunate indeed that the friend they selected was so deserving, and one that I should have been very happy to have been useful to on his own and his brother's account. I shall feel great pleasure in cultivating your kind acquaintance.'* Contemporary comment was less flattering, Farington writing that the Chancellor had ignored 'many old and most respectable claimants to his favour' when awarding the £600 rectory.* And another version of Erskine's reply was recorded by Samuel Rogers: 'Don't thank me, Mr. Smith. I gave you the living because Lady Holland insisted on my doing so; and if she had desired me to give it to the devil, *he* must have had it.'*

Except for the welcome stipend, the presentation for a time made no difference to Sydney's life in London. As he had written to Jeffrey, explaining the technicalities: 'I am exempted at present from residence, as preacher to the Foundling Hospital; had it been otherwise, I could, I think, have lived very happily in the country, in armigeral, priestly, and swine-feeding society.'* The parochial duties at Foston were accordingly performed by a respectable clergyman sent out from York. Sydney gained a characteristic reputation amongst his Yorkshire colleagues from the time of his induction and his first discussions of residence with the Archbishop. An old friend later recalled the brilliance of Sydney's conversation which he had first heard at Bishopthorpe: 'When he went away, the old Archbishop, I could see, though struck with his extraordinary abilities, did not half like, or understand, how one of the inferior clergy should be so much in possession of his faculties in the presence of his diocesan.'*

He was less resigned to moving to the country than his letter to Jeffrey suggested. His first thought after appointment had been to exchange his living for one more convenient to London. As early as December 1806 the playwright Edward Topham was writing to the Prince of Wales's secretary that 'the Revd. Sydney Smith, Lecturer at the Royal Institution, has lately had presented to him the Rectory of Foston. As preferment in Yorkshire does not suit him, I am given to understand he would readily exchange it, if he could get a living in the south, in its place.'* Apart from the general difficulties of exchanging, there was some feeling that Sydney had been lucky to have acquired even Foston. He approached Lord Chancellor Eldon through his brother Sir William Scott in 1807, in case any Chancery incumbent wished to exchange a living in the South for one in the North. 'I could have no objection to gratify his wishes,' Eldon replied: 'I fear, however, that it will be no easy matter. His living in Yorkshire is a very good one, *if he resided*; *such* don't often fall: and when they do *in the South*, all the world is applying for them.'*

An exchange would have been convenient, but Sydney was hampered by the patron's general ruling that a Chancery living might only be exchanged for another Chancery living of similar income, and that the incumbents should be of similar age. The triple restriction—of patron, age, and value—meant that Sydney had to turn down several possibilities which the Hollands suggested to him. Discovering that a private chaplaincy to a peer might permit him to hold a second living, he tried to attach himself nominally to the households of several noble friends, starting with the Hollands: 'Is Lord Holland's number [of chaplains] full? If not, will he do me the honour of appointing me and will your Ladyship trust me with your spiritual concerns? I am severe but steady—and safe.'* But such schemes came to nothing, and he remained without a second benefice.

He had to make occasional visits to Yorkshire, however, notably to vote in the 1807 election. He had pledged himself to Wilberforce in the spring, remarking in a letter of February:

I hope now you have done with Africa you will do something for Ireland—which is surely the greatest question and interest connected with this empire. There is no man in England who from activity, understanding, character and neutrality could do it so effectually as Mr Wilberforce. And when this Country conceded a century ago an establishment to the Presbyterian Church, it is horrible to see millions of Christians of another persuasion instructed by ragged priests and praising their creator in wet ditches. I hope to God you will strive in this great business—and then we will vote for the Consulship for life: and you shall be perpetual Member for Yorkshire.'*

The election, when it came in May, was something of a disappointment. 'An election out of Westminster is sad work', he wrote to Creevey, '—at the moment of the greatest ferment, York was, in the two great points of ebriety and pugnacity, as quiet as average London at about 3 o'clock in the morning.'* Sydney reported having voted for Lord Milton ('one of the most ungainly looking young men I ever saw'), and giving his other vote for Wilberforce 'on account of his good conduct in Africa, a place returning no members to parliament, but still, from the extraordinary resemblance its inhabitants bear to human creatures, of some consequence.'*

The first effect of the Foston income on the Smiths' Orchard Street ménage was to enable Sydney to take his family away to Sonning-on-Thames, near Reading. He took a house there where the children received their first taste of the country—'the first breath of air, free from carpet-shakings, that we had inhaled', as Saba put it.* 'Mrs S. is quite delighted with her country box', Sydney reported to Lady Holland, '—so am I. I have seen a great number of thrushes hopping before the window this evening—but their conduct was by no means innocent or decorous.'* One of their near neighbours in the village was Sir William Scott (later Lord Stowell), Lord Chancellor Eldon's elder brother. Although a political enemy, the prominent Tory lawyer enjoyed Sydney's company and regretted his loss to his own party. 'Ah, Mr. Smith, you would have been in a different situation, and a far richer man, if you would have belonged to us,' Saba records him as saying, mentioning her father's gratification at this recognition of his talents from so unexpected a quarter.*

The fall of the Ministry of All the Talents, which had at least provided Sydney with his Yorkshire living, gave him an opportunity to give full expression to his skills as a controversialist. Compared with the abolition of the slave trade which stands to the credit of the short and oddly assorted administration of 1806, the emancipation of Roman Catholics from their many civil disabilities was to prove exceptionally difficult to manage. Even though some measure of Catholic relief had weighty support from the ministry (and there was even a short-lived attempt to allow Roman Catholics to hold commissions in the army up to the rank of Colonel), the whole highly sensitive and controversial

issue foundered on the King's personal opposition. Nor was it merely the peace of the royal mind which led to the collapse of the ministry in March 1807; the general outcry of 'No Popery' after the dissolution was taken up by the country as a whole, and some of the successors to the Talents showed a rigidly Protestant fervour which combined with the royal opposition to block the Whigs' hesitant moves towards Catholic emancipation. Patriotism, protestantism, and placemanship ran disagreeably in parallel, even at a time of national peril and the threat of Napoleonic invasion. The confused history of Catholic disabilities had given rise to many anomalies, and the speciously patriotic defence of them by Tory churchmen provided even more inconsistencies. Here was a splendid opportunity for a clear-headed polemical writer to show his colours, to argue the matter before militant Catholic groups under O'Connell had begun to show their power in a way that was to alter the whole complexion of the emancipation campaign later on. Sydney Smith had just made an effective public avowal of his opinions in *A Sermon on Toleration preached at the Temple Church*, 'my *infamous* discourse' as he called it in a letter to Lady Holland announcing its publication in July 1807.*

About the same time there began to appear *Letters on the Subject of the Catholics, to my brother Abraham, who lives in the country*, by one Peter Plymley. Ten short letters were to appear in groups in the next few months. The authorship of them seemed at first a mystery, and the author was until late in life to deny having written them (latterly avowing repentance of some of their personal attacks). But no amount of deliberate mystification, no ill-disguised letters from 'Peter Plymley' to his rather shady printer,* could conceal the early and widespread impression that the *Letters* were the work of the Reverend Sydney Smith.

Controversial tracts are very much a fugitive literary form, and there is a great deal of topical allusion in *Peter Plymley* which would require ponderous elucidation to set the letters fully in their historical context. But they are so well conceived and executed that they lift the argument beyond the ephemeral and contain so many good things well put, so many general points about political administration and about Irish affairs, that they have had a following long after the Catholic question and the Irish problem (of the nineteenth century, that is) had been settled. And from a literary point of view *Peter Plymley's Letters* show Sydney working at a length which particularly suited his talents, and with the extra seasoning of recklessness which formal pseudonymity allowed him.

Peter Plymley addresses himself to his brother Abraham, an honest, devout, philoprogenitive country parson, not unreasonably alarmed by all he has heard of current events. He is careful to respect the rural pastor's point of view, but regards it as misguided. In fact, as Peter's first letter opens, 'A worthier and better man than yourself does not exist, but I have always told you, from the time of our boyhood, that you were a bit of a goose.'* Abraham's misinformation is patiently corrected: the Pope had *not* landed, and such fears exist only in the mind of the Chancellor of the Exchequer (which 'though they reflect the highest honour upon the delicate irritability of his faith, must certainly be considered as more ambiguous proofs of the sanity and vigour of his understanding').* Arguments are supported by domestic analogies adapted to the fictional brother's way of life: 'You may not be aware of it yourself, most reverend Abraham, but you deny their freedom to the Catholics upon the same principle that Sarah your wife refuses to give the receipt for a ham or a gooseberry dumpling: she values her receipts, not because they secure to her a certain flavour, but because they remind her that the neighbours want it:—a feeling laughable in a priestess, shameful in a priest; venial when it withholds the blessings of a ham, tyrannical and execrable when it narrows the boon of religious freedom.'* Abraham Plymley's worthy dimness enables him to be squashed all the more tellingly: 'When I hear any man talk of an unalterable law, the only effect it produces upon me is to convince me that he is an unalterable fool.'*

Peter's exasperatedly considerate tone of his brother contrasts well with the direct attacks on the Tory politicians, particularly George Canning and Spencer Perceval. 'You tell me, I am a party man,' Peter wrote to Abraham: 'I hope I shall always be so, when I see my country in the hands of a pert London joker and a second-rate lawyer. Of the first, no other good is known than that he makes pretty Latin verses; the second seems to me to have the head of a country parson, and the tongue of an Old Bailey lawyer.'* Neither was spared throughout the *Letters*. The Chancellor, who comes in for some specially unfair treatment from Peter Plymley, was mocked for his churchy interests, his 'strictest attention to the smaller parts of ecclesiastical government, to hassocks, to psalters, and to surplices; in the last agonies of England, he will bring in a bill to regulate Easter-offerings;

and he will adjust the stipends of curates, when the flag of France is unfurled on the hills of Kent.'* The Foreign Secretary was similarly taunted, attacked not 'from the love of glory, but from the love of utility, as a burgomaster hunts a rat in a Dutch dyke, for fear it should flood a province.'* It is however Perceval who comes off worst: 'If I lived at Hampstead upon stewed meats and claret; if I walked to church every Sunday before eleven young gentlemen of my own begetting, with their faces washed, and their hair pleasingly combed; if the Almighty had blessed me with every earthly comfort,—how awfully would I pause before I sent forth the flame and the sword over the cabins of the poor, generous, open-hearted peasants of Ireland!'* Personal attacks in controversy often fail to be remembered because of their force of malice, but the case gradually built up against Perceval in *Peter Plymley* makes it difficult now for us to think of him outside the satirical context of stewed meats and claret.

By turning arguments upside down and giving contrary examples, Sydney is able to indulge in digs against Wilberforce, whom he had tried to turn towards Irish affairs after the slave trade had been dealt with, and 'the patent Christians of Clapham'. He saw the latter as a greater threat to the Church than the Catholics, and warned against 'that patent Christianity which has been for some time manufacturing at Clapham, to the prejudice of the old and admirable article prepared by the Church. I would counsel my Lords the Bishops to keep their eyes upon that holy village, and its hallowed vicinity.'* Such a view of the evangelical sects and the Methodists was not unfamiliar from Sydney's contributions to the *Edinburgh Review*; here it made an odd antithesis. Not that it should be thought that Sydney had any sympathy for the practices of Roman Catholics, though he acknowledged them 'Christians, though mistaken Christians'.* He saw their beliefs as absurd, and 'as for the enormous wax candles, and superstitious mummeries, and painted jackets of the Catholic priests, I fear them not'.* A defensive tone when Catholic faith was under discussion led him into vulgarities about 'the thumbs and offals of departed saints' which match later passages on the result of blocking the export of cathartics to Napoleonic Europe. Even the Papal threat belonged more to folklore than reality: 'I thought that the terror of the Pope had been confined to the limits of the nursery, and merely employed as a means to induce young master to enter into his small clothes with greater speed, and to eat his breakfast with greater attention to decorum. For these purposes, the name of the Pope is admirable; but why push it beyond?'* Such a bluff, no-nonsense view of catholicism at least helped to ensure that the emancipation problem was seen as a secular one, with a strategic importance at a time of national danger.

Sydney saw England as being unprepared for defence against an enemy with whom disaffected Irish Catholics would all too readily ally themselves: 'it is now three centuries since an English pig has fallen in a fair battle upon English ground, or a farmhouse been rifled, or a clergyman's wife been subjected to any other proposals of love than the connubial endearments of her sleek and orthodox mate'.* The French threat was new and urgent, and a national emergency was no time to be debating theological niceties as a qualification for commissions in the army. 'Are we', Peter Plymley asked, 'to stand examining our generals and armies as a bishop examines a candidate for holy orders? and to suffer no one to bleed for England, who does not agree with you about the second of Timothy?'* He pictures Perceval as the captain of a frigate attacked by a corsair:

He calls all hands upon deck; talks to them of King, country, glory, sweethearts, gin, French prison, wooden shoes, Old England, and hearts of oak: they give three cheers, rush to their guns, and, after a tremendous conflict, succeed in beating off the enemy. Not a syllable of this; this is not the manner in which the honourable Commander goes to work: the first thing he does is to secure 20 or 30 of his prime sailors who happen to be Catholics, to clap them in irons, and set over them a guard of as many Protestants; having taken this admirable method of defending himself against his infidel opponents, he goes upon deck, reminds the sailors, in a very bitter harangue, that they are of different religions ... and postively forbids every one to sponge or ram who has not taken the Sacrament according to the Church of England.*

Throughout *Peter Plymley's Letters*, Ireland is seen as the key to the problem: from the strategic, economic, educational, and generally humanitarian points of view, some measure of conciliation towards the Roman Catholic population there is held to be essential. And yet, Peter tells Abraham, 'you know, and many Englishmen know, what passes in China; but nobody knows or cares what passes in Ireland'.* British conduct to Ireland throughout the war is likened to 'that of a man who subscribes to hospitals, weeps at charity sermons, carries out broth and blankets to beggars, and then comes home and beats his wife and children.

We had compassion for the victims of all other oppression and injustice except our own.'* Even Scotland had been brought prosperously within the commonwealth by religious concessions, a point argued with the familiar references to thistles, oatmeal, and sulphur. The broad view which is taken of the Irish question, not merely as a possible military and naval threat during the Napoleonic period, nor merely as a problem of Catholic emancipation, helps to account for the popularity of the *Letters* throughout the nineteenth century.

The letters had a keen readership amongst all parties at the time of their publication. Lord Holland wrote to Sydney in October 1809 of a conversation he had had with Lord Grenville at Dropmore, when the obvious parallel with Swift came to mind. Grenville spoke of Peter Plymley in a warm and enthusiastic way; 'I did not fail', Holland reported 'to remind him that the only author to whom we both thought it could be compared in English, lost a bishopric for his wittiest performance; and I hoped that if we could discover the author, and had ever a bishopric in our gift, we should prove that Whigs were both more grateful and more liberal than Tories. He rallied me upon the affectation of concealing who it was, but added that he hoped Peter would not always live in Yorkshire, where he was persuaded he was at present; for, among other reasons, we felt the want of him just now in the state of the press, and that he heartily wished Abraham would do something to provoke him to take up his pen.'* But even with such high approval and interest it was to be long before the author was brought back from the north of England, and even then a bishopric was not to be his reward.

Events were soon to force Sydney to take up regular residence in Yorkshire. Some of the acerbities about Perceval's punctiliousness in ecclesiastical legislation came home to roost, and the minister had indirect revenge for the mockery. One of the ecclesiastical measures in which he had been keenly interested was the Clergy Residence Act of 1803. Archbishop Markham, who had not enforced the Act, died in 1807, and Sydney wrote apprehensively to Jeffrey that 'I am waiting to see who is to be my new master in York. I care very little whether he make me reside or not, and shall take to grazing as quietly as Nebuchadnezzar.'* Edward Vernon (later Harcourt) was appointed to the Archbishopric and eventually decided to put the Residence Act into force throughout his diocese, requiring Sydney to leave London and take charge of the parish himself.

Sydney obtained permission, but only temporarily, to remain in London, and reported to his father in February 1808 after discussing the matter with the Archbishop, that 'at all events I shall gain leave for two years and he has not made up his mind whether he shall consider my case as a permanent excuse for absence'.*

Meanwhile Sydney made the best of what were to be his final months before being tied down to a long period of country residence. In the autumn of 1808, he paid a brief visit to Edinburgh, which foreshadows two of his most important friendships in the North of England. Lord and Lady Carlisle and their eldest son Lord Morpeth, who were to become some of Sydney's closest friends, are discussed in his correspondence for the first time. He explained to Lady Holland why he did not intend to visit them on his journey north: 'I have no doubt of Lord Morpeth's good disposition towards me, but he is afraid of introducing such a loquacious personage to his decorous parents. This, however, is very fair,—and I hope my children will have the opposite dread of introducing very silent people to me in my old age. I like Lord Morpeth—a man of excellent understanding, very polished manners, and a good heart; but I should suspect very irritable and very sensitive—the last to a fault.'* He was soon to have an ample opportunity of confirming his impression of Morpeth's kindness and understanding, and of getting to know his parents at Castle Howard, quite near his parish of Foston. The Edinburgh visit also gave him a chance to develop a Holland House acquaintance by spending a couple of days on the journeys up and down with Lord and Lady Grey at Howick. 'An excellent man, Lord Grey, and pleasant to be seen in the bosom of his family', Sydney wrote to Lady Holland from Grey's Northumberland seat in September.* His intimate friendship with the future Prime Minister and his family was to continue until the end of their lives.

He much enjoyed his visit to Edinburgh. To his regret, a few friends such as Archibald Alison were out of town, but he saw Jeffrey and many others and wrote to Alison when 'staying a day with the Stewarts—Dugald fat and agricultural—fond of indecent stories as ever'.* The literary circles of Edinburgh were little changed. 'I found a great number of philosophers in Edinburgh in an high state of obscurity and metaphysics. The itch this year has been extremely severe and the professors and others were just recovering their outer or scarf skin as I left the place. Poor Dugald Stewart is extremely alarmed by the repeated assurances I made that he was the author of Plymley's Letters—generally so considered to be.'* Sydney was in high glee at the thought of his metaphysical friends. As soon as he returned to London he sent some game out to Holland House with a note saying 'I take the liberty to send you two brace of grouse, curious, because killed by a Scotch metaphysician; in other and better language they are mere ideas, shot by other ideas, out of a pure intellectual notion called a gun.... The modification of matter called grouse which accompanies this note is not in the common apprehension of Edinburgh considered to be dependent upon a first cause, but to have existed from all Eternity. Allen will explain.'*

The expedition to visit his old friends in Scotland was only a diversion from the anxieties of waiting for the Archbishop's decision about residence in Yorkshire. As late as October 1808, opinion at Bishopthorpe was still unsettled, but it seemed to be moving rather against him: 'I have heard nothing yet of the doubts and scruples of the Archbishop of York, and hope they may be dying away', Sydney wrote to Lady Holland.* During the summer he had again attempted to obtain a living in the south, but was becoming resigned to exile. 'If by exchange, or in addition, I can get any thing *tolerable* in the South, I shall esteem myself very fortunate' he wrote to Lady Holland in June, 'if not, my situation there is not destitute of many advantages, and I must content myself as well as I can.'* He rejected the chance of a small living at Harefield in Middlesex ('bad society—no land—no house—no salary—dear as London—neither in London, nor out of it'*) and at the end of October decided to settle in Yorkshire. 'My lot is now cast and my heritage fixed—most probably. But you may choose to make me a Bishop, in which case I shall return to town in the tenth or fifteenth year of the Hegira with great shouting and glory. If you do make me a Bishop I think I shall never do you discredit; for I believe that it is out of the power of lawn and velvet, and the crisp hair of dead men fashioned into a wig, to make me a dishonest man; but if you do not, I am perfectly content, and shall be ever grateful to the last hour of my life to you, and Lord Holland. I leave London the 25th of March next.'*

Having once made up his mind, Sydney became quite happy at the prospect of moving north, writing immediately to a Yorkshire friend to find a house near the parish, and travelling up to York soon afterwards to examine properties. 'I am by no means grieved at quitting London', he wrote to Jeffrey on this visit; 'sorry to lose the society of my friends, but wishing for more quiet, more leisure, less expense, and more space for my children. I am extremely pleased with what I have seen of York.'* 'I have bought a book about drilling beans, and a greyhound puppy for the Malton meeting. It is thought I shall be an eminent rural character'—so he wrote to Lady Holland when he was making preparations for his move.* And to prove his contentment, he wrote to her nearly a year later, when he was settling down, that

I hear you laugh at me for being happy in the country, and upon this I have a few words to say. . . . I am not leading precisely the life I should choose, but that which (all things considered, as well as I could consider them) appeared to be the most eligible. I am resolved therefore to like and to to reconcile myself to it; which is more manly than to feign myself above it, and to send up complaints by the post, of being thrown away, and being desolate and such like trash. I am prepared therefore either way. If the chances of life ever enable me to emerge, I will show you that I have not been wholly occupied by small and sordid pursuits. If (as the greater probability is) I am come to the end of my career, I give myself quietly up to horticulture, and the annual augmentation of my family. In short, if my lot be to crawl, I will crawl contentedly; if to fly, I will fly with alacrity; but as long as I can possibly avoid it I will never be unhappy.*

CHAPTER III

❈

SYDNEY's first visit to his new living of Foston-le-Clay had scarcely been promising. To the amazement of his prospective parishioners, who rarely saw such finery, he arrived well-dressed and in a four-wheeler. He was met by the ancient parish clerk, who showed him the poor church and worse parsonage—'one brick-floored kitchen with a room above it'. The old man looked Sydney over very carefully and after a long conversation on parish affairs felt moved to pay his new rector a taciturn Yorkshireman's compliment which Saba recorded in her poor phonetics: ' "Muster Smith, it often stroikes my moind, that people as comes frae London is such *fools* ... But you", he said (giving him a gentle nudge with his stick), "I see you are no fool." '*

The so-called parsonage could not be lived in. 'When first I was presented to the Chancery living of Foston,' Sydney wrote to Lord Eldon in 1820 when stating his case for another preferment, 'I had a cottage valued at £50, by way of parsonage house, 300 acres of glebe land entirely exhausted, styles and gates all in ruins, and not a single farm building for my tenants. From my foolish moderation and from my ignorance of country matters, I received £30 for dilapidations.'* There had been no resident pastor for a hundred and fifty years, hence the hovel of a rectory. Sydney therefore obtained leave to reside outside the parish and found a suitable house nearer York in the village of Heslington. It was convenient for the city—'just sufficient', as Sydney remarked of the distance, 'to enable me to stem the torrents of tea by which I should at a nearer distance be overwhelmed. I have read much in books of *simple* pleasures and am about to try whether there be any such pleasures or not.'*

He paid for the move to Heslington by publishing his sermons in two volumes, for which he received £200 from Cadell and Davies. (They were a straightforward batch which were received with predictable scorn by the recently founded *Quarterly Review*.) Aided by the fee, the family soon established itself in the rented house, which is now (appropriately enough) the Roman Catholic chaplaincy of York University, where Sydney's bedroom has become the chapel and his closet a confessional. Sydney wrote of Heslington and its squire that

I fixed myself meantime at a small village two miles from York, in which was a fine old house of the time of Queen Elizabeth, where resided the last of the squires, with his lady, who looked as if she had walked straight out of the Ark, or had been the wife of Enoch. He was a perfect specimen of the Trullibers of old; he smoked, hunted, drank beer at his door with his grooms and dogs, and spelt over the county paper on Sundays. At first, he heard I was a Jacobin and a dangerous fellow, and turned aside as I passed: but at length, when he found the peace of the village undisturbed, harvests much as usual, Juno and Ponto uninjured, he first bowed, then called, and at least reached such a pitch of confidence that he used to bring the papers, that I might explain the difficult words to him; actually discovered that I had made a joke, laughed till I thought he would have died of convulsions, and ended by inviting me to see his dogs.*

This reminiscence is one of many given to his daughter Saba late in life, and used in the *Memoir* of her father in which her happy memories of her Yorkshire upbringing are mingled with his own and the evidence provided by his correspondence. Sydney's period in Yorkshire—a sizeable part of his life—is therefore amply documented, with plenty to confirm his daughter's view that his high spirits soon returned once he had resigned himself to leaving London. York, too, was pleasing, and not too outlandish a place, as he explained to Lord Valentia when returning a book to him in July 1809: 'I shall enquire of its reception from such persons skilful in books as travel to these parts. The people here are converted to the Christian faith, wear clothes, and understand the principles of truck, or barter. Justice can generally be obtained by applying to the Sheikh or Mayor of York, and the stories of cannibalism are utterly without foundation. Provide yourself with looking-glasses, and nails, and make a journey among us; and if you do, allow me to regale you after the fashion of the country and to assure you in person how much I consider myself obliged by your polite attention.'*

The Smiths soon established a comfortable and hospitable home at Heslington, where their early visitors included London lawyer friends in York for the Assizes, and some old friends from

Edinburgh stopping on the London road. 'We are about equal to a second rate inn, as Mrs Smith says,' Sydney remarked in an invitation to Lady Grey, 'but I think myself we are equal to any inn on the North Road except Ferry Bridge.'*

Sydney frequently rejoiced in having had 'a brisk run on the road',* and the house was often filled with visitors. He commended 'two Scotch ladies' to Lady Holland (who had been in Spain) as suitable recipients of Henry Fox's attentions, 'for love, though a very acute disorder in Andalusia, puts on a very chronic shape in these high northern latitudes; for first the lover must prove *metapheezically* that she ought to yield; and then in the fifth or sixth year of courtship, or rather argument, if the summer is tolerably warm, and oatmeal plenty, the fair one yields'.* And Lady Holland herself came to stay; in 1810 Sydney urged her to avoid the week of York Races for her intended visit, adding that 'We have now another bed in which a maid or a philosopher, or a maid with a philosopher, might be put. God grant in this latter event that they may both merit their respective appellations the ensuing morning.'*

The three young children the Smiths had brought with them from London (a fourth was born in 1813) were a source of great enjoyment. Except for their prolonged vacation at Sonning-on-Thames in 1807, it was their first escape from the confinement of the city. They took to the country eagerly and their obvious happiness did much to reconcile Sydney to an unfamiliar way of life. He took great delight in teaching and in teasing them, and proudly observed their progress; his happy, growing family was a distinctive part of his life in the country.

It was always Sydney's intention, after being sent to Yorkshire, to build a rectory at Foston, but the final decision to 'brick down' his money in a parsonage took several years to mature. Late in 1812 and in the early months of 1813 he discussed the matter with the Archbishop and with his friends in London. He sent John Allen at Holland House a long letter of explanation:

You may easily imagine that I have reflected a good deal upon the expediency of an undertaking so very serious as that of building. I may very likely have determined wrong, but I have determined to the best of my judgment anxiously and actively exerted. I have no public, nor private, chance of changing my situation for the better. Such good fortune may occur, but I have no right to presume upon it. I have waited and tried for six years, and I am bound in common prudence to suppose that my lot is fixed in this land. That being so, what am

I to do? I have no great certainty of my present house. The distance is a great and serious inconvenience. If I am turned out of it, it will be scarcely possible in so thinly inhabited a country to find another. I am totally neglecting my parish. I *ought* to build. If I were Bishop, I would compel a man in my situation to build, and should think that any incumbent acted an ungentlemanlike part who compelled me to compel him and who did not take up the money which is lent by the Governors of Queen Anne's Bounty for the purpose of the building.

Such I conceived would be the Archbishop's opinion of me had I availed myself to his good-nature to apply to him for perpetual absence from my living, and for permission to live on in hired houses. In all conversations I have had with him, he has never discouraged the idea of building, but on the contrary always appeared to approve and promote it.... To brick down all the money I have been saving for my family has cost me a great deal of uneasiness, and at one time I thought of resigning my living. Having now decided according to the best means of an understanding extremely prone to error, nothing remains but to fight through my difficulties as well as I can.*

Holland House, of course, interpreted the Archbishop's view differently, taking the view that although Sydney was expected and encouraged to build, His Grace was not disposed to compel him to do so. Indeed, their interest went so far as to secure for Sydney the Archbishop's formal permission to avoid building altogether. In the course of a complicated correspondence with his London friends, Sydney maintained that he could not postpone building indefinitely, and wrote to Allen that 'I should have thought it mean and shabby to have been perpetually excusing myself from this burthen'.* He acknowledged Lady Holland's good intentions in negotiating with the Archbishop, but was soon able to report that 'I had burnt my bricks, bought my timber, and got into a situation in which it was more prudent to advance than to recede'.* Sydney thought that the Archbishop might perhaps have been 'misled by my light manner of talking of these matters, and never imagined me to be in earnest', but he himself took very seriously the promise to reside and to committing himself finally to remaining at Foston for a long period. 'When I say that I shall pass my life at Foston,' he added, 'I by no means intend to take any desponding view of my situation.'*

He was able to draw on a special fund of Queen Anne's Bounty, established by the eighteenth-century 'Gilbert Acts', which permitted the Bounty to lend money for the improvement of parsonages on the security of the parochial revenues and to be repaid by successive incumbents.* Sydney, one of the first to borrow under the scheme, received a loan of £1,600, and later recalled the total cost of building and equipping Foston Rectory and its adjacent farm-offices as about £4,000. Sydney repaid the Bounty £130 a year, this coming from an income which he told Lady Holland in 1816 was only £900 a year and insufficient to support a prolonged visit to London with his family.* Later in life, as a well-placed Canon of St. Paul's, he was to draw on this experience when in controversy over cathedral endowment, showing how heavy were the burdens placed on his first substantial professional earnings.

The Foston building accounts and plans have survived in the York diocesan archives and add some details to Sydney's own picturesque tale of the construction of his house. There is a plan of a rectory proposed 'for the Revd Sydney Smith, arranged under his immediate direction and drawn by Peter Atkinson of the City of York, Architect, Sept. 21, 1812'.* It is similar to the building as finished, but not quite the same, and may well be the plan which Atkinson, a member of the well-known family of York architects, submitted with an estimate for £3,000. It 'would have ruined me', Sydney recalled; 'I made him my bow. "You build for glory, Sir; I, for use." I returned him his plans, with five-and-twenty pounds, and sat down in my thinking-chair, and in a few hours Mrs Sydney and I concocted a plan which has produced what I call the model of parsonage-houses.'*

Mrs Sydney recalled that her husband had said to her: ' "We both know what we want, the number and size of rooms we wish to have. Can not you take your ruler and compasses and so arrange these by a scale that we may do without this great man?" This I did, and we sat in judgment over our plans, hired an excellent carpenter, and a mason, and our house was begun! When finished we had not made *one mistake*!"* The building work was not, however, without incident, as Sydney remembered:

I then took to horse to provide bricks and timber; was advised to make my own bricks of my own clay; when the kiln was opened, all bad; mounted my horse again, and in twenty-four hours had bought thousands of bricks and tons of timber. Was advised by neighbouring gentlemen to employ oxen; bought four—Tug and Lug, Haul and Crawl; but Tug and Lug took to fainting, and required buckets of sal–volatile, and Haul and Crawl to lie down in the mud. So I did as I ought to have done at first, took the advice of the farmer instead of the gentleman; sold my oxen, bought a team of horses, and at last, in spite of a frost which delayed me six weeks, in spite of walls running down with wet, in spite of the advice and remonstrances of friends who predicted our death, in spite of an infant of six months old, who had never been out of the house, I landed my family in my new house, nine months after laying the first stone, on the 20th of March [1814] ... a feat, taking ignorance, inexperience and poverty into consideration, requiring, I assure you, no small degree of energy.*

Saba was only twelve years old at the time, but she vividly recalled the move forty years later:

It was a cold, bright March day, with a biting east wind. The beds we left in the morning had to be packed up and slept on at night. Waggon after waggon of furniture poured in every minute; the roads were so cut up that the carriage could not reach the door; and my mother lost her shoe in the mud, which was ankle-deep, whilst bringing her infant up to the house in her arms. But oh, the shout of joy as we entered and took possession. It was the first time in our lives that we had inhabited a house of our own ... We thought it a palace; yet the drawing room had no door, the bare plaster walls ran down with wet, the windows were like ground glass from the moisture which had to be wiped up several times a day by the housemaid.*

The damp of the new house was a source of constant worry. So many friends had warned him of the dangers that Sydney began to think they wished him ill. 'I dare say my new house will cost something in apothecaries' bills,' he wrote to Lady Holland, 'but some risk must be run in order to get in as soon as I can.'* The move was the culmination of months of tireless activity, but Sydney remained buoyant, as Saba recollected:

But then was the time to behold my father! Amid the confusion, he thought for everybody, encouraged everybody, kept everybody in good humour. How he exerted himself! How his loud, rich voice might be heard in all directions, ordering, arranging, explaining, till the household storm gradually subsided ... In a few days, through my father's active exertions, everything was arranged with tolerable comfort in the little household and it began to assume a settled appearance.*

'I am very much pleased with my house,' Sydney wrote to Allen in April 1814; 'I aimed at making it a snug parsonage, and I think I have succeeded.'* Foston Rectory (which was gutted by fire in 1962 but has been sympathetically restored) remains a light, spacious, and comfortable house, well placed for a fine view of the surrounding countryside and built in a pleasant local rose-coloured brick. Architecturally it is regular and plain, with a fairly low-pitched roof and well-grouped chimney stacks. The bedroom walls are coved into the roof-space—an economical and pleasing feature. Outside the elevation is dominated by the large bay-window of the long drawing-room and principal bedroom above it; the drawing-room window-sashes reach nearly to the floor and give access to the lawns. They also add to the general impression of lightness and cheerfulness which must have been part of Sydney's directions to the architect and are certainly a feature of his own realization of the professional plans. One of Sydney's unfinished sketches, 'Of Cheerfulness', gives some idea of the atmosphere of Foston Rectory: 'Persons subject to low spirits should make the rooms in which they live as cheerful as possible, taking care that the paper with which the wall is covered should be of a brilliant, lively colour, hanging up pictures or prints, and covering the chimney-piece with beautiful china. A bay-window looking upon pleasant objects, and, above all, a large fire whenever the weather will permit, are favourable to good spirits, and the tables near should be strewed with books and pamphlets.'*

Sydney considered himself an expert on fireplaces, and those at Foston are noteworthy. The surrounds were erected to his own design in Portland stone (to save the expense of marble) and the grates are fed by air-tubes—'Shadrachs'—of his own invention, let into the outer walls. Another novel device secured the fire-irons, which he commemorated in verse:

> The poker, tongs and shovel—rebels three,
> Whom on my hearth suspended firm you see,
> Who for four centuries mankind defied,—
> Have bent to me; I checked their noisy pride,
> I hooked their noses, I reduced their reign;
> Ne'er shall you see them tumble down again;
> Ne'er shall you hear their cursed outrageous din:
> With me, your peace, and their repose begin.*

The Foston fireplaces were particularly successful, and in 1820 Sydney ordered one of the firebacks he had himself designed to be copied by the York foundry for Lady Grey. He told her that 'I have these iron backs to every fireplace in my house, now six years old: I am notorious also for having the warmest house in this part of Yorkshire.'*

By the time he had settled in at the end of 1814, Sydney was able to write to Jeffrey with reasonable contentment: 'I like my new house very much; it is very comfortable, and after finishing it, I would not pay sixpence to alter it; but the expense of it will keep me a very poor man, a close prisoner here for my life, and render the education of my children a difficult exertion for me. My situation is one of great solitude, but I preserve myself in a state of cheerfulness, and tolerable content, and have a propensity to amuse myself with trifles.'*

Contemporary reminiscences confirm the family memories and the impression gained from Sydney's letters that his domestic life at Foston was contented and gay. One of the best descriptions is that contributed by an anonymous clerical correspondent (possibly Bishop Stanley of Norwich) to Saba's *Memoir* of her father. The clergyman concerned visited Foston in 1827 and the letter he then wrote to his wife shows the quality of domestic life very well indeed:

A man's character is probably more faithfully represented in the arrangements of his home than in any other point; and Foston is a facsimile of its master's mind from first to last. He had no architect, but I question whether a more compact, convenient house could well be imagined. In the midst of a field, commanding no very attractive view, he has contrived to give it an air of snugness and comfort, and its internal arrangements are perfect. The drawing-room is the colour you covet, the genuine chromium, with a sort of yellow flowering pattern. It is exquisitely filled with irregular regularities—tables, books, chairs, Indian wardrobes; everything finished in thorough taste, without the slightest reference to smartness or useless finery, and his inventive genius appears in every corner; his fires are blown into brightness by *Shadrachs*, tubes furnished with air from without, opening into the centre of the fire; his poker, tongs and shovel are secured from falling with that horrid crash which is so disturbing to the nerves and temper. His own study has no appearance of comfort; but as he reads and writes in his family circle, in spite of talking and other interruptions, this is of less consequence... His bedrooms are counterparts of the lower rooms; in mine there were twenty-eight large Piranesi prints of ancient Rome, mounted just as we do ours, but without frames; and, indeed, in every vacant part of the house he has them hung up. His store-room is more like that of an Indiaman than anything else, containing such a complete and well-assorted portion of every possible want or wish in a country establishment. The same spirit prevails in his garden and farm: contrivance and singularity in every hole and corner.*

The whole household was permeated with its master's gaiety. Sydney delighted in the company of his family, of whom the three eldest spent all their remembered childhood in Yorkshire. Sydney himself taught his sons until they went to their public schools, and with his wife saw to the entire education of his daughters Saba and Emily. One of the most memorable features of Saba's life of her father is the chapter of affectionate reminiscence in which she recalled her father's interest in their childhood pursuits:

He never lost an opportunity of showing us whatever could instruct or amuse, that came within his reach. He loved to exercise our minds; and I remember that often, in childhood, he gave my elder brother and myself subjects on which to write essays for him. He encouraged the ceaseless questions of childhood; he was never too busy to explain or assist; and as we grew older, he endeavoured to stimulate us to exertion by shame at ignorance. He loved to discuss with us, met us as his equals, and I look back with wonder at his patient refutation of our crude and foolish opinions. As we grew up we became his companions; we were called in to all family councils, and his letters were common property.*

Macaulay remarked that Sydney seemed to regard it as the greatest of luxuries to keep his family in fits of laughter for several hours each day. Saba recalled that 'in an evening, often with a child on each knee, he would invent a tale for their amusement, composed such ludicrous images and combinations as nobody else would have thought of, succeeding each other with the greatest rapidity. They were devoured by them with eyes and ears, in breathless interest: but at the most thrilling moment he always terminated with "and so they lived very happy ever after", a kiss on each fat cheek, "and now so to bed".'*

Sydney delighted in making the Foston servants laugh when visitors were present, and he constantly teased them. Jack Robinson, a carpenter who originally turned up in search of parish relief, was set to make furntiure for the new house and became the regular odd-job man, waiting at table on grand occasions. 'He sometimes naturally makes a mistake,' Sydney remarked, 'and sticks a gimlet into the bread instead of a fork.'* The regular 'butler' was one of the best-remembered of the household, Bunch. Sydney recalled of her that 'a manservant was too expensive; so I caught up a little garden-girl, made like a milestone, christened her Bunch, put a napkin in her hand, and made her my butler. The girls taught her to read, Mrs. Sydney to wait, and I undertook her morals; Bunch became the best butler in the county.'* It was Bunch who performed the solemn ritual of shaving her master, or at least preparing his shaving-soap with a large painter's brush in a wooden bowl. Mrs Marcet remembered hearing Sydney ask her whether she preferred roast duck or boiled chicken, and how delighted he was to hear her answer immediately 'roast duck': he had spent a long time training her to develop such decision of mind instead of giving a characteristic Yorkshire 'A's sur ai don't knaw, Sir.'* Bunch went on to repeat her 'crimes' to Mrs Marcet in a little catechism Sydney had taught her. They were ' "plate-snatching, gravy-spilling, door-slamming, blue-bottle fly-catching, and curtsey-bobbing" ', these last two being explained as 'standing with my mouth open and not attending' and 'curtseying to the centre of the earth'.*

Another favourite with the family (and with all their visitors) was Annie Kay, who joined the household at the age of nineteen. Saba recalled that 'she officiated first as nurse, then as lady's-maid, afterwards as housekeeper, apothecary's boy, factotum and friend'.* Annie moved with the family to Somerset and lived to nurse her old master on his death-bed in 1845. The main out-door woman was the cheerful and active Molly Mills, who dealt with cows, pigs, poultry, the gardens, and the posts. 'With her short red petticoat, legs like millposts, high cheek-bones red and shrivelled like winter apples; a perfect specimen of a "yeo-woman"; a sort of kindred spirit too, for she was the wit of the village, and delighted in a crack with her master, when she could get it.'* She and her two sons ruled the farm, and with Jack Robinson, Bunch, Annie Kay, a pet donkey, a tame fawn, and a lame pet goose made up the domestic establishment. Some of the servants moved to Combe Florey, and Sydney recalled that 'When I took my Yorkshire servants into Somersetshire, I found that they thought making a drink out of apples was a tempting of Providence, who had intended barley to be the only natural material of intoxication.'*

Visitors to Foston included friends from the Smiths' early married life in London and Edinburgh, and later many of the nota-bilities Sydney met at Holland House. Lord and Lady Holland themselves condescended to visit when on tour, Samuel Rogers and Henry Luttrell came, Francis Jeffrey and John Murray were among the travellers from Scotland who stopped on their way south. There were innumerable philosophers and scientific literati. Sydney wrote to Lady Mary Bennet in August 1822 that 'I have had a great run of philosophers this summer—Dr and Mrs Marcet, Sir Humphry Davy and Mr Warburton, and divers small mineralogists and chemists. Sir Humphry Davy was very agreeable—neither witty, eloquent, nor sublime, but reasonable and instructive.'* The Marcets—the Swiss chemist–physician and his wife Jane, writer of popular educational works—came up to Sydney's requirements for stimulating guests. 'She is always rational and informed,' Sydney wrote to the bluestocking Lydia White; 'he is a very clever man, and to me a very agreeable one. I like live men to be alive, and dead men to be dead. It is impertinent in a ghost to walk, and unpardonable in an intelligent being to be as stupid as if the apothecary had killed him, and the parson buried him.'* That other chemical couple, Humphry Davy and his ebullient wife, had visited Foston a few years previously, provoking the comment that 'Davy is as he always was, a very foolish coxcomb out of his crucibles. My lady wore her summer manners and was agreeable enough. I cannot think they will go on together to the end without being decomposed.'*

Sydney's noble friends also came to stay and were assured of 'a very comfortable parsonage house, and an hearty welcome',* and members of the Holland family were particularly welcome. At a busy time, Sydney wrote to Miss Elizabeth Vernon in August 1817 that 'we are about to condense all these good people into our parsonage next week—a process requiring some ingenuity on our part and some indulgence on theirs. It would give us pleasure if the inhabitants of Little Holland House were of the number; in that case the packing would be perfect, and the parsonage house might travel behind Lady Holland's carriage without the danger of internal friction or the derangement of parts.'* At this time Sydney was preparing to accommodate his father, brother, and brother's family, which he admitted was a tight fit— they would have to be 'packed by Sabatier's condensing machine'—and when they had gone he told Lady Mary Bennet that 'a house emptied of its guests is always melancholy for the first three or four days'.*

Scottish friends were always pressed to stay at Foston on their way south. Mrs Sydney wrote to the Edinburgh publisher Archibald Constable: 'Between Edinburgh and London this is an halfway house, that I wish our Scots friends found out more frequently; for the goodness of its accommodation I must refer you to Mr Leonard Horner who has been so good as often to visit our "Hostelrie".'* On one of his visits, Francis Jeffrey rode on the rectory's donkey, Biddy, who 'was almost considered a member of the family'. On seeing the diminutive Whig critic so oddly mounted, Sydney burst into laughter and produced this impromptu:

Witty as Horatius Flaccus,
As great a Jacobin as Gracchus,
Short, though not as fat, as Bacchus,
Riding on a little jackass.*

The young Thomas Babington Macaulay was one of the many lawyers who visited Foston while attending the York Assizes. In July 1826, he reported to his father that his York landlady had announced a Mr Smith to him as he was dressing. Macaulay had no idea who it could be, as he wrote in a letter to his father:

Of all names by which men are called there is none which conveys a less determinate idea to my mind than that of Smith.... Down I went, and to my utter amazement beheld the Smith of Smiths, Sydney Smith, alias Peter Plymley. I had forgotten his very existence till I discerned the queer contrast between his black coat and his snow-white head, and the equally curious contrast between the clerical amplitude of his person and the most unclerical wit, whim and petulance of his eye.... I am very well pleased at having this opportunity of becoming acquainted with a man who, in spite of innumerable affectations and eccentricities, is certainly one of the wittiest and most original writers of our times. I shall see him indeed in those situations in which he displays his best and his worst peculiarities most strongly, at the head of his own table and in his pulpit. How strange an instance of self-love it is that the man who possesses perhaps the finest sense of the ridiculous of any person now living, should not perceive the exquisite absurdity of his own style of preaching.*

Sydney pressed the young barrister to stay for a few days between Court sessions and Macaulay was favourably impressed when he got to Foston. ' "Fifteen years ago," said he to me when I alighted at the gate of his shrubbery, "I was taken up in Piccadilly and set down here. There was no house, and no garden, nothing but a bare field." One service this eccentric divine has certainly rendered to the Church. He has built the very neatest, most commodious, and most appropriate rectory that I saw. All its decorations are in a peculiarly clerical style, grave, simple and Gothic.' (This opinion of Foston Rectory as 'Gothic' is eccentric, to say the least.) He attended Church on the Sunday, rightly condemning it as 'a miserable hovel', but was less disposed to continue his priggishness about Sydney's forceful delivery: 'He preached a very queer sermon—the former half too familiar and the latter half too florid, but not without some ingenuity both of thought and expression.'*

Macaulay left Foston the following day, having taken a great liking to his host, recognizing his shrewdness as well as his humour. Sydney had given the young *Edinburgh* contributor some useful, and much-needed, advice against 'a tone of too much asperity and contempt in controversy' in his reviews,* and the foundation was laid for a close friendship and a long rivalry in conversation. Lord Houghton had it from one present when Macaulay took his leave then that Sydney gave 'a look of ludicrous relief exclaiming "I am now like Zacharias, my mouth is opened".'* Many years later, Sydney recalled in conversation that 'I take great credit to myself; I always prophesied [Macaulay's] greatness from the first moment I saw him, then a very young and unknown man on the Northern Circuit ... He is like a book in breeches ... but now he has occasional flashes of silence, that make his conversation perfectly delightful.'*

The 'sporting clergy of Malton', as he characterized his brethren, did not share his tastes or his sensibilities. When a newcomer among them he had reminded them in a Visitation sermon of their clerical duties and asked 'Are there no decencies, and proprieties, which we owe to our situation in society? Is a minister of God to lead the life of a gamekeeper, or a groom?'* Colleagues who needed such warnings were unlikely to be congenial companions and local clerical society had little to offer: hence the welcome he gave to the visitors who provided a relief from the ennuis of country life. Years later he had memories of bad meals and worse conversation.* The local sense of humour was scarcely up to his polished urban wit; as he remarked:

A joke goes a great way in the country. I have known one last pretty well for seven years. I remember making a joke after a meeting of the clergy, in Yorkshire, where there was a Rev. Mr Buckle, who never spoke. When I gave his health, saying that he was a buckle without a tongue, most persons within hearing laughed, but my next neighbour sat unmoved and sunk in thought. At last, a quarter of an hour after we had all done, he suddenly nudged me, exclaiming 'I see *now* what you meant Mr Smith; you meant a joke'. 'Yes,' I said, 'Sir, I believe I did.' Upon which he began laughing so heartily that I thought he would choke, and was obliged to pat him on the back.*

York itself provided regular diversions, particularly when the children were growing up. Sydney usually took lodgings there for the whole family during the Assizes. In 1821 he wrote to Edward Davenport that 'I have taken lodgings in York for myself and family during the Assizes, to enable them to stare out of the window, there being nothing visible where we live but crows'.* When Scottish families came to York, like Mrs Eliza Fletcher's, Sydney remarked that it was for them 'no bad place for change, cheapness, and comparative warmth'.* Circuit lawyers provided friends, and entertainment. During his 1821 visit Sydney wrote to Lady Grey that: 'We have been at the Assizes at York for three weeks, where there is always a great deal of dancing, and provincial joy. Brougham was much employed and constantly opposed to Scarlett [another friend, from their London days]. He was silent, sufficiently humble, and in good health. The prudence of Scarlett in conducting a cause Brougham can never attain, his knowledge and acuteness he will never surpass, but he excels him in force, and in wit and humour. In singleness of heart and suavity of disposition, I will make no comparison.'* The previous year's Assizes had been dominated by the trial for sedition of the radical politician Henry Hunt. Sydney was most impressed with Hunt's ability, and wrote to Davenport that he was 'much struck with his boldness, dexterity and shrewdness. Without any education at all, he is the most powerful barrister this day on the Northern Circuit; of course I do not mean the best instructed, but the man best calculated by nature for that sort of intellectual exertion.'* Though he admired Hunt's forensic skill, Sydney did not approve of the man. He wrote to Lord Grey that 'Hunt I hope will have six [years] if it is possible to inflict so many—not for his political crimes but for himself; he is such a thorough ruffian. But he acquitted himself with great ability on his trial.'* Hunt was sentenced to two years' imprisonment.

The York Musical Festival, held regularly in the 1820s, was another local diversion. Sydney each year ridicules the proceedings. In 1823: 'Nothing can be more disgusting than an oratorio. How absurd, to see 500 people fiddling like madmen about Israelites in the Red Sea. Lord Morpeth pretends to say he was pleased, but I see a great change in him since the music-meeting.'* In 1825: 'The music went off very well, £20,500 was collected. I did not go once. Music for such a length of time (unless under sentence of a jury) I will not submit to. What pleasure is there in pleasure, if quantity is not attended to, as well as quality? I know nothing more agreeable than a dinner at Holland House, but it must not begin at ten in the morning and last till six.'* And finally, in 1828: 'The festival seems to be at a discount. Mr Dickson is said to have written to Catalani to know if her voice was *really* as good as it used to be. No answer, perhaps no Catalani. Two or three of their other female singers are (it is said) in the family way, and expect to be confined about the musical week; nevertheless, they will come, though their medical advisers are rather apprehensive of the effects of grand choruses, but I hope all will go off quietly.'*

Sydney acted as Chaplain to the High Sheriff at the York Assizes in 1824, and was at some pains to observe the sartorial proprieties of the office. He wrote to Archdeacon Wrangham, who had held the chaplaincy before, that 'there is an hatter at the corner of Ousegate; be so good as to give him advice upon the important question of an hat for the Assizes for me. It should I fancy be a mere manual hat: *I will not have a shovel*, so pray direct about the instrument. I presume it is a Chapeau de Bras.'* Sydney preached two Assize sermons in York Minster. The first, 'The Judge that smites contrary to the law', was addressed very directly to the two presiding judges, and contains an eloquent plea for the proper administration of justice by disinterested men who trust in God and temper their justice with mercy. At the next Assize, Sydney's sermon on 'The Lawyer that tempted Christ' is pointed just as directly at the bar, insisting on high Christian standards in advocacy, and stressing the importance of public and private duty before God in the establishing of justice and truth. Sydney thought highly enough of these two discources on the principles of Christian justice to include them in his *Collected Works* in 1839.

When James Tate was Chaplain to the High Sheriff in 1825, Sydney advised him on his religious and social duties. He explained the procedure of the cathedral service, remarking 'always remember that of what you say in the Minster not one syllable can be heard. Do not let your sermon be the less treasonable on that account ... Seriously speaking, the only advice I can give you is to avoid politics. Odd advice by me. Be learned in your sermons—everybody knows you are strong there.' Sydney's advice to Tate on his social functions is interesting: 'When you dine at these official dinners you always appear in gown and cassock, and at the Sheriff's dinner he sits at the head of the table, and you at the bottom, where you act as deputy toast-master. At a certain time after dinner when the conversation becomes too secular as to border on impropriety, you retire and return (if you choose to return) out of canonicals. In the absence of the Chaplain certain toasts are given allusive (as I am told) to the generation of the human race, but what they are I could never distinctly learn. Your health is drunk once or twice and a speech of the neat and appropriate kind expected.'*

The chance of occasional visits to London and other parts of the country did much to reconcile Sydney to his exile and to keep him a cosmopolitan *in partibus*. As early as 1809 he wrote to Lady Holland: 'I mean to come to town once a year, though of that I shall soon be weary, finding my mind growing weaker and weaker and my acquaintance gradually reduced to very much neglected aunts and cousins, to whose proferred tea I shall crawl in, a penitent and Magdalene kinsman. I shall by that time have taken myself again to shy tricks, pull about my watch-chain and become (as I was before) your abomination.'* Needless to say, he remained a popular and vivacious visitor, usually managing to spend several weeks in London each spring. When in London he usually stayed at Holland House, and his name is recorded in the Dinner Books many times each year. Inviting himself in 1810, Sydney wrote to Lady Holland: 'I need not say I shall spend as much time with you as from our mutual engagements will be agreeable to you and possible to me. Some of the best and happiest days of my life I have spent under your roof, and though there may be in some houses, particularly those of our eminent prelates, a stronger disposition to pious exercises and as it were devout lucubrations, I do not believe all Europe can produce as much knowledge, wit and worth as passes in and out of your door under the nose of Thomas the porter.'*

He was sometimes able to take his family to London in spite of heavy expense and worrying preparations. At the end of 1819 he turned down an invitation to Lambton, explaining to John George Lambton that 'I am going with all my family to London at the end of next week, and though you perform this with as much ease as a ball quits a cannon, you cannot conceive the blunders and agony, the dust and distraction, the roaring and raving with which a family like mine is conveyed through three degrees of latitude to its place of destination.'* The children were thrilled by their visit. 'They are, as you may suppose, not a little entertained and delighted,' Sydney wrote to Lady Mary Bennet: 'It is the first time they have ever seen four people together, except on remarkably fine days at the parish church.'* Sydney felt that such trips were an essential part of his family's education, and was later to urge the relaxation of residence requirements for country clergymen whose children had to acquire civilized accomplishments which could only be learnt in towns.*

More often, however, he went up to London by himself, and the family at Foston were often to regret his absence. At the time of his visit to Holland House in 1810, Mrs Sydney wrote to Jeffrey reporting that little Saba had said to her when they were wondering why they were all feeling so miserable: ' "*I'll* tell you what the matter is; you are so melancholy and dull because papa is away; he is so merry, that he makes us all gay. A family doesn't prosper, I see, without a papa!" ' Mrs Sydney agreed with these sentiments and, 'suspecting that the observation would please him quite as well as that of any of his London flatterers', passed the remark on to her absent husband.* But Sydney did not—indeed he could not—go away too often, for reasons he explained to Jeffrey in 1819 when declining an invitation to Edinburgh: 'A clergyman can by law be absent only three months from his living and is liable to be informed against, and to heavy penalties, if he is so. I should certainly be informed against, I know that I am watched. I have very little money, and the expense of travelling is an object to me. All my relations live in the South.'*

Besides these regular visits to London, Sydney found time to travel north. He revisited Scotland in 1820, making his usual comments on the condition of the skin of his learned friends. He went back in 1827, making similar jokes (about 'those compositions of itch, oatmeal and metaphysics, the Scotch philosophers')* and hoping to visit the Deanery at Durham on the way: 'I have some curiosity to see a Golden Prebendary, a being described by Linnæus, but whom I have never yet seen.'*

His family was able to accompany him on many of these trips in the north. He visited Lambton Castle and the Greys at Howick, his friend the cotton magnate Sir George Philips near Manchester and Lord Derby at Knowsley; or, nearer home, the Beilby Thompsons at Escrick, who became particular friends. These country house trips often gave him an experience of opulence greater even than that he encountered in London. Sydney reported a return journey from Edinburgh at the end of 1820 in a letter to Lady Mary Bennet, whose father, Lord Tankerville, owned the wild cattle of Chillingham:

From thence to Lambton. And here I ask, what use of wealth so luxurious and delightful as to light your house with gas? What folly, to have a diamond necklace or a Correggio, and not to light your house with gas! The splendour and glory of Lambton Hall make all other houses mean. How pitiful to submit to a farthing-candle existence, when science puts such intense gratification within your reach! Dear lady, spend all your fortune in a gas-apparatus. Better to eat dry bread by the splendour of gas than to dine on wild beef with wax candles.*

He often travelled in Yorkshire, and an itinerary for 1823 is characteristic: 'We are going to make a tour of visits: Mr York, uncle to Mr Lascelles, William Herbert, M. A. Taylor, Lord Harewood, Walter Fawkes, and shall be out about three weeks.'* This visit to Harewood was critically reported to Lady Morpeth:

I was pleased with my visit to Harewood. Lady Harewood I found extremely agreeable, his Lordship straightforward, sensible, unaffected and good natured, the young ladies very amiable and polite, the place beautiful, the dinners too good, and Lady Louisa Lascelles a lively, clever person. The house was warm also, which was more than I expected, but they have bad potatoes—I mean not mealy—which is a dreadful oversight, and the salads were poor and insignificant till I gave them a lesson, which (considering it was the first visit) was a strong measure. But it is difficult for a person like myself, who has turned his attention to salads, to witness without instruction and remonstrance the mistakes and follies which are every day committed with salads.*

Throughout his life, Sydney reckoned himself an authority on salads. Like many gastronomists of consummate fastidiousness but little practical ability, he was prepared to lay down the law on various articles of diet: Sydney had the advantage of being able to pontificate in verse. His classic statement on the concoction of a winter salad, no doubt the fruit of prolonged meditation and research, was so popular that by the late 1830s he had to have copies printed to satisfy the many enquirers; it probably belongs, however, to his Foston years:

> To make this condiment your poet begs
> The pounded yellow of two hard-boiled eggs;
> Two boiled potatoes, passed through kitchen sieve,
> Smoothness and softness to the salad give.
> Let onion atoms lurk within the bowl,
> And, half-suspected, animate the whole.
> Of mordant mustard add a single spoon,
> Distrust the condiment that bites so soon;
> But deem it not, thou man of herbs, a fault
> To add a double quantity of salt;
> Four times the spoon with oil of Lucca crown,
> And twice with vinegar procured from town;
> And lastly o'er the flavoured compound toss
> A magic soupçon of anchovy sauce.

Oh, green and glorious! Oh, herbaceous treat!
'Twould tempt the dying anchorite to eat;
Back to the world he'd turn his fleeting soul,
And plunge his fingers in the salad-bowl!
Serenely full, the epicure would say,
'Fate cannot harm me, I have dined today'.*

Sydney's skill as a gourmet provided another link between Foston and London, as he was able to repay some of the hospitality of Holland House by sending special tributes of country produce up to town. A large ham of between twenty and thirty pounds was sent down each New Year, the weight specified so that any exchange on the journey could be detected. Their dispatch was usually accompanied by some banter. In 1814: 'I have taken the liberty to send you an ham upon which I have as it were a notion that my benefice at Foston depends.'* In 1819: 'We have taken the liberty to send you two hams in token of your seignorage over Foston and its inhabitants. They are, I understand, of domestic manufacture and we shall feel exalted above the neighbouring clergy if they are approved of at Holland House.'*

In the Visitation sermon which he had delivered in 1809, Sydney had reminded his clerical colleagues that 'the most inveterate disease to which a clerical life is exposed, is that of indolence: we are apt to see admirable understandings dwindling away into absolute insignificance from the want of some adequate object, and men who at school or college held forth the fairest promise of distinction, lulled into the tamest mediocrity by the gradual effects of solitude and retirement.' He urged the pursuit of knowledge as a corrective and recommended proper clerical activity to his fellow ministers.* He certainly practised what he preached. He later recalled of his life at Foston that, in addition to educating his children and his many other domestic cares, he was 'village parson, village doctor, village comforter, village magistrate and Edinburgh Reviewer; so you see' (he explained) 'I had not much time left on my hands to regret London.'* In 1820 he expounded his roles to Lord Holland as 'doctor, justice, road-maker, pacifier, preacher, farmer, neighbour and diner-out.'* It is possible from the ample correspondence of his Yorkshire years to study each of his chosen roles in turn.

First, the parson. Foston Church had been described by Macaulay as a 'miserable little hovel with a wooden belfry'. It was restored in 1911 (when a north aisle was added) and can now be seen as a pleasing, plain building, notable for its two decorated Norman doorways. The pulpit is of the eighteenth century, with a velvet cushion and a pair of brass candleholders. It is the same as that of which Sydney said: 'When I began to thump the cushion of my pulpit on first coming to Foston, as is my wont when I preach, the accumulated dust of a hundred and fifty years made such a cloud, that for some minutes I lost sight of my congregation.'* A clerical friend later reminisced about a service he shared with Sydney at Foston, riding over from the rectory in the family chariot, the 'Invincible': 'About fifty people were assembled; I entered the reading-desk; he followed the prayers with a plain, sound sermon upon the duty of forgiving injuries, but in manner and voice clearly proving that he felt what he said, and meant that others should feel it too.'*

Most of Sydney's surviving sermons were written for special occasions, like that preached at the Visitation of 1809. This he had described to Allen as 'a sermon against horse-racing and coursing, judiciously preached before the Archbishop and the sporting clergy of Malton',* but its more serious purpose was explained to Lady Grey: 'I publish the Sermon merely to take the opportunity of saying in a note that I am a great stickler for the doctrine of the Trinity—which they [the *Quarterly Review*] accuse me of attacking, whereas I am a perfect bigot about it, and have a sort of natural antipathy to it, as some have to cats, others to cheese.'* Sermons which were printed or collected may have been very different from his ordinary parochial discourses, which seem to have been based on the simple and energetic presentation of basic moral teachings, not very inspiring and not very exacting, but showing Low Church piety at its best,* and fairly well suited to his unsophisticated parishioners. Macaulay, as we have seen, noted the mixture of familiarity and floridity in his manner, and Sydney himself confirms such an impression in the rhymed refusal of invitation to a ball which he once sent to Lady Woodhouselee:

> 'Tis mine, with all my consecrated dress on
> To read the evening and the morning lesson;
> With band bi-forkèd, and with visage calm
> To join the bawling, quav'ring Clerk in Psalm.
> With brawny fist the velvet lump to beat,
> And rouse the faithful, snoring at my feet!*

The presence of a large dissenting population in the area provided Sydney with an opportunity of putting his theories into practice. His attitude to dissenters was very mixed. He was openly contemptuous of extreme evangelical enthusiasm, and reserved some of his most biting wit in the *Edinburgh Review* for the Methodists. But he was sympathetic to beliefs which he felt were genuinely held and found to be oppressed in some way. The Catholic emancipation question is the main example of his coming to the support of those whose faith involved much that appeared to him to be ridiculous, or even grotesque, but whose sincerity he saw to be unfairly oppressed by political disabilities. The Unitarians provided another cause for him to fight. He correctly regarded the imposition on Unitarians (abolished by Act of Parliament in 1819) of a Trinitarian marriage service as an infringement of liberty of conscience. He first wrote on the subject to William Smith MP, for whom he had considerable admiration. 'You know my unfortunate zeal for civil and religious liberty,' he remarked, asking what he might read and if possible review on the subject of 'heterodox nuptials'; but the member could provide only periodical publications and 'magazines are not proper subjects for reviews'.* He also asked Charles Wellbeloved, a leading Unitarian minister and Principal of Manchester College, York, securing the pamphlets which served as a 'peg' on which to hang Sydney's article on 'Dissenters' Marriages' in the *Edinburgh* of 1821. 'I have and can have no other motive for meddling with it' [he wrote to Wellbeloved] than the detestation of anything like persecution in religious opinions, and it is gross persecution to say to any man "your only method of getting married shall be by listening to, repeating and appearing to acquiesce in doctrines which in your conscience you do not believe to be scriptural". I write this to you in confidence, though I should not on proper occasions object to preaching it at the Market Cross—indeed I have done so before now.'* Sydney took a good-humoured view of local religious differences, and wrote to Wellbeloved five years later: 'Your Unitarian preachers have stolen away four of my congregation who had withstood Ranters and Methodists. I shall make reprisals and open a chapel near the College, but it shall be generous and polite warfare, such as is the duty, not the disgrace, of Christian divines.'*

In spite of his once having told a humourless neighbour at dinner that his one secret desire was 'to roast a Quaker', Sydney was particularly sympathetic to the Society of Friends, who were very strong in the neighbourhood. He found them an obvious subject for banter: 'A Quaker baby? Impossible! There is no such thing; there never was; they are always born broad-brimmed and in full quake',* but his residence near York gave him many opportunities of seeing active Quaker piety at work. He greatly admired the efforts of the local Quakers during an epidemic at Thornton in 1816, and once visited Newgate with Mrs Fry—a deeply moving experience which he commemorated in an eloquent sermon and in his essay on 'Prisons' in the *Edinburgh Review* of 1821.* He remarked of Elizabeth Fry after the publication of his article: 'She is very unpopular with the clergy; examples of living, active virtue disturb our repose, and give birth to distressing comparisons: we long to burn her alive.'* He once called on Joseph Rowntree, his York grocer, 'and asked him to provide a Quaker nursemaid for the rectory at Foston: her faith should in no way be interfered with while resident in a clergyman's family'. Sydney, who respected the Friends' practical and spiritual qualities, said 'you obtain something which we do not', an eloquent statement of his practical broadmindedness.*

The parish registers of Foston were conscientiously enough kept, and show the usual regular entries for births, marriages, and deaths. But Sydney never thought of such formal duties as the whole of his pastoral responsibility. 'Village doctor' and 'village comforter' were two of the roles Sydney regarded as an essential part of his duties in the parish. He once joked to Dr John Allen about 'my absurd affectation of knowing something about medicine', but he had been well trained in elementary treatments. He had attended some of Sir Christopher Pegge's lectures at Oxford and the clinical classes at the Royal Infirmary of Edinburgh to prepare himself for the work of a country parson. His widow wrote in her 'Narrative': 'The poor *intirely* confided their maladies to him and he had the satisfaction of being to them eminently useful. All his drugs were got from London, a record was kept of each case of sickness, of the remedies applied. These were all written down, dated, and filed, so that they could be immediately referred to, if any doubt arose.'*

There was, of course, humour as well as method in Sydney's doctoring. Annie Kay, one of the most delightful of the rectory servants, acted as Sydney's 'apothecary's boy', making up the medicines which Sydney taught her in his own fashion: 'There is the Gentle-jog, a pleasure to take it; the Bull-dog, for more serious cases; Peter's puke; Heart's delight, the comfort of all the old women in the village; Rub-a-dub, a capital embrocation; Dead-stop, settles the matter at once; Up-with-it-then needs no explanation; and so on. Now, Annie Kay, give Mrs Spratt a bottle of Rub-a-dub; and to Mr Coles a dose of Dead-stop and twenty drops of laudanum.'*

Turning to Mrs Marcet, who recorded this pharmacopoeia, Sydney explained:

This is the house to be ill in; indeed everybody who comes is expected to take a little something; I consider it a delicate compliment when my guests have a slight illness here. We have contrivances for everything. Have you seen my patent armour? No? Annie Kay, bring me my patent armour. Now look here: if you have a stiff neck or a swelled face, here is this sweet case of tin filled with hot water, and covered with flannel, to put round your neck, and you are well directly. Likewise, a patent tin shoulder in case of rheumatism. There you see a stomach-tin, the greatest comfort in life, and lastly, here is a tin-slipper, to be filled with hot water, which you can sit with in the drawing-room, should you come in chilled, without wetting your feet.*

Sydney was able to act quickly and effectively at times of medical necessity. He described to John Allen how he treated his son Douglas for a severe attack of croup. 'I darted into him all the mineral and vegetable resources of the shops, cravatted his throat with blisters, and fringed it with leeches, excited now the peristaltic, now the antiperistaltic motion, like the *strophe* and *antistrophe* of the tragedies, and set him in five or six hours to play at marbles, breathing gently and inaudibly.'* Small wonder, then, that with such skill and resourcefulness, Sydney was very pleased when a small child in the parish identified him as 'the Parson Doctor'.*

His medical talents were put to good general use in 1816, a year of severe agricultural distress in the county. 'Corn is rather bad than dear', Sydney wrote to Horner at the end of the year, 'but makes good unleavened bread; and the poor, I find, seldom make any other than unleavened bread, even in the best seasons.'* His daughter recalled that even the rectory had to make do with an unwholesome diet based on the poor flour of the 1816 harvest. The poor fared very badly, and a fever epidemic broke out in Thornton. Sydney's work is described in a letter from his wife to Lady Morpeth:

Three people died of it, and I believe fully sixteen were ill of it; Sydney visited them all *constantly every day*, but never approaching them, standing at the door, and from thence put his various *medical* questions. I must add he did not undertake to administer any other than medicine which had been prescribed by the apothecary, and to take care that all such nutriment as *he* directed was regularly received and taken by the patients; but the disease was of too fearful a nature for *him* to venture on the responsibility of. As you know, he never was in the slightest degree affected by it.*

He wrote in verse of his medical work in the parish:

> I know all drugs, all simples and all pills;
> I cure diseases, and I send no bills.
> The poor old women now no lameness know;
> Rheumatics leave their hand, the gout their toe.
> Fell atrophy has fled from Foston's vale,
> And health, and peace, and joy and love prevail.*

Sydney was also much concerned for the general welfare of the poor in his parish. While at Edinburgh, with many opportunities of comparing the common diet of the poor in England and Scotland, he had thought carefully about providing cheap, nourishing food and had written that 'I am in hopes to carry these ideas into execution at some future time, and become master cook, as well as master parson, of my village'.* He was convinced by his Scottish experience that the best means of helping them to better their condition was by educating them in the best use of available resources rather than by charitable doles of food.

One of the practical ways in which he helped his parishioners was by dividing several acres of his glebe into sixteenths, and letting them out cheaply—a very early example of a beneficial scheme which later became widespread. His daughter wrote of these plots for the poor (to which Sydney later added 'Dutch gardens for spade cultivation') that 'It becomes quite a pretty sight afterwards to see these small gardens (which were just enough to supply a cottager with potatoes, and sometimes to enable him to keep a pig) filled at dawn with women and children cultivating them before they went to their day's labour.'* Late in the century, they were still gratefully remembered as 'Sydney's orchards'.*

Sydney once remarked on being presented to another living that 'my examination ... ought to be in Burn's Justice and the Farmer's Calendar, if respect were had to that kind of life which my situation at Foston has compelled me to lead'.* When he was made a county magistrate in 1814, he wrote rather guiltily to John Allen at Holland House: 'Pray tell Lady Holland that I am a Justice of the Peace one of those rural tyrants so deprecated by poor Windham. I am determined to strike into the [Benthamite] line of analogous punishments, but what am I to do in cases of bastardy—how can I afflict the father analogously? Help me in this difficulty.'*

How he dealt with one of the bastardy cases which came before him is explained in a letter (probably of 1816) to Francis Cholmeley, a fellow magistrate:

It is right enough that a mole catcher should have his relaxations, and there is more excuse for persons of that business than any other, from the effects of association. You are not perhaps aware that the mole of all four footed animals has the largest member of generation, and is supposed by Buffon to enjoy the greatest pleasure; his venereal endowments have drawn from the pen of that naturalist a most splendid and eloquent eulogium, to which I refer you. I have just heard the cause and am sorry to be compelled to give it against the fair one—I will explain on what grounds when I see you.*

Sydney's methods of preventing unlawfulness were sometimes as unorthodox as his judicial reasoning. When he first went to Foston he was much troubled by the farmers' savage dogs. 'I scolded, preached, and prayed, without avail; so I determined to try what fear for their pockets would do. Forthwith appeared in the county paper a minute account of the trial of a farmer, at the Northampton Sessions, for keeping dogs unconfined; where said farmer was not only fined five pounds and reprimanded by the magistrates, but sentenced to three months' imprisonment. The effect was wonderful and the reign of Cerberus ceased in the land.' Years later he recounted this to Lord Spencer, who always attended the Northamptonshire Sessions but had been puzzled never to have come across the celebrated dog case.*

His general correspondence often deals with matters arising from his work as a magistrate. Thus he wrote to Sir Robert Peel in 1824:

I took up a man for poisoning cattle, and sent the constable to search the house of the suspected person for poison. Poison he found (arsenic in a paper), brought it to my house in his pocket, and to shelter the prisoner denied that any had been found: I have his own confession of the fact, signed by himself. If I prosecute this man it will cost me £60 or £70, nor is there any power in the Quarter Sessions to allow me my expenses. The man therefore escapes with impunity. Surely it would be a great improvement, if two magistrates concurring in the indictment of a constable could be allowed their expenses at the Q. Sessions, unless the indictment was found to be vexatious and frivolous.*

Eighteen months later he reverted to the subject after Peel had mentioned the case in a speech. He explained that he had said in the earlier letter not that he had indicted the constable and been subject to expense, but that the fear of expense had prevented him from making any indictment. Peel received the suggestion very sympathetically.

Another example of the way in which he put his local experience at the service of friends in the south is a series of proposals he sent to Lord Lansdowne in 1827 for changes in the procedure for licensing alehouses. The theme was developed in the *Edinburgh Review*, and Sydney maintained that the proceedings on the bench should be more open, with the names of objectors revealed, and that an appeal against refusal should be allowed to the Quarter Sessions.* He took the matter up with Peel early in 1828, pointing out the corrupt practices of interested parties in rejecting licensing applications. 'Nobody ever *thinks* of the accommodation of the public,' he wrote. 'In a road within my knowledge in Yorkshire there are between two cities precisely the same number of public houses as there were seventy years past, and the magistrates obstinately refuse to increase their number, though the turnpike tolls and the posthouse duties show that traffic has been quadrupled within that period.'*

Prison administration was a matter of constant concern to Sydney while he was on the bench. His admiration for the work of Elizabeth Fry has already been mentioned. He was so far aware of the corrupting influence of the contemporary prison system that he was always reluctant to send a young offender to gaol. As he put it in one of his *Review* articles on the subject: 'There are, in every county in England, large public schools, maintained at the expense of the county, for the encouragement of profligacy and vice, and for providing a proper succession of housebreakers, profligates and thieves.'* Some of the contemporary evils are revealed in two letters he sent to Lord Lansdowne in 1819, at a time when Parliament was considering Criminal Law reform. His practical suggestions were based on his own observation of the evils, and he took advantage of a change in contemporary opinion to press them. 'It is very singular to find the public so humane and reasonable that they will listen to these subterraneous miseries, and very good and wise in you to derive from this spirit a law of permanent humanity which will outlive it.' Sydney asked for a public record of the names and work of the visiting magistrates, to secure full supervison. The separation of accused and committed, and of old and young offenders, was essential. Compulsory worship was not to be enforced against the prisoner's conscience. The diet of the prisoners was to be contolled, with the minimum decreed, and there should be a limit of ten hours in night confinement.* A few weeks later he expanded some of his views: 'Coarse men should be made sorrowful by plain food. A jail is not an object of terror if men have friends who send them money and so purchase roast veal and porter. Spiritous liquors and dangerous tools are let down from the windows of debtors. The weekly allowance is meant for food, but spent in a very different way.'*

It should not be thought, however, that Sydney was in favour of lighter punishment, however anxious he was to see conditions in prisons improved. As he wrote to Peel:

A sentence of transportation to Botany Bay translated into common sense is this: 'Because you have committed this offence, the sentence of the Court is that you shall no longer be burthened with the support of your wife and family; you shall be immediately removed from a very bad climate, and a country overburthened with people, to one of the finest regions of the earth, where the demand for human labour is every hour increasing, and where it is highly probable you may ultimately regain your character, and improve your fortune. The Court has been induced to pass this sentence upon you in consequence of the many aggravating circumstances of your case, and they hope your fate will be a warning to others.'*

Peel admitted the justice of this argument and replied that 'we are at this moment occupied in devising some means of giving to transportation some degree of salutary terror as a punishment'. The whole question of secondary punishment was rendered very difficult by 'the vast harvest of transportable crime that is reaped at every assize'. 'The real truth', Peel concluded, 'is the number of convicts is too overwhelming for the means of proven and effective punishment. I despair of any remedy but that which I wish I could hope for—a great reduction in the amount of crime.'*

Sydney was pleased with Peel's attitude and wrote in his reply:

If unfortunately for mankind the reins of internal government were placed in my hands, I *suspect* I should put an end to transportation, hulks, and penitentiary, and use no other secondary punishment than the tread mill, varying in all degrees from a day to a life. . . . The punishment would be economical, certain, well administered, little liable to abuse, capable of infinite division, a perpetual example before the eyes of those who want it, affecting the imagination only with horror and disgust, and affording great ease to the Government.... The wheel should go round whether it ground anything, or nothing. I suspect that to grind nothing would be more terrible to the grinder, and cheaper to the master. I will follow out these notions in the Edinburgh Review.*

He had an opportunity of putting into practice some of his ideas on prison reform. In the same letter to Peel, he remarked that 'you will be glad to hear that after long combats against mistaken economy, it is resolved to build a very superior jail for the County of York, and it is actually begun upon'. Sydney was one of the magistrates on the Building Committee set up in 1825 to consider plans for enlarging the county prison. They eventually recommended the construction of a tall battlemented gritstone wall around the jail, which took years to build and proved very expensive. These castellations were demolished in 1935 and were known as Sydney Smith's hardest joke.*

The magistrates were much occupied with the administration of roads, which Sydney found very troublesome when he had to make frequent journeys to Malton on turnpike business. After he had left Yorkshire for Somerset, Sydney wrote to Jonathan Gray of York, a prominent local lawyer, asking for his name to be withdrawn from the list of turnpike trustees. 'Nobody can more sincerely wish the prosperity of the road from York to Oswaldkirk than I do. I wish to you hard materials, diligent trustees, gentle convexity, fruitful tolls, cleanly gutters, obedient parishes, favouring justices, and every combination of fortunate circumstances which can fall to the lot of any human highway.' Sending his apologies for absence, he continued: 'I shall think on the 15th of my friends at the White Bear, Stillington. How honourable to English gentlemen that once or twice every month half the men of fortune of England are jammed together at the White Bear, crushed into a mass at the Three Pigeons, or perspiring intensely at the Green Dragon!'*

Road business at the Malton magistrates' meeting was the cause of a lively dispute which is well covered in the Castle Howard archives. The volume of Sydney's letters there contains a slip of paper reading: 'Words stated by Mr Read to Lord Carlisle to have been used by Mr Smith at a Justice Meeting at Malton— "Sir, if you raise your voice and do not hold your noise I shall say something which you will not easily forget".' This refers to a minor but exaggerated altercation between Sydney and the

Revd C.R. Read of Sand Hutton in the autumn of 1824. Lord Carlisle was asked to act as mediator, and the opinions of several witnesses were collected. The original complaint which produced the 'words' seems to have been the charge that Sydney had referred to some of his fellow Turnpike Trustees as 'the nine enemies of McAdam' in the press. 'There can be little doubt,' Read opined to Lord Carlisle (without special perspicacity), 'but the intention was to exhibit [us] in some ridiculous view or other—to effect which, and suit his own purposes, he spares no one.' Sydney was alleged to have replied very brusquely when challenged by Read, but the bench differed in their recollections of the precise words used. There was some feeling that Sydney was exceeding his station. Colonel Cholmeley of Brandsby wrote to Read that 'I think a clergyman residing in the county, without an acre of land in the county belonging to him, ought to know better than to attempt to be a leading character in county business.' Sydney showed his own indignation in his letters to Lord Carlisle, reporting that Read was habitually troublesome at public meetings. As for the rest of Read's correspondence—which is as bulky, and as angry, as Sydney's own—Sydney concluded: 'I pass over the expressions of violent and unmannerly abuse in Mr Read's letter, so common among quarrelling clergymen. As I cannot risk my life for this sort of language, I never use it.' The affair eventually faded away, thanks to Lord Carlisle's rather amused intervention. The tone of his mediation may be judged from a copy of one of his letters to Read: 'A sad mistake prevails somewhere. Until the saddle is put upon the right horse, I own I do not see my way towards successful mediation.'*

Sydney was quite correct to consider his work for the *Edinburgh Review* as part of his life as a country parson. Remoteness of residence perhaps gave him a greater objectivity—and a greater daring of manner—as he joked to Lady Grey when announcing that he would be writing on female education: 'You will be astonished at my presumption—but what has [one] to fear who lives in a little [village] in Yorkshire—he is as safe and intangible as the dead.'* Sydney contributed to the *Review* less and less frequently and gave up altogether when he was made a dignitary of the Church in 1828, but until then Jeffrey continued to rely on him for a lightness of touch in his articles to offset heavier matter in the rest of the journal: Sydney was proud, as he reminded the editor, that 'lightness and flimsiness are my line of reviewing'*. The articles he wrote in Yorkshire include some of his best-remembered periodical contributions—for example the essays on public schools, on boy chimney-sweepers, and on the proceedings of the Society for the Suppression of Vice. He continued to give some attention to Ireland and of course devoted much time and energy to the Catholic question. By 1827 he had begun to feel that both he and his readers were becoming exhausted by the latter. He wrote to George Lamb that 'I am writing for the Edinburgh Review an article upon the Catholics which of course nobody will read—but something should be said about them from time to time—and I am so mixed up with the subject that to write upon it ... is only a necessary evacuation.'*

Many of his articles on other subjects reveal his growing knowledge and understanding of rural life and administration. Some of these are very obviously local—like the essay on 'Mad Quakers' (1814), containing a complimentary account of The Retreat at York, or that on 'Cruel Treatment of Untried Prisoners' (1824), attacking pamphlets published by the North Riding Bench in support of the compulsory working of prisoners before trial. Many others, however, have a generally rural flavour, such as the several articles on the Game Laws or on the licensing of alehouses, which were strengthened by references drawn from his experience as a county magistrate.

He kept a critical eye on the general progress of the *Review*, counselling some intending contributors like Edward Davenport of Capesthorne, whom he steered away from economics to literary subjects, remarking that 'Political Economy has become, in the hands of Malthus and Ricardo, a school of metaphysics. All seem agreed what is to be done; the contention is how the subject is to be divided and defined. Meddle with no such matters.'* To the editor himself Sydney sent comments on each issue, briskly assessing the length or competence of articles. Of a phrenological essay by Jeffrey in 1826 he wrote that 'Your review of the Bumpists destroys them—but it is temendously long for such a subject. I cannot tell what the Scotch market may require but Bumpology has always been treated with contempt among men of sense in England and the machinery you have employed for its destruction will excite surprise.'* He occasionally sent the editor accounts for his work ('Francis Jeffrey Esq Debtor to the Rev S. Smith Clerk'), detailing his contributions: 'To an attack upon a Bishop in No 74, said Bishop being a bigot and a tyrant, and for making said Bishop ridiculous and so improving him. ...

all executed in the best manner—good language, witty and clear of Scotticisms, and very provoking according to order.'*

His longstanding literary connection with Edinburgh was maintained not just through the *Review* but by parcels from Constable in Edinburgh, which kept him in touch with literature, just as visits to London kept him in touch with society. Letters written to friends while the Waverley novels were appearing provide a good commentary on the series, on which Sydney sometimes took a line independent of his friends. On *The Heart of Midlothian*, published in 1818, he wrote to Lady Mary Bennet that 'At Holland House it is much run down: I dare not oppose my opinion to such an assay or proof-house; but it made me cry and laugh very often, and I was sorry when it was over, and so I cannot in justice call it dull.'* Many of his comments on later novels refer to a repetitiveness of characterization, but they are generally free of his usual 'Scotch' joking. Sydney wrote to Jeffrey about *The Pirate* (1822) that 'It is certainly one of the least fortunate of Sir Walter Scott's productions. It seems now that he can write nothing without Meg Merrilies and Dominie Samson! One other such novel, and there's an end; but who can last for ever? Who ever lasted so long?'*

CHAPTER IV

❄

IN addition to all his other rural occupations, Sydney had been obliged to turn farmer. His widow recalled in the 'Narrative' she wrote for her grandchildren that his predecessor at Foston had let the land at the beginning of the American War for £250, but that Sydney immediately raised this to £500 from Mr Horner, the farmer. The Foston glebe was an extensive one, and Sydney had to farm much of it himself. About seventy years before Sydney's time, 'a large tract of common land had been enclosed, and in lieu of tithe 310 acres of excellent wheat and bean land was allotted to the clergyman'.* The neighbouring township of Flaxton, of about 900 acres, was titheable. Although Sydney was 'fresh from London, not knowing a turnip from a carrot',* Mrs Sydney remembered that 'he was very fond of farming, and understood it well. I believe he made it answer as well as any gentleman ever does.'*

Sydney supervised his farm energetically. As a visiting friend later wrote, 'Not to lose time, he farms with a tremendous speaking-trumpet from his door; a proper companion for which machine is a telescope, slung in leather, for observing what they are doing.'* His labourers obviously needed encouragement as well as eccentric supervision. In July 1811 he wrote to Francis Cholmeley that he could not accept an invitation: 'on Tuesday the haymaking begins, from which I cannot possibly be absent—having nobody but bad servants everything would go to ruin but for my presence.'* On one occasion, one of the labourers blundered so much that Sydney lost his temper and called the man a fool. ' "God never made a fool," growled the transgressor. "That is true," was the immediate retort, "but man was not long in making a fool of himself." '*

Another noteworthy feature of Sydney's fields was his 'Universal Scratching Post'. He reasoned thus: 'I am all for cheap luxuries, even for animals. Now all animals have a passion for scratching their backbones: they break down your gates and palings to effect this. Look, there is my universal scratcher, a sharp-edged pole resting on a high and a low post, adapted to every height from a horse to a lamb; even the Edinburgh Reviewer can take his turn. You have no idea how popular it is; I have not had a gate broken since I put it up. He comme-morated this ingenious benefaction to his livestock in his 'Imita-tion of Virgil's Sixth Eclogue':

> That learned scratching-pole that yonder stands
> Owes its existence to my curious hands;
> Framed for all animals, or great or small,
> It perfect satisfaction gives to all;
> Their rumps, their tails, their flea-bit backs confess
> How e'en in scratching-poles a priest may bless.*

Sydney came to reckon himself a tolerable farmer, and his let-ters are full of seasonal agricultural intelligence. In 1820 he wrote to Malthus: 'When do you mean to come ... and see me and my cultivation of land? I am beginning to gain reputation in the agriculture line, and have (which you will scarcely believe) kept myself remarkably clear of gentleman's farming nonsense.'* Each year he reported on the (usually poor) harvest to his friends. For example, on 1818: 'The harvest is finished here, and is not more than two-thirds of an average crop. Potatoes have entirely failed; there is no hay; and it will be a year of great scarcity.'* In 1820: 'We have had about three or four inches of rain here, that is all. I heard of your being wet through in London, and envied you very much. The whole of this parish is pulverized from long and excessive drought. Our whole property depends upon the tran-quillity of the winds: if it blows before it rains, we shall all be up in the air in the shape of dust, and shall be *transparished* we know not where.'* And in 1821: 'A very wet harvest here, but I have saved all my corn by injecting great quantities of fermented liquors into the workmen, and making them work all night.'*

Soon after he settled at Foston, Sydney started holding annual dinners for the most respectable of the local farmers. They were jolly affairs, well-managed. Saba recalled that 'without lowering his own dignity or appearing to descend to the level of his more humble guests, it was interesting to observe how he drew out the real sense and knowledge they possessed, how he discussed their opinions, and with what tact he gave a tone of general interest to the conversation.'* The dinners were profitable to host and to guest alike: he increased his agricultural knowledge and influence in the community, and they came to know and respect their parson all the more.

His farming ability was used to his friends' advantage when he bought some Scotch sheep on a commission from Lord Holland. He first discussed the matter in 1810 with Lady Holland: 'Lord Holland is quite right to get a stock of eatable sheep; but such sheep are not exclusively the product of Scotland, but of every half-starved, ill-cultivated country; and are only emphatically termed *Scotch*, to signify *ill-fed*, as one says *Roman* to signify *brave*. They may be bought in Wales in any quantities; and every November at Helmsley, Yorshire, in any quantities; the mutton you eat at my house was from thence. Helmsley is 200 miles from London.'* When a purchase was eventually made two years later, Sydney had some doubts—'as they are Scotch sheep, I think the Presbyterian Pastor of York would buy them to better advantage'*. Unfortunately the sheep did not come up to expectation after the long journey to London, and Lord Holland protested at their poor quality. Sydney replied:

You are a statesman, a scholar, and a wit, but no butcher ... It is not unamusing to see you deciding upon the nationality of sheep. When an human creature is lean, lousy and logical we know him to be a Scotchman, but how does this apply to sheep? The meaning of Scotch mutton is old, small mutton fed on poor pastures—these requisites attended to, the register of birth is idle. Lastly, without joke, if the sheep are bad I am very sorry. I employed a very intelligent, honest cattle dealer to buy them and we both did our best, and as such in your good nature I am sure you take it.*

Scotch sheep provided material for Sydney's only contribution to agricultural literature. In 1819 he wrote a letter to the *Farmer's Magazine*, a journal run by his friend Archibald Constable of the *Edinburgh Review*, in which he repeated his arguments against the undisciplined and omnivorous Scotch sheep, which never fattened. 'Five to six times they all assembled and set out upon their return to the North. My bailiff took a place in the Mail, pursued, and overtook them half way to Newcastle.'

'My ploughing oxen', Sydney continued, 'were an equal subject of vexation. They had a constant purging upon them, which it was impossible to stop. They ate more than twice as much as the same number of horses. They did half as much work as the same number of horses. They could not bear hot weather, nor wet weather, nor go well down hill. It took five men to shoe an ox. They ran against my gate-posts, lay down in the cart when they were tired, and ran away at the sight of a stranger.' The solution was obvious: 'I have now got into a good breed of English sheep, and useful cart-horses, and am doing very well. I make this statement to guard young gentlemen farmers against Arthur Young and the pernicious nonsense of brother gentlemen, for whose advice I am at least poorer by £3 or 400.'*

Sydney's ingenious mind naturally turned to agricultural experiments. In 1818 he wrote a long letter to William Vernon, son of the Archbishop and a considerable scientist, in which he pointed out that all agricultural experiments are 'very slow in their results, very expensive and from the prodigious variety of circumstances very uncertain in their conclusions'. He remarked that when liming his own lands in a fallow year, he had long been careful to leave one strip unlimed to compare the difference. After a long discussion of the necessary duration of manuring tests and their general application, and a passage in which he reveals a detailed knowledge of the food consumption of his cattle, he concludes that 'the useful object in farming is as you well know to reduce everything to value, and an experimenter should fling various sums of money into a cow's mouth and see what it comes out of the teats'*.

He tried to improve his farming and sent a long questionnaire to his neighbour Francis Cholmeley, who was staying in Kent at the time, asking about the best methods of sowing beans used there.* Such practicalities showed how anxious he was to avoid what he called 'gentleman's farming nonsense'. Equally, he had no aspirations to the country pursuits of the gentry. The first rule he had made for himself on going to live in the country, he said, was 'not to smite the partridge, for if I fed the poor, and comforted the sick, and instructed the ignorant, yet I should do nothing worth, if I smote the partridge. If anything ever endangers the Church, it will be the strong propensity to shooting for which the clergy are remarkable. Ten thousand good shots dispersed over the country do more harm to the cause of religion than the arguments of Voltaire and Rousseau.'* On another occasion he remarked that 'if you do shoot, the squire and the poacher both consider you as their natural enemy, and I thought it more clerical to be at peace with both'.* His aversion to shooting was related to his opinion of the contemporary Game Laws, against which he conducted a long campaign in the *Edinburgh Review*. He hated them because 'for every ten pheasants which fluttered in the wood, one English peasant was rotting in gaol'.* He was known to be lenient towards any poacher who appeared before him on the Bench.

Many of his clerical neighbours were great riders, as Sydney remarked in a letter to Brougham. 'I see so little of any clever men here, that I have nobody to recommend; but if you have any young horses to break I can find some and indeed many clergymen who will do it for you.'* The Archbishop himself was a skilled horseman, and once said to Sydney, 'I hear, Mr Smith, you do not approve of much riding for the clergy.' 'Why, my Lord,' was the answer, 'perhaps there is not *much objection*, provided they do not ride too well, and stick their toes out professionally.'* Sydney rode none too well himself, being much prone to accidents. 'I have had six falls in two years,' he recalled, 'and just behaved like the three per cents when they fall—I got up again, and am not a bit the worse for it, any more than the stock in question. I left off riding for the good of my parish and the peace of my family; for, somehow or other, my horse and I had a habit of parting company. On one occasion I found myself prostrate in the streets of York, much to the delight of the Dissenters.'* The first of the several horses bred on the rectory farm, where his later foals were much admired, had to be called Calamity. It was inelegant and had a huge appetite, and so slow that Sydney devised a 'patent Tantalus' consisting of a small sieve of corn attached to the shafts just beyond the horse's nose, to encourage it.*

The family carriage was an important appendage to the household.

After diligent search, I discovered in the back settlements of a York coachmaker an ancient green chariot, supposed to have been the earliest invention of the kind. I brought it home in triumph to my admiring family. Being somewhat dilapidated, the village tailor lined it [with green cloth], the village blacksmith repaired it; nay, but for Mrs Smith's earnest entreaties we believe the village painter would have exercised his genius upon the exterior; it escaped this danger, however, and the result was wonderful. Each year added to its charms: it grew younger and younger; a new wheel, a new spring; I christened it the *Immortal*. It was known all over the neighbourhood; the village boys cheered it, and the village dogs barked at it; but 'Faber meæ fortunæ' was my motto, and we had no false shame.*

The family travelled all round the locality in this conspicuous vehicle: it must have been 'one of those Shem-Ham-and-Japhet buggies, made on Mount Ararat soon after the subsidence of the waters' which Sydney depicted in his *Third Letter to Archdeacon Singleton*. Because of the many preliminary interruptions to travel in the 'Immortal', Sydney established what he called a 'Screeching Gate' a little way from the house, deriving its name from the Smith ladies' exclamations about things left behind. There they were to pause for recollection, and then proceed complete.*

The main public issue to occupy Sydney while he was in Yorkshire was that of Catholic emancipation.* His involvement in the later stages of the dispute is the nearest he ever came to direct, practical political activity. He had made a prominent (and formally anonymous) contribution to the earlier stages of the emancipation movement in *Peter Plymley*, but his task was by no means finished. Discussions, petitions, and dissensions continued sporadically. Early in 1813, for example, he wrote to Lady Holland that 'We have had meetings here of the clergy upon the subject of the Catholic petition, but none in my district; if there is, I shall certainly give my solitary voice in favour of religious liberty, and shall probably be tossed in a blanket for my pains.'* Although it had been checked by the death of Pitt, the movement towards Catholic emancipation had never collapsed, but it took the exertions of the Catholic Association and of Daniel O'Connell to bring the issue into prominence in the 1820s. The clergymen of the Church of England—Abraham Plymleys almost to a man—took fright. Meetings were organized all over the country to petition Parliament to preserve their protestantism from attack. The clergy of the Archdeaconry of Cleveland met at Thirsk on 24 March 1823 to petition against emancipation. Sydney prepared a counter-petition and spoke eloquently against the main motion.*

His speech began by regretting that the meeting had been called at all—silence would have been preferable—but he felt bound in conscience to attend it and to speak out. He apologized for his inexperience in oratory (it was, he said, the first public political meeting he had attended), but he proceeded with great skill to dispose of the traditional anti-Catholic arguments. This was ground he had already covered in the *Peter Plymley Letters*, but the emphasis was altered to suit changed conditions: national security was not so prominent an issue as in 1807, and more of his speech was taken up with Ireland and its problems. At the

Thirsk meeting he deftly considered the accusations that a Catholic was not to be trusted on oath, that his religion was one of immutable bigotry and persecuting cruelty, and that any concession to him would endanger the Church of England. Instead of the North Riding clerical petition, he presented one of his own, and ended his speech roundly by saying:

I am sick of these little clerico-political meetings. They bring a disgrace upon us and upon our profession, and make us hateful in the eyes of the laity ... Here we are, a set of obscure country clergymen, at the Three Tuns at Thirsk, like flies on the chariot-wheel; perched upon a question of which we can neither see the diameter, nor control the motion, nor influence the moving force. What good can such meetings do? They emanate from local conceit, advertise local ignorance; make men, who are venerable by their profession, ridiculous by their pretensions, and swell that mass of paper lumber, which, got up with infinite rural bustle, and read without being heard in Parliament, are speedily consigned to merited contempt.*

Sydney's own petition was short and moderate, stressing the loyal intentions of its promoters, and asking Parliament to consider 'whether all those statutes, however wise and necessary in their origin, may not *now* (when the Church of England is rooted in the public affection and the title to the throne undisputed) be wisely and safely repeated ... We feel the blessing of our own religious liberty, and we think it a serious duty to extend it to others, in every degree in which sound discretion will permit.'* Sydney sent a copy to the Duke of Devonshire shortly before the Thirsk meeting, saying that its framers would submit it if they obtained ten signatures, but others thought this number insufficient; 'whereas three clerical signatures to a liberal petition appear to me a sort of *infinite* ... You will perceive that the petition is of the *Aqueo-Lacteous* kind, which fluid I thought upon the whole to be the best adapted to our profession.'* Sydney's motion won only two other supporters, but these two were locally important colleagues—Francis Wrangham and William Vernon, the archbishop's son. As Sydney wrote to Allen: 'to get an Archdeacon and the son of an Archbishop to appeal in favour of the Catholics is worth while'.* The petition received some further lay support, but seems to have been too delayed in submission to Parliament to have been at all effective.*

Two years later, a similar meeting was held at Beverley by the clergy of the East Riding. Public opinion was generally turning in favour of emancipation, as Sydney wrote when asking the date of the meeting from Wrangham: 'I am inclined to think from all I hear from Town that Government are somehow or other softening towards the Catholics—so let the clergy beware they vote not on the losing or unprofessional side.'* A few days later he berated Wrangham for his part in organizing the meeting: 'I regret extremely that you have called this meeting, which I do not with you consider as unimportant, but as very mischievous. Nor ... do I understand why you were induced by your presence to countenance a purpose which you state to be so much at variance with your principles ... Having admired your conduct before, in resisting the folly of the North Riding clergy, I am proportionately sorry that you have judged it right to give way.'*

However much he disapproved of the organization of the meeting, Sydney felt it his duty to attend and speak, which he was entitled to do by his temporary tenure of another rectory, of Londesborough in the East Riding archdeaconry. Once again his case was simply and effectively stated. The arguments are similar to those used at Thirsk and by Peter Plymley, but they are supported by new rural examples, such as this characteristic sustained analogy:

If you go into a parsonage-house in the country, Mr Archdeacon, you see sometimes a style and fashion of furniture which does very well for us, but which has had its day in London. It is seen in London no more; it is banished to the provinces; from the gentlemen's houses of the provinces these pieces of furniture, as soon as they are discovered to be unfashionable, descend to the farm-houses, then to cottages, then to the faggot-heap, then to the dung-hill. As it is with furniture so it is with arguments. I hear at country meetings many arguments against the Catholics which are never heard in London: their London existence is over—they are only to be met with in the provinces, and they are fast hastening down, with clumsy chairs and ill-fashioned sofas, to another order of men.*

He cut short his detailed arguments 'from compassion to my reverend brethren, who have trotted many miles to vote against the Pope, and who will trot back in the dark, if I attempt to throw any additional light upon the subject'.* He was even less successful than he had been at Thirsk, and found himself (as he had feared) in a minority of one. Amongst those in the majority was Sydney's own curate at Londesborough, Mr Milestones (or Maylestone). Sydney remarked in his speech that 'Mr Milestones, indeed, with that delicacy and propriety which belongs to his character, expressed some scruples upon the propriety of voting against his rector, but I insisted he should come and vote against me. I assured him nothing would give me more pain than to think I had prevented, in any man, the free assertion of honest opinions.'* Sydney was not, however, totally without some support. 'A poor clergyman whispered to me', he reported after the meeting, 'that he was quite of my way of thinking, but had nine children. I begged he would remain a Protestant.'*

The year 1826 was an important year in the Catholic campaign, as the question was a major issue in the general elections. 'Terrible work in Yorkshire with the Pope,' Sydney wrote to Lady Grey early in the year; 'I fight with beasts at Ephesus every day.... This week I publish a pamphlet on the Catholic question with my name to it. There is such an uproar here, that I think it gallant and becoming a friend of Lord Grey's (if he will forgive the presumption of my giving myself that appellation), to turn out and take a part in the affray.... What a detestable subject— stale, threadbare, and exhausted; but ancient errors cannot be met with fresh refutations.'* A *Letter to the Electors upon the Catholic Question* (which Sydney later published in his *Collected Works*) manages to maintain the freshness of the controversy. Beginning with the question 'Why is not a Catholic to be believed on his oath?', Sydney discusses the legal and political anomalies which exclusion of the Catholics has given rise to. His remarks are again addressed to a country audience, for it is in the provinces that old bigotries have lingered long after they have been given up in the inner circles of government. Many of the prejudices are 'confined to provincial violence, and to politicians of the second table'; rabble-rousing is easy, for 'a little chalk on the wall and a profound ignorance of the subject, soon raises the cry of No Popery'. Some of the restrictions on Catholics have already been removed—why, then, not take away the rest? Sydney has the Irish situation always in mind, and discusses the historical, political, and religious aspects of Irish Catholicism with knowledge and force. He makes the characteristically frank statement that 'It is no part of my province to defend every error of the Catholic Church: I believe it has many errors, though I am sure these errors are grievously exaggerated and misrepresented ... The question is not, Whether there shall be Catholics, but the question (as they do exist and you cannot get rid of them) is, What are you to do with them?... I join in the cry on No Popery, as lustily as any man in the streets, who does not know whether the Pope lives in Cumberland or Westmorland ...' Equally characteristic is his technique of standing commonplace arguments on their heads. 'My cry then is, *No Popery*; therefore, emancipate the Catholics, that they may not join with foreign Papists in time of war. *Church for ever*; therefore, emancipate the Catholics, that they may not help to pull it down. *King for ever*; therefore, emancipate the Catholics, that they may become his loyal subjects.' He runs through the whole range of popular slogans, ending up with a plea for 'no chains, no prisons, no bonfires for a man's faith; and, above all, no modern chains and prisons under the names of disqualifications and incapacities, which are only the cruelty and tyranny of a more civilised age ... no oppression, no tyranny in belief: a free altar, an open road to heaven: no human insolence, no human narrowness, hallowed by the name of God'. The whole argument is bolstered by skilled and amusing analogies drawn from his rural observation—driving swine, preserving game, and the like.*

Altogether, the *Letter to the Electors* is (in the words of one of Sydney's biographers) a 'tremendous missile against the tottering fortress of bigotry'.* It created a minor pamphlet war. His 43 pages were answered by 72 in *The Elector's True Guide*, based by 'An East Riding Freeholder' upon 'the good old protestant principle of NO POPERY'. This lengthy pamphlet discusses Sydney's Catholic arguments in detail, with many dismissive phrases, interesting mainly when they refer to their antagonist's humorous propensities. 'We meet him again, as at Thirsk and Beverley, exhibiting, in the cause of catholic emancipation, the same flow of eloquence and wit, the same boldness of assertion, the same love of paradox, the same studied antithesis, the same irrelevancy of simile, the same confusion of principles, and the same false reasoning; and at all times you find him in merry mood, and making up in banter what he wants in argument.' Except for this fair isolation of some of the better features of Sydney's campaigning style, the pamphlet (which displays a controversialist's decent knowledge of Roman Catholic canon law and history) is dull enough stuff.

Sydney was one of the organizers of a petition asking Lord Morpeth (Lord Carlisle's heir) to stand in the Catholic interest in the 1826 elections; but he did not form one of the party which presented it, feeling that 'it would give the deputation a jejune appearance if an accidental parson (who had no tap root in the soil) constituted any part of it; that the importance of a deputation depended on measure and value, and was only to be estimated by a land surveyor"*. He was able to send Lord Carlisle a detailed account of Leeds politics, which he had gathered in 1826 on a visit to Harewood, where he had met the editor of the *Leeds Mercury*: 'Baines stated to me that the No Popery cry had not answered the expectation of the parties, and that in his opinion there was in the trading countries little general feeling on that subject, but a pretty general belief among the people that the cry had been set up for party purposes.' Sydney passed on the views of the local newspaper editor and political negotiator, discussing the various candidates and concluding that 'His opinion certainly is that there is liberality enough in the County to bring in a second Whig, but at the same time he did not pretend to speak with confidence on the subject.'*

Sydney's active work for the Catholic cause was drawing to an end. He wrote to the Duke of Devonshire in November 1827 that 'without giving up one tittle of my opinions respecting the Catholics, I intend for the present (unless called upon to express my opinion at any meeting of the clergy) to be silent upon that subject'.* Repeal was to come before very long. The Test and Corporation Acts were removed from the Statute Book in 1828, after bitter opposition from Lord Eldon and the extreme Protestant Tories, and the Roman Catholic Relief Bill was passed in 1829. The latter stages were more a matter of high political negotiation than of local dispute, but Sydney had done much to change the climate of opinion at all levels. Locally it had led him into much by no means ungratifying professional opposition, which gave him the pleasure of seeing the goose-like Abraham Plymleys acting true to form. And the satisfaction of having, as he put it, worked as a bricklayer's labourer'* at the temple of Toleration, was to be deep and lasting.

Sometimes because of—and sometimes in spite of—his work for the cause of Catholic emancipation, Sydney made a number of important and lasting friendships in Yorkshire, some neighbourly, some clerical, some noble. The correspondence has survived from them and shows the different qualities of his country friendships, and how ecclesiastical, squirearchical, noble, and even gastronomic associations were treated in the same good-natured, teasing manner.

On going to Heslington, Sydney was able to renew his acquaintance with Francis Cholmeley of Brandsby, a neighbouring

Catholic squire. Eighteen letters which he and his wife wrote to Cholmeley between 1808 and 1822 have been preserved and tell something of their friendship. Cholmeley was married shortly after the Smiths moved to Yorkshire, much to Sydney's delight, though he spared him the 'many established jokes and pleasantries about marriage with which it is the fate of the Neogamist to be assailed'. 'Pray tell me if Mrs Cholmeley and you are likely to come to York soon,' he continued, 'if not, Mrs S. and I must get the buggy repaired, give our broken-winded horse some asthmatic cordial, and resolutely perform a visit to Brandsby.'* Sydney and his wife were frequently invited to stay by the Cholmeleys, but could not always accept, Sydney fearing that 'Mrs S. could not be prevailed upon to stay out more than one night, as she would be by that time thoroughly convinced of the death and burial of all her children.'*

Sydney and Francis Cholmeley were soon exchanging domestic information. Sydney wrote for a receipt for cleaning boot tops—'The request would appear trifling to some persons, but you have lived too much the world and observed it too well not to know that human beings are valued in proportion to the goodness of their boot tops—though I am far from denying that integrity and moral worth come in as very good seconds to this ocreal splendour.'* The reply was accompanied by the gift of a cake, much to Sydney's surprise: 'I was much alarmed at first, thinking the tops were to be cleaned by the cake.'* When Cholmeley's first child was born, Sydney told him 'It is the greatest of all possible mistakes for a mother to nurse her own child, though it is more poetical. Do not fall into this error—or if fallen in, do not persevere too long.'*

Cholmeley was one of the very few Yorkshire neighbours who were suitable guests at Sydney's table along with Lord John Russell, Lady Davy, and other friends from London. This was partly because he was a moderate and intelligent Catholic. 'I wish you would inspire those Irish Catholic Bishops with a little of your understanding—they have marred their own cause most miserably',* Sydney wrote in the first surviving letter to Cholmeley. He later urged his friend to write a pamphlet on the Catholics, and asked him to remind his bride that 'I never joined in the cry of No Popery.'* Sydney greatly enjoyed the company of his Brandsby neighbours, and asked to be allowed 'to cultivate Mrs Cholmeley and yourself as much as you will allow an heretic to do so—

A lawless priest who dares to eat
Twice in a week forbidden meat
And gratify carnivorous desire
In spite of everlasting fire.*

'If I have left an horsewhip at Brandsby,' Sydney wrote to these tolerant Catholics in 1815, 'be so good as to take care of it for me: but you are welcome to horsewhip any violent bigot with it—of either persuasion—till I reclaim it.'*

Mrs Sydney wrote to Francis Cholmeley with her usual breathlessness in 1818: 'I thank you very much for your letter and for the details respecting my *beloved Angelica*. I shall be extremely obliged to you if you would have the goodness to send me some when it is fit for cutting ... If I make love to your gardener, do you think he will at the right time be induced to send me some of the seeds?' Her letter was full of general chatter mixed with her basic shrewdness and humour, as in a comment on Byron: 'I have not yet seen Beppo, but Mr Thompson has promised it me; Sydney says the verses are excessively ill-natured, that he would not have written them for £1000!! That however is a *large* sum.'* She later sought Cholmeley's help in placing Signor Denarchi, and Italian refugee, in a teaching post at Ampleforth or at the York Nunnery.*

It is a pity that no letters from Sydney survive in the Cholmeley papers after 1822, as the correspondence has a lightness of tone uncommon in Sydney's local friendships in Yorkshire. Reproving Cholmeley for his mis-spelling of a local place-name, Sydney wrote: 'I am excessively annoyed at your method of spelling *Spittal Bridge*—according to you Saliva Bridge, as if officers of the dragoons were quartered there.'*

Richard York of Wighill Park, near Tadcaster, was another Yorkshire squire with whom Sydney established a friendship. Although their extensive correspondence only survives from 1817, it continues until the end of their lives (York died in 1843) and shows that they had already known each other for some time. It was one of his Yorkshire friendships which continued into Sydney's old age, ripening over the years. Sydney and York shared an interest in food as well as similar occupations on the bench and on the land: one of the earliest letters tells York that 'next year [1818] my little boy will go to school, and one use of my leisure will be to hold a great Session in the Moor of *manger et parler*, or General Larder Delivery—so look to your corner dishes'.* York obviously took a technical interest in the table and

Sydney wrote to him on return from a trip to Paris in 1835, reporting ecstatically his new discoveries in French cooking, including a new recipe for Tartare Sauce ('excellent with bread as well as cold meat') of good clerical provenance: Beauvilliers had it from a dying uncle, Canon of Tours, who 'gave him the receipt, hiccupped, and died'. The mixture depended on the vinegar: 'and here let me beg you always to use *L'Huile d'Aix* and *Vinaigre d'Orleans*, not the liquid tallow and cut throat acidity with which salads are made in England'.* Sydney relished his friend's hospitality and soon after leaving Yorkshire he was to send his regrets to York in a letter showing the easy terms on which the Smith family had been with their neighbours: 'I shall not easily forget the many hearty laughs we have had together, and your amiable toleration of my incessant nonsense'. Wighill was a house of which the Smiths were often to 'make warm and honourable mention'.*

Many of Sydney's later letters to Richard York—some of them unusually long for their period—refer to his life in London and Somerset, and will be quoted in later chapters. There are others, however, which look back with amusement to Foston. Richard York, a Colonel in the local volunteer cavalry, was a keen horseman. Sydney, with a wide experience of disasters on horseback, liked to think of him as an unsuccessful rider, and there is much rather heavy joking each time a fall is reported. 'I hope that young Mrs Edward rides to hounds—or at least that she is a good kennel lady' was Sydney's comment when York's son was married, 'I never saw any lady prosper in Yorkshire who had not this turn.'* After the daughter-in-law produced a first child, Sydney wrote: 'I wish you joy; it is now proved that Edward is a sure foal getter—the next must be a colt.'* A later birth produced the comment that 'It is a singular thing that all Yorkshire boys can ride as soon as they are born, and it has never been properly explained. Give him plenty of brandy and water, and if he is indisposed let him smell to a fox and lisp Tallyho as his first sounds.'*

There were many opportunities for gossiping about old friends from Yorkshire. 'The Fairfaces of Gilling have been here (Fairfaces is the plural of Fairfax)', Sydney wrote in 1834:

What a mad and absurd match Harriet is about to make. She is going to espouse Mr Frederick Worsley, a gentleman who is in possession of a clear income of £100 per annum, the lady having an income equally clear of the same amount—and upon this they set down to farm, and to procreate. A young lady who has lived upon cream and sugar, been wrapped up in cotton, who has taken lessons in singing from Squallini and been taught the Italian language by Conjugatelli, wholly ignorant of those distinctions which nature has made between turnips and carrots, and believing in the slenderness of her agricultural acquirements that the ram suckles the young ones and the ewe begets them—Alas! Alas!*

York was apparently a Tory, and was easy game for Sydney's teasing. 'A pretty business you and your friends have made of the Queen.' he wrote in 1820, '—that chaste, injured and spotless woman.'* Five years later he wrote from Brougham Hall, telling York's wife Lady Mary that 'I am come here to escape from the loyalty of your neighbourhood, and to refresh myself with a little treasonable conversation.'* He wrote from London in 1834 that 'everything is going on well and quietly here, the Whigs increasing in strength and favour. I put it to you as a man of the world whether you had better not turn and buy a blue-and-buff coat.'* No change was made, but Sydney's affection for his friend continued undiminished. During York's prolonged illness in 1839–41, Sydney wrote to him frequently, sending long letters brimful of gossip and nonsense, based on a serious concern for York's failing health.

They did not meet often in the country after 1829, but frequent invitations to Combe Florey were sent to Wighill. In December 1835 Sydney wrote: 'I wish Edward and his wife and you would come down here next month. We will get some butchers' dogs and will turn out a curate. I will answer for the scent—but what are we to do for a brush?'* The comment is typical of a firm friendship of which Sydney wrote soon after settling in his Somerset parish: 'I shall not easily forget the many hearty laughs we have had together and your amiable toleration of my incessant nonsense.'*

One of the few Yorkshire clergy with whom Sydney became particularly friendly was Francis Wrangham, Vicar of Hunmanby from 1796 and Archdeacon successively of Cleveland from 1820 and of the East Riding from 1828. Wrangham is remembered as a classical scholar, a minor poet in several languages, and as the collector of a large and important library. Sydney once advised Mrs Wrangham 'If there be a single room which you wish to preserve from being completely surrounded by books, let me advise you not to suffer a single shelf to be placed in it; for they will creep round you like an erisypelas till they have covered the whole.'* Like Sydney, Wrangham was much interested in parochial improvements—for example establishing an early parish library—and unusually for one in high local office was in favour of Catholic emancipation. When the question was settled in Parliament, Sydney wrote to Wrangham, forgiving his inconsistency in the two clerical meetings—'As to the Catholic question I dare say you have on all occasions done what you thought was right; happy the man who can look back to it and believe that he has always been liberal, and consistent.'*

Their friendship began, while Sydney was still living at Heslington, with an exchange of printed sermons and elegant compliments: 'Let us both agree to like each others' discourses,' Sydney wrote, 'a very advantageous contract for me.'* They soon passed from such courtesies to a more serious discussion of their work, Wrangham, using a favourite method, pointed out to Sydney a string of errors in his essay on public schools. Acknowledging another letter in 1810, Sydney wrote: 'I am obliged to you, my dear Sir, for your praise, but I assure you I pretend to nothing but honesty and liberality—I do not think I would advocate a bad cause for any advantage whatever. I believe I would hazard a good cause at much hazard and risk to myself, and I think I would give up any opinion whatever if any man would show me it was wrong—beyond this you will find me a sleepy, commonplace country parson.'* Wrangham's profound learning spilled over into his general writings, and Sydney pointed to this defect in an undated letter acknowledging one of his sermons: 'Don't use hard words and say odd things in the pulpit. As you ask for my Critique it is this: and I say it because no man respects more your attainments and liberal sentiments than I do; but, in words, you have peregrinity and sesquipedality.'* The Archdeacon was fond, too, of imparting his knowledge to his correspondents, as Sydney pointed out when sending him an enquiry about some ecclesiastical business: 'I am sorry to give you trouble, but to apologise to you for asking for information is as it were to beg pardon of a cow for milking, or of the pump for taking water from it.'*

The Archdeacon and Sydney obviously enjoyed a very pleasant and humorous friendship. We can only regret that Wrangham's letters to Sydney have not survived, as his rather elaborate humour would have contrasted with Sydney's jollity. When they were both in London in June 1814 they planned to share a coach for the return journey. 'We shall be better all our lives for 200 miles of serene discussion,' Sydney wrote; 'you shall talk for 140 miles and only listen for 60. My first proposition shall commence at Bawtry.'* Earlier in the year, Sydney had acknowledged one of Wrangham's sermons: 'I will read you, and judge you as uncharitably as I can to lessen the pains of that envy which your Assize glory naturally inspires me with, but I will promise not to print my severity.'* When Sydney was himself preparing to be Sheriff's Chaplain ten years later, it was to Wrangham that he turned for sartorial advice.*

In his last letter to Wrangham in 1842, Sydney remarked 'I wish you had been a Bishop';* this has been a constant theme in his earlier letters to the Archdeacon. In 1812 Sydney had written 'I saw six weeks ago the mitre hanging over your head by a very slender thread. The agreeable vision has fled, and you must return to churchwardens and overseers till the Whigs learn to avail themselves with greater dexterity of the overtures which fortune makes to them.'* A year later another vacancy produced the remark: 'Why are you an honest man? You might have been Bishop of London. Will no time and no example cure you? Repent and do not go unmitred to your tomb.'*

Sydney liked to talk of Wrangham as a place-seeker, and frequently joked about him. He once remarked to James Tate (sometime Master of Richmond School and later a colleague of Sydney's as Canon of St. Paul's): 'Wrangham, Sir, asks for everything. On a distant rumour of a vacancy lately, he asked to be made Dey of Algiers.'* In 1828, Sydney reported to Lady Carlisle on a day spent on the Castle Howard lake: 'We had a miraculous fishing, catching 105 perch, each longer than any of Mr Wrangham's fingers, and quite as rapacious.'* Lady Copley (later Lady Lyndhurst) asked Sydney to secure Wrangham's graduate vote for her husband in the Cambridge University election of 1826. Sydney did so, though not quite as he told Lady Copley. 'Mr Wrangham,' he reported to her (with some justice), 'is a great respecter of persons bearing authority ... the avenues to [his] heart are the Granthams, the Duke of Leeds, the Archbishop of York. I have told him (Heaven forgive me) that I have repeatedly seen his works lying on your table, with an elegant silk string in them, and highly perfumed, that the Attorney General and yourself had an insatiable anxiety respecting every thing he did and said, and that I had a sort of commission from you to collect his fugitive verse and prose.'*· Wrangham was, of course, innocent of ecclesiastical avarice; he was snugly placed at Hunmanby and none of his extensive correspondence shows him seeking for office.

Sydney found the Archdeacon's official knowledge of ecclesiastical preferments very useful when he was seeking an exchange of livings in 1828, at a time when (following a promotion) he found himself 'in constant danger of another living from the Cathedral of Bristol—a peril which haunts me day and night'.* He wrote several letters to the Archdeacon on the subject. One of them asks about a recent local appointment which might alter his own chances of preferment: 'If I were to interrogate you respecting the celebrated dispute on the use of the first aorist in the Third Idyll of Theocritus, if I were to ask you where I could find Loubens' *Fugitive Thoughts on the Digamma*, I have no doubt I should receive accurate information—but my humble question in the present instance is to know the age of Mr Butler of Nottingham. Is he in the spring, autumn, or summer of life; has he any other preferment?'* It is amusing to see Sydney himself fretting about livings with the vigour he often ascribed to Wrangham.

The great event at Foston Rectory of the year 1815 was a first visit from Lord and Lady Carlisle, which led to a great intimacy between Sydney's family and what he later called 'the little cottage of Hinderskelf'—the great mansion of Castle Howard.* Saba recalled the circumstances of this first encounter:

Our infant colony was still in so rude a state, that roads, save for a cart, had hardly been thought of. Suddenly, however, a cry was raised, that a coach and four, with outriders, were plunging about in the midst of a ploughed field near the house, and showing signals of distress. Ploughmen and ploughwomen were immediately sent off to the rescue; and at last the gold coach (as Lady Carlisle used to call it), which had mistaken the road, was guided safely up to the house, and the kind old Lord and Lady, not a little shaken, and a little cross at so rough a reception, entered the parsonage. The shakes were soon forgotten, and good-humour restored; and after some severe sarcasms on the state of the approach to our house on the part of the old Earl, and promises of amendment on the part of my father, Lord Carlisle drove off, and made us promise to come and stay with him at Castle Howard.*

Sydney reported to Lady Holland that Lord Carlisle 'has broke out this year into a fit of most extraordinary politeness towards his neighbours. Among the rest he paid a visit to a family whom he had not visited since the capture of the Bastille, and apologized for not having called before; in the meantime the estate had passed through two different races. We have stayed at Castle Howard for two or three days ... I soon found myself at my ease at Castle Howard, and if he is not capricious, which I suppose he is, Castle Howard will make an agreeable variety to my existence.'* The Earl and the rector were soon visiting each other regularly. Sydney was given the run of the library while Lord Carlisle was in town—a great blessing, as he was able to buy but few books at this time—and he benefited generally from the delicate kindness of the whole Howard family. He was equally solicitous in return. When Lord Carlisle was ill in 1821, Sydney wrote to his daughter-in-law: 'How is Lord Carlisle? Pray do not take it for inattention that I do not call oftener, but it is rather too far to walk and I hate riding. Next year I shall set up a gig, and then I shall call at Castle Howard twice a day all the year round, like an apothecary.'* Sydney and his wife became as familiar with the house as with its inhabitants. He wrote to the Duke of Somerset (a brother of his Edinburgh friend Lord Webb Seymour) in 1824: 'If you ever travel in the North and will look at our parsonage, we will take great care of her Grace and you, and show you Castle Howard, which we are reckoned to do better than the housekeeper, Mrs Flinn.'*

It should not, however, be thought that Sydney's attitude to all this aristocratic benevolence was wholly uncritical. In 1838, George Ticknor, a discerning young American visitor, breakfasted with Sydney in London. 'The conversation', he reported, 'fell on the influence of the aristocracy in England ... To my considerable surprise, both [Henry] Hallam and Smith, who have been to a singular degree petted and sought by the aristocracy, pronounced its influence noxious. They even spoke with great force and almost bitterness on the point. Smith declared that he found the influence of the aristocracy, in his own case, "oppressive", but added, "However, I have never failed, I think, to speak my mind before any of them; I hardened myself early".'* Sydney was fortunate in his aristocratic friendships, from which he derived great benefits, social and intellectual. His long association with the Hollands, the Greys, and the Carlisles was of incalculable importance in his life. But he was always determined neither to be overwhelmed by the blandishments of his friends, nor to be tempted into toadying. His early row with Mrs Hicks Beach shows something of this, and he was able to resist Lady Holland's celebrated imperiousness. His relationship with the fifth Earl of Carlisle nicely illustrates the attitude which so surprised Ticknor.

Lord Carlisle was himself an author of repute. Byron classed him as 'Lord, rhymster, petit-maître, pamphleteer' when referring to 'the paralytic puling of Carlisle' in *English Bards and Scotch Reviewers*, but later regretted his acerbity. In 1819 Carlisle presented Sydney with his collected works. They were acknowledged elegantly on 29 August: 'The pursuits of an English nobleman should be politics, elegant literature, and agriculture. Your three volumes are surely a proof of time wisely and gracefully employed.'* But he sent more detailed comments a few days later: 'I think both the tragedies very good, and there are many parts in *The Stepmother* of very considerable power. I am decidedly against *The Sisters*, and I think the end of *The Stepmother* might be a *little* changed for the better. The prologue I like very much, but if I had been young Aristarchus, I would have urged you to correct or exhange some expressions worn out in poetry – "tuneful nine", "awake the British Lyre", "the sounding shell", and so forth ... I respect you and myself too much to make any apology for my frankness.'*

As if in return, Lord Carlisle later found himself commenting on Sydney's writings. Worried by Sydney's increasingly strident critical tone in the *Edinburgh Review*, Lord Carlisle wrote to him in October 1824:

A friend alarmed at Pope's indulgence of severe satire, says to him
'When every Grace and every Muse is thine
Why choose the least attractive of the nine?'
When you are so capable of giving us both instruction and pleasure, why run amuck at every component part of society: Order, Class, Profession, the Bar, the Bench, rural residents, West Indian proprietors, youthful sportsmen, brother Magistrates? These perhaps you think you are only tickling with a straw, but your friends too well know, by the writhings of the wounded, you have occasioned many an ulcer that is mining all within ... What is your present situation? Well received wherever a kind reception can be made acceptable to you, no hesitating acknowledgement of your talents, as much indulgence from society as can be bestowed for vivacious sallies, hurrying you sometimes to a verge overwhich you would grieve to be carried. But these ebullitions of spirits, even should a tinge of gall be detected in them, immediately disappear under the indian rubber of partiality, and a friendly leaning towards you and the house of Foston. What can you desire more? For God's sake consider that what often is forgiven from the *tongue* is not endured from the *pen* ... Retire from the dangerous

enterprise. Why prepare for yourself a bed of thorns for that hour when one of down might hardly invite repose?*

Lord Carlisle's long remonstrance, replete with metaphors and cushioned with many assurances of kind intention, provoked a strong but basically good-humoured reaction in Sydney. He replied on 30 October, recognizing Lord Carlisle's benevolent intention but arguing at length in favour of the salutary use of comic gifts:

Presuming for a moment (which I assure you I do not claim) that I have any powers of wit and ridicule, you do not deny that they give force and popularity to the attack, but you contend that by multiplying enemies they accumulate materials for unhappiness. There is no doubt of the truth of this, but the advantages on the other side of the question must not be overlooked.

Continue the same gracious and unfounded hypothesis, that those attacks are made with a mixture of argument and pleasantry which commands attention and produces a strong effect—what are the advantages to the writer? The successful exercise of power in the promotion of truth and justice; the advancement of good principles and the destruction of bad ones; emersion from darkness and obscurity; the sincere friendship of many good men, who agree with his opinions, honour his courage, respect his honesty and are grateful to him for the triumphant statement of their own argument and the successful developemnt of their own thoughts ...

What am I doing at this moment? I am writing familiarly to a nobleman of the most cultivated talents and of the highest rank, about myself and my own concerns. How should I ever have become acquainted with you, if you had not known something about me by reviews, by Peter Plymley, falsely ascribed to me but really by Lord Morpeth?

I can not agree with you that it is more dangerous and more injurious to the character and peace of mind of the writer to attack classes than individuals. I believe if Pope had confined himself to classes and not drawn portraits of individuals he would have been less abhorred—but though I think it useful and creditable to attack what ought to be attacked, and expedient to use such weapons in attack as God has given us, gravity or gaiety, sense or sarcasm, yet there is moderation to be used in the frequency of attacks and in the bitterness of attacks, and in both these points I believe I have sinned.*

Sydney promised to remember Lord Carlisle's advice and to amend his faults in future, but pointed out that 'a severe article upon the Catholic Question' had been sent off before the letter came. He was therefore annoyed when Lord Carlisle continued his protest after the review in question had been published. He retorted at enormous length, repeating his undertaking to be less severe, but stating that 'My opinions, and the free expression of them, I will surrender to no man alive—nor will I hold myself *accountable to any man* for the exercise of this right.'*

Several further letters were exchanged on specific points objected to in this essay, but the dispute seems to have ended his correspondence with Lord Carlisle. No further letters survive up to the time of the death of the old earl in September 1825. Sydney then lamented the loss of 'so good a neighbour and so kind a friend', and praised his kindness, immediately forgetting the acrimonious dispute of the previous year.* The quarrel is not characteristic of either party, but it is important in that it produced Sydney's longest mature discussion of the nature, use, and control of satirical gifts.

More typical of Sydney's relationship with the fifth Earl of Carlisle are his earlier letters, which are much more domestic and humorous. They discuss such local matters as the dispute on the bench or the price of coal at Malton, and often acknowledge the frequent gifts of vension, game, cucumbers, pineapples, or cauliflowers which passed from Castle Howard to Foston Rectory. Lord Carlisle quizzed Sydney on his articles on the Game Laws in the *Review*, provoking the reply that 'your attack upon me is a very fair one. It never occurred to me in indicating the rights of humanity that my neighbours might be so literal as not to send me game. What a rash man I have been! Had I not better publish an advertisement stating that I never meant to push matters to such a disagreeable extremity, that I was only theorising and never intended to proceed to practical abstinence from such delicacies? As for you, my dear Lord, I never had the slighest belief that you put bullets in your guns ... Thank you for the game, at whatever expenditure of human life obtained.'* Early in their friendship, Sydney reported that 'the old Earl is young, athletic, beautiful, and merry', and that 'he has many good points, and I must do him the justice to say that he keeps his bad ones tolerably well out of sight. He is fond of quizzing me, but I give him as good as he brings, so all goes on very well.'*

Sydney was a near contemporary of Lord Morpeth (1773–1848), who succeeded to the earldom of Carlisle in 1825. He was on intimate terms with him and with his wife, Lady Georgiana Morpeth. He enjoyed visiting them—'you have no idea how splendidly lugubrious Castle Howard appears when you are all away',* he once remarked—and took a benevolent interest in the entire family ('no mean part of the population of Yorkshire').* When the next generation decided to make their home on the Yorkshire estate, Sydney wrote rejoicingly to Lady Grey: 'I am very pleased that the Howards intend to live at Castle Howard. They will be rich enough to do so. They are excellent people, and I am truly fortunate in having such agreeable neighbours.'* He continued his frequent visits, usually staying overnight after dining, when he once left behind his gloves, blue wristbands, some letters, his *Morning Chronicle*, and a slate-coloured linen umbrella.* He sometimes found ways of repaying the hospitality he had received. Thus in 1828 he wrote to Lady Carlisle: 'I send you what I think is the model of all potatoes—a large basketfull. Pray do not let Flinn eat them in the Steward's Room. If your happiness depend upon potatoes as much as mine does, you will desire to know where they are procured—it is at Huttons Ambo, William Horsley's, near you.'*

Sydney was on intimate enough terms with Lady Georgiana Morpeth to be able to discuss her religious and personal problems. She confessed to him a tendency to despair which Sydney— who himself suffered from the constitutional melancholy of the jovial—discussed with understanding. In September 1819 he wrote to her that 'Everybody is haunted with spectres and apparitions of sorrow, and the imaginary griefs of life are greater than the real. Your rank in life exposes you the more to these attacks.' He continued with a typical statement of his religious beliefs. 'I like in you very much that you are a religious woman, because, though I have an infinite hatred and contempt for the nonsense which often passes under and disgraces the name of religion, I am very much pleased when I see anybody religious for hope and comfort, not for insolence and interest.' Sydney realized that Lady Georgiana required reassurance in her (unspecified) complaint, and this and the succeeding letters nicely balance counsel and jocularity: 'As for me, I will promise never to quizz you— that is, only a very little, and to your face, and in a low voice, and not before strangers; and for the rest, you will always find me a discreet neighbour and a sincere friend.'*

The following February Sydney sent his friend his well-known advice on low spirits:

Nobody has suffered more from low spirits than I have done, so I feel for you. 1. Live as well and drink as much wine as you dare. 2.

Go into the shower-bath with a small quantity of water at a temperature low enough to give you a *slight sensation of cold*—75 or 80°. 3. Amusing books. 4. Short views of human life not farther than dinner or tea. 5. Be as busy as you can. 6. See as much as you can of those friends who respect and like you; 7. and of those acquaintance who amuse you. 8. Make no secret of low spirits to your friends but talk of them fully: they are always the worse for dignified concealment. 9. Attend to the effects tea and coffee produce upon you. 10. Compare your lot with that of other people. 11. Don't expect too much of human life, a sorry business at the best. 12. Avoid poetry, dramatic representations (except comedy), music, serious novels, melancholy sentimental people, and everything likely to excite feeling or emotion not ending in active benevolence. 13. Do good and endeavour to please everybody of every degree. 14. Be as much as you can in the open air without fatigue. 15. Make the room where you commonly sit gay and pleasant. 16. Struggle by little and little against idleness. 17. Don't be too severe upon yourself, or underrate yourself, but do yourself justice. 18. Keep good blazing fires. 19. Be firm and constant in the exercise of rational religion. 20. Believe me dear Lady Georgiana very truly yours, Sydney Smith.*

From time to time Sydney also gave some good-natured advice to the sixth Earl of Carlisle. For example, he wrote in 1826: 'as I am an adviser by trade, allow me to recommend moderation in pursuing the pleasures of the chase. The fox was given to mankind not for business, but for amusement.'* Other letters deal with the Catholic question and the state of the parties in county politics. Sydney's later correspondence with Lord Carlisle parallels that with his father, when his friend deplored the tone of Sydney's writings on the problems of ecclesiastical finance in the 1830s. *The Letters to Archdeacon Singleton* showed that Sydney had lost none of his skill in pungent argument; but the discussion of principles with Lord Carlisle was more restrained and more amicable than it had been with the old Earl fifteen years before.

Sydney was on affectionate terms with all the Howard children. His rhymed pharmaceutical advice, 'The Poetical Medicine Chest', which he addressed to the Hon. Mrs Henry Howard, shows his general affection for the family as well as his skill and humour in basic medication:

> With store of powdered rhubarb we begin;
> (To leave out powdered rhubarb were a sin),
> Pack mild magnesia deep within the chest;

And glittering gum from Araby the blest;
And keep, oh lady, keep within thy reach
The slimy surgeon, blood-devouring leech.
Laurel-born camphor, opiate drugs prepare,
They banish pain, and calm consuming care.
Glauber and Epsom salts their aid combine,
Translucent streams of castor-oil be thine,
And gentle manna in thy bottles shine.
If morbid spot of septic sore invade,
By heaven-sent bark the morbid spot is stayed;
When with black bile hepatic regions swell,
With subtle calomel the plague expel.
Anise and mint with strong Æolian sway,
Intestine storms of flatulence allay,
And ipecacuanha clears the way.
I know thee well, thou antimonial power,
And to thee fly in that heart-rending hour,
When feverish patients heave their laden breath,
And all is sickness, agony, and death!
Soda and potash change with humours crude,
When hoven parsons swell with luscious food.
Spare not in eastern blasts when babies die
The wholesome vigour of the Spanish fly.
From timely torture seek thy infant's rest,
And spread the poison on his labouring breast.
And so, fair lady, when in evil hour,
Less prudent mothers mourn some faded flower,
Six Howards valiant and six Howards fair,
Shall live and love thee, and reward thy care.*

In 1828 Sydney, by then Canon of Bristol Cathedral, wrote to
Lady Carlisle that 'I begin to fear the patronage of this Chrurch
may lure me from Foston. I will struggle all I can to be virtuous,
but you have read in novels an account of ladies upon whom
Lotharios and Lovelaces *begin* to make an impression ...'* He
succumbed, and in one of his first letters to Lady Carlisle from
his new parish he wrote to her: 'Castle Howard is a perpetual
sorrow to us. I often say "Here are woods, and hills, and a fine
climate, but where is Castle Howard and its inhabitants?" And
yet do not imagine me of a generally discontented disposition,
for I bear the distance from Wrangham like an ancient Stoic.'*
Their correspondence continues up to the end of Sydney's life,
and his letters are always full of affectionate interest in the family.
'I should be very glad to hear how all is going on at Castle

Howard, dear Lady Carlisle,' Sydney wrote in one of his late letters,'—and whether my Lord and you keep up health and spirits
with tolerable success—a difficult task in the fifth act of life, when
the curtain must ere long drop and the comedy or tragedy be
brought to an end.'*

The story of some of Sydney's most important Yorkshire
friendships has anticipated some of the events of his later years
at Foston. His domestic and professional circumstances gradually improved. While he was still recovering from the burden of
paying for the rectory building, his financial postion had never
been easy, but there were better prospects ahead. In Autumn
1821, when he was fifty years of age, Sydney received an unexpected legacy from his aunt Mary. He had not had any hopes
of a bequest. 'I have employed the greater part of my life in quizzing her and I thought she would take a testamentary revenge of
me. However she behaved very well and is now in heaven.'* The
legacy consisted of city property in Coleorton Street and of the
Guildhall Coffee House and Tavern. 'It puts me a little at my
ease. I have few wants and am not a bad manager,' Sydney wrote
to Lady Morpeth, acknowledging her congratulations and suggesting a dinner and ball in the tavern.* Lord Carlisle wrote from
Castle Howard to congratulate his friend on his good fortune:
'Foston, in neatness and ostensible comforts, will hardly perceive
the benefit of this addition to your income; but I trust this augmentation will extend to objects of nearer interest to you. I have
ever regarded the establishment at Foston with admiration and
surprise, not being above knowing to a shilling the monthly consumption, and expenses, of this house; and then I have thought
of my friend Fitzwilliam who has erased the word Comfort out
of the Wentworth Dictionary, as neither he nor any one about
him could ever comprehend its meaning.'*

Sydney was himself prepared, as he had advised Lady Morpeth, to 'take short views of life'. An undated fragment, 'A Little
Moral Advice . . . on the cultivation and improvement of the animal
spirits' refers to his early economic despondency, relieved by a
timely inheritance, and counsels a friend with the advice that
'Every one has uncles and aunts who are mortal; friends start
up out of the earth; time brings a thousand chances in
your favour; legacies fall from the clouds. Nothing so absurd
as to sit down and wring your hands because all the good
which may happen to you in twenty years has not taken place
at this precise moment.'* It was in the 1820s that Sydney's

fortunes began to improve, not least through the death of his father.

Maria Smith, Sydney's much-loved sister and useful go-between in his acrimonious dealings with their father, had died in 1816, with her brother lamenting that 'The loss of a person whom I would have cultivated as a friend, if nature had not given her to me as a relation, is a serious evil.'* Sydney had, however, kept up occasional visits to his father. In 1821, for example, he wrote to Jeffrey: 'I wish at such an age you and all like you may have as much enjoyment of life; more you can hardly have at any age. My father is one of the very few people I have ever seen improved by age. He is become careless, indulgent, and anacreontic.'*

Robert Smith's vigour of mind and body continued into old age, with flashes of his old belligerent spirit. At the age of eighty-four he complained to Bobus of a lawyer who 'wrote me a very rude insolent letter ... and either did not know how to address a gentleman or thought he was writing to a blackguard'.* But it was not long before Bobus and young Cecil had to make arrangements for the administration of his property. Sydney agreed to visit his father again, 'though he has never been much of a father to me'. Ancient resentments welled up in Robert Smith's lucid spells; an incoherent draft to Bobus mentions that 'Sydney never writes me, whether he is affronted at the truth I told him, *that his wife wanted good temper*, I know not.'* The trustees found the old man's papers in confusion, with credit and debit accounts still muddled by the elder Cecil's Indian estate, which had never been tidied up. Sydney visited his father's house at Bishop's Lydeard in Somerset and examined the papers in June 1826, methodically docketing them and reporting on them to Bobus. He estimated his father's total estate between £40 and £50,000.* This was ample for his comfort, even though Bobus and Courtney had discontinued their allowances—their father had never revealed that they had long been unnecessary. Robert Smith's wills were examined, and a private letter to Cecil was found, providing for a bastard son begotten of a respectable housemaid when he was well over seventy.* A formal codicil intimated the bequest of £10,000 to Sydney, which was to give him his first taste of affluence. The situation remained delicate while the old man still lived, but Sydney and his nephew came to a pleasant working arrangement after a little preliminary friction: they were soon to become neighbouring clergymen and close friends. Robert Smith died in August 1827 in his 88th year, and Cecil saw to the obsequies. Sydney was offered a memento, but replied that

I loved my father in spite of his numerous faults and imperfections, and any memorial of him would fill me with melancholy. My plan is to have no memorial of the friends I loved—they make me wretched; therefore I will accept nothing of any sort or kind however trifling.*

His aunt's legacy and the prospect of a substantial capital enabled him to feel enough at ease financially to allow the family some relief from the strict economy which had governed their lives, and in 1826 he was able to fulfil a long-cherished wish to visit Paris, where the Hollands were spending a season. His letters to his wife have survived to show how he tried to share his enjoyment of the trip with the family at Foston. From the time when he lost 'above a pound of liquid flesh', puffing and blowing up the new staircase in the cliff at Dover, every detail was recorded for their pleasure, Civil servants and shopkeepers, fine food in good hotels, and the amenities of Anglo-French society all appealed to him, although he wanted mainly to see the sights of Paris rather than make acquaintance with his fellow-countrymen. There were of course frequent confusions with Admiral Sir Sidney Smith, the hero of Acre, who lived in Paris, with letters crossing and proposals of social visits confused. When Sydney preached at the Embassy chapel, his namesake commended the sermon highly to Mrs Hurt Sitwell, who had been sitting near by. 'Yes,' she said to him, 'I think it should make you proud of your name.' 'You may easily guess how this was relished by the vainest man in Europe', the preacher commented.* He bought plenty of silks, ribbons, bonnets, and wallpapers, and a cookery book—the *Cuisinier Bourgeois*: 'I think we may attempt one or two dishes. We shall not be perfect at first, but such an object will ensure and justify perseverance. I meant when first I came to have bought all Paris; but finding that difficult, I have for *myself* only spent six shillings.'*

Small luxuries such as continental travel show how prosperous Sydney was becoming—and feeling—in his late fifties. It remained for him to be awarded—and to seek as actively as possible—the professional advancement which his age and talents qualified him. He was fully aware of his own extensive parochial experience, and of his ecclesiastical requirements. As he put it to William Smith, the Dissenting politician, in February

1820: 'I am enjoying that *otium sine dignitate* which is the ordinary lot of country clergymen—by which you must not understand that my pursuits are low or my character dubious, but that I am not a prebendary, for I mean *sine dignitate ecclesiastica*.'* His earlier attempts on another Yorkshire living (Wigginton, near York), for which he pressed Lord Holland to intercede with the Lord Chancellor, apparently fell through because of the continuing health of the rector, a Mr Dealtry, whom Sydney liked. When Dealtry was recovering from his illness, his disappointed successor wrote that 'The incumbent is proceeding by slow stages to Buxton. I wish him so well, that under other circumstances I should often write to know how he was going on; at present I must appear unfriendly, to avoid appearing hypocritical.'* There were, however, other reasons behind his lack of success over Wigginton. Thanking Lord Holland for his friendly exertions, Sydney was bound to admit that 'The Chancellor is quite right about political sermons, and in this I have erred; but I have a right to preach on general principles of toleration, and the fault is not mine if the congregation apply my doctrines to passing events. But I will preach no more on political subjects; I have not done so for many years, from a conviction it was unfair.'*

No such political objections stood in the way of one temporary but none the less welcome piece of Yorkshire patronage. In 1823 the Duke of Devonshire, at Lord Carlisle's suggestion, presented him to the living of Londesborough, to hold until the Duke's nephew William Howard came of age and took orders to hold it himself. Sydney said that the 'living . . . while it lasts, will make me (accustomed to little), rather a rich man',* and sent a graceful acknowledgement to the Duke of Devonshire: 'I have always been poor, and am of course glad to be richer, but I assure you it is a real increase of my pleasure to receive this favour from the hands of one who sustains a great part in life so honourably and so well; and this I would not say, if I did not think it, for all the wealth the Church could bestow.'* The living was worked by a curate—the Mr Milestones whose anti-Catholic opinions Sydney had been so careful to respect—and Sydney was able to draw most of the income. Sydney preached occasionally in his new parish, and wrote to Lady Carlisle in January 1829 (shortly before he resigned the living): 'Pray tell the Duke that it is not my fault if there are so many poachers at Londesborough. I have preached several sermons about the Birds in the Air, and the

Beasts of the Field, stating that they all belong to His Grace. I shall be under the painful necessity of mentioning the pheasants by name. I have no doubt however that with three or four sermons I can disperse the whole gang.'* Londesborough did not, however, represent the substantial and permanent Dignity which Sydney was seeking. When Richard Heber wrote asking him to become a founder member of the Athenaeum in 1824, he received the reply that 'When my merits are properly understood and rewarded in the Church, I will subscribe to the Athenaeum, or any other club you please—but I have not risen at present (nor shall I ever rise) beyond Mutton Chops and the Gray's Inn Coffee House.'*

Sydney was the first to recognize that promotion was a chancy business, and that his characteristic political concerns and irrepressible manner were a disadvantage in the search for preferment. There were the usual mischances of fickle patronage to be reckoned with. 'You are to have the command of the Channel fleet,' he wrote to Dr Headlam of Newcastle in August 1827, 'and I am to be Bishop of Carlisle—the two events I assure you are of equal probability. If the administration remain in three years, which is not probable, and I am alive, and not forgotten, and no great Lord comes across me for his son's tutor—or the brother of his harlot—I may possibly get a stall in some Cathedral—but upon the whole I really think it most probable I shall get nothing.'*
And to his nephew Cecil a few months earlier he had written humorously, in June 1827, balancing the political and personal elements of promotion:

You suppose I am to be made a bishop, or something with a petticoat; but I will lay you a bet of a sovereign, if you please, that I am not made a dignitary of the Church before Christmas 1827. Dignitary means a fellow with rose shovel, petticoat knee and shoe buckles of ormolu. Canning is very well. There is no chance of the Catholic question being carried this year, or next year either. I have put myself so forward about the Catholic question, that they will be very reluctant to promote me. I have very serious doubts if it will be done, so I offer the Elizabeth, or Bett.*

Sydney won his bet, but only by a month (and Canning had died in August). Promotion in the Church came sooner than he expected, and the place and patron were both unexpected.
Lord Lyndhurst, politically an opponent but personally a friend, bestowed on Sydney a prebend of Bristol Cathedral,

attached to the Devonshire living of Halberton. Sydney, who had just had to cope with letters congratulating him on ill-founded rumours of his being made Rector of St George's, Bloomsbury, treated premature congratulations on the Bristol appointment circumspectly, and it was not until the end of January 1828 that he received an informal intimation from his friend Lady Lyndhurst (whom he was known to refer to as 'Zenobia'). He took up residence for one of the statutory periods soon afterwards, and reported to Lady Holland that he had 'An extremely comfortable prebendal house, seven-stall stable, room for four carriages, so that I can hold all your cortege when you come.'* His colleagues seemed agreeable; one, Dr Randolph, was described as 'deaf, tottering, worldly-minded, vain as a lawyer, noisy and perfectly good-natured and obliging'.* They were small men, from prebends to Bishop. 'It is supposed that one of these ecclesiastics elevated upon the shoulders of the other, would fall short of the summit of the Archbishop of Canterbury's wig,' Sydney wrote delightedly: 'The Archbishop of York is forced to go down on his knees to converse with the Bishop of Bristol just as an elephant kneels to receive its rider.'*

He reported himself to Lady Carlisle as marching through the Minster 'preceded by a silver rod, the very type of dignified gravity—they say I am a severe solemn-looking man',* and during his October residence of 1828 described his excellent prebendal house to her:

I am living quite alone in a large gothic room with painted glass, and waited upon by an old woman with only one gothic tooth. About six o'clock when it is dark the various ghosts by which this house is haunted come into the room, and converse with me—dead deans the colour of Rogers, and ancient sextons of the Cathedral, prebendaries now no more, elderly ladies who lived near, and came regularly during their lives to morning-service. I have very little pleasure in their conversation, they seem to be limited foolish people, much the same as people still alive—the deceased clergy are particularly inquisitive about preferment, and the elderly ladies enquire about patterns. When I am tired of their company I order tea and candles and they hobble away.*

Sydney would not have been Sydney if he had resisted the glorious opportunity of using the sermon at the annual civic service on 5 November both to tease the Mayor and Corporation ('the most protestant Corporation in England')* by delivering a resounding discourse on Toleration to the assembled burgesses.

Many years later Mrs Catherine Crowe recalled the crowded occasion for Sydney's daughter:

Although we went to the Cathedral long before the doors were open, we found a crowd already established there; and when the doors *were* opened, it was a rush like entering the pit of a theatre on the night of a new play.... He preached very finely and very bravely—in direct opposition to the principles and prejudices of the persons in authority present—and ended by the beautiful apologue from Jeremy Taylor, illustrating charity and toleration. And yet never did anybody look more like a high Churchman! As he walked up the aisle to the altar, I always thought of Cardinal Wolsey, there was an air of ... proud dignity. At Clifton and Bristol, you may readily conceive that he was much more wondered at, than liked. All their prejudices were against him; and they were totally incapable of appreciating his talents, or comprehending his character.*

Sydney was of course delighted with the result. 'I told you I would make a splash at Bristol ... and accordingly I let off in the Minster no ordinary collection of squibs, crackers and *Roman* candles', he reported to E.J. Littleton: 'In short I gave the Mayor and Corporation ... such a dose of toleration as will last them for many a year.'* His sermon was in fact a revised version of *A Sermon on Religious Charity* which he had delivered and published at York in 1825. It was in various forms to remain a favourite for the rest of his life, and is included in his *Collected Works*. As revised for Bristol, it begins deceptively with a few comfortable sentences suited to tastes of the civil dignitaries, but soon gathers controversial momentum with recommendations such as 'We should not judge any sect of Christians from the representations of their enemies alone, without hearing or reading what they have to say in their own defence.' There was a warning, too (which he himself ought sometimes to have heeded when writing about Dissenters) not 'to represent the opinions of the most violent and eager persons who can be met with as the common and received opinions of the whole sect'. The sermon ended with the extract from Jeremy Taylor, which followed specifically Catholic references that made the aldermen stare with horror. 'I cannot discuss the uses and abuses of this day,' he told them, without touching upon the errors of the Catholic faith from which we have escaped; but I should be beyond measure concerned if a condemnation of theological errors were construed into an approbation of laws so deeply marked by the spirit of intolerance.'* He sent an extract to Lady Holland, remarking that

'I know your taste for sermons is languid, but I must extract one passage for Lord Holland to show that I am still as honest a man as when he first thought me a proper object for his patronage.'* No wonder the civic dignitaries were, as he put it, scarcely able to keep the turtle on their stomachs.

Almost as soon as he was installed, Sydney began to devote as much attention to preferment and exchanges and livings as had those ghostly clergymen who chattered in his drawing-room at dusk. The Lord Chancellor's rules for the exchange of livings, which might enable Sydney to give up Foston for a similar living near Bristol tenable with the prebendal parish, were complicated and strict. An anxious correspondence ensued, with several unsatisfactory possibilities being rejected, but at last he was able to come to an arrangement which Mrs Sydney explained in her 'Narrative' written for her grandchildren: 'The Chancery Living of Combe Florey was about fifty miles from [Bristol]. The incumbent, Mr Escott, a gentleman of large fortune, who resided on his own property five miles from it and never inhabited the parsonage, had appointed his son his curate, who rode over from his father's house to serve the Church ... [Sydney] requested the Chancellor would permit him to exchange Foston for Combe Florey and that he would nominate Mr Escott's *son* to Foston, in which case Mr Escott (the father and possessor of the living) would most thankfully vacate Combe Florey for him. This was done.'*

A greater promotion was soon to come his way, but Sydney's move to Somersetshire in the summer of 1829 proved to be as important a break in his life as the move to Yorkshire had been twenty years before. It came at a time when his family, now grown up, was beginning to disperse. Saba was to remain at home for some five years more, but in January 1828 her younger sister, Emily, married Nathaniel Hibbert, a Northern Circuit barrister— 'well bred, liberal, spiritual and affectionate'*—with the prospect of inheriting a substantial property in Hertfordshire. Wyndham, much younger than the others, was at the Charterhouse, and his elder brother Douglas Smith had done well at Westminster, where he was head of the school, and at Christ Church. But early in 1829, soon after he had decided on a legal career, Douglas suddenly became ill and died in mid-April leaving his parents shattered by what Sydney described as 'the first real misfortune which ever befell me'.* 'I have experienced a shake from which I think I shall never thoroughly recover,' he wrote to Lady Mary

York; 'I have fits of spirits come across me after my manner—but I am very often and very suddenly overpowered'.*

The transfer to Somerset was therefore a welcome distraction as well as a geographical break. It was a good time to move. The new rectory had its advantages, which Sydney described in an affectionate letter to the Archbishop of York in August 1829:

I am very sorry to quit old friends—that I need not say—but in other respects I have mended my position. Nothing can exceed the beauty of this country, and I really think Combe Florey the prettiest place in it. I shall at no great expense make a better house at Florey than at Foston: and am proceeding with my usual rapidity.... I have seen many civil gentlemanlike persons, and many convex ladies, but nothing that has particularly struck me—all very fair, but nothing remarkable. Castle Howard and Bishopthorpe I cannot of course replace—but generally speaking the flat of York was not a land of prodigies.... Pray say to any of the other Vernons that if they come to the West, and will do me the favour to make the experiment, they will find a better sort of Foston at C. Florey.*

CHAPTER V

❋

PARISH and rectory at Combe Florey were soon found to be 'a better sort of Foston', and Sydney described his new house to Lady Grey as 'a most parsonic parsonage, like the parsonages described in novels'.* The rectory itself was larger than Foston, with three or four acres of woodland near the house and a glebe of some sixty acres nearby. As at Foston twenty years before, a fair amount of building work was necessary. Sydney told his friends that he was building 'not from the love of architecture but from the fear of death',* to remedy dilapidations, and the builders had to be watched: 'I consider that every day's absence from home costs me £10 in the villainy of carpenters and bricklayers; for as I am my own architect Clerk of the Works, you may easily imagine what is done when I am absent.'* 'Nothing so vile as the artificers of this country!' he remarked to Lady Morley, 'A straight line in Somersetshire is that which includes the greatest possible distance between the extreme points.'*

Soon after arrival Sydney reported that 'the only acquaintance I have made here is that of the Clerk of the Parish, a very sensible man with great *Amen*-ity of disposition'.* The people he described as 'civil (very civil), drunken, wretched and degraded' and he seems to have been little prepared for the importance of cider in the recreational life of the county. 'This is the most beautiful country in England,' he told George Tierney in November 1829, 'and nature in imitation of the shepherd Paris has given it the apple—an accursed gift: every body is drunk from the first of January to the last of December—in every other respect it is enchanting.'* In less than a year Parliament was to repeal the Beer Tax, a measure which took effect while Sydney was staying with the Philips at Chipping Norton; it produced one of his better-known sayings (in a letter to Sir John Murray): 'The new Beer Bill has begun its operations. Everybody is drunk. Those

149

who are not singing are sprawling. The sovereign people are in a beastly state.'* Undeterred by rural inebriation, Sydney continued the attentive ministry he had begun in Yorkshire, with his nephew Cecil (son of his Indian brother) acting as curate. And as at Foston there was a medical as well as a spiritual aspect to his work. In 1833 he told Lady Grey that 'our evils have been want of rain, and scarlet fever in our village where in three quarters of a year we have buried fifteen instead of one per annum. You will naturally suppose I killed all these people by doctoring them, but scarlet fever awes me, and is above my aim. I leave it to the professional, and graduated, homicides.'*

The neighbouring gentry were declared to be much the same as in other neighbourhoods ('red wine and white, soup and fish, bad wit and good nature'),* but perhaps because of his regular visits to London, Sydney never seems to have struck up such close friendships with the Somerset gentlefolk as he did in Yorkshire. As he put it to Richard York of Wighill, 'Our neighbours here are in the common line, port and sherry for dinner, hail rain and snow for conversation, but the best people in any place come slowly to light and lie, like maccaroon cakes the bottom of an Italian cream, last and best.'* Not long after he arrived, he reported a 'calamity' to Lord Bathurst: 'My next door neighbour is dead, so much the better for he was a perfect devil—but he has left his estate (£4,000 p.a.) to a little linen draper in a very small town in Dorsetshire; and my merchant of linen has 8 grown up sons all brought up to low professions, and they are all coming to live here. What can this be but a visitation of Providence for my Whig principles? This is indeed a severe dose of the People.'*

Taunton never provided the provincial excitements which the family had found at York, even at electiontide (though in 1835, when Disraeli was standing for Taunton, 'the boys called out "Old Clothes!" as he came into the town, and offered to sell him sealing-wax and slippers').* Instead, Sydney was inclined to devise local amusements and neighbour-teases, such as tying oranges to his bay-trees at Christmas ('finer than the Ludovician orange-trees of Versailles*,) or more elaborate artifices, which he told Richard York about in 1840: 'You would laugh to see the lawn round my house: fat deer looking upon us with fine branching horns—more magnificent than those of the most ample cuckold. How could I have done this? Not by buying deer—I am not such a fool—but I have had the horns fixed on to leather caps and they are buckled on to the heads of the don-

keys who became instantly as glorious as newly created peers—
and have a truly venison appearance.'*

Combe Florey provided opportunities for 'aristocratic visits',
to Lord Bath at Longleat, for example, or Lord Lansdowne at
Bowood. Sydney's old friend Sir George Philips had moved from
the outskirts of Manchester to Weston House, Chipping Norton,
whence Sydney reported that 'The evils of old age, gout, and pro-
lixity of narrative, are invading the worthy and recent Baronet.'*
It was at Bowood that Sydney observed of Henry Luttrell that
'he had not his usual soup-and-pattie look; there was a forced
smile upon his countenance which seemed to indicate plain roast
and boiled and a sort of apple-pudding depression as if he had
been staying with a clergyman'.* Sydney never tired of twitting
Luttrell on gastronomic matters which he took so very seriously:
'he was very agreeable, but spoke too lightly, I thought, of veal
soup. . . . Luttrell is not steady in his judgments on dishes. Individual failures with him soon degenerate into generic objections,
till, by some fortunate accident, he eats himself into better
opinions.'*

Country-house visits, particularly to old Whig friends, were
to continue to the end of Sydney's life, when the 'derangeable
health' of old age made such journeys inconvenient. 'The bread,
the water, the hours, the bed, the change of bolster—everything
puts me out,' he wrote in 1843. 'I recover in two or three days,
and then it is time to depart. This made the wise man say that
a man should give over arguing at thirty, riding at sixty, and visiting at seventy.'*

Visitors were always eagerly welcomed at Combe Florey.
William Smith, MP, was pressed to pay a visit and assured that
'We will receive you with as much honour as if you were an uncle
from whom a large legacy might speedily be expected.'* Jeffrey
was one of the very first to visit the new home, Sydney reporting
him to Lady Grey as 'a man of rare talent and integrity, who
has been honest even in Scotland, which is as if he were temperate
and active at Capua. . . . [He] wanted to persuade me that myrtles
grew out of doors in Scotland; upon cross examination it turned
out that they were prickly and that many had been destroyed
by the family donkey.'* The tide was beginning to run in favour
of the Whigs in Scotland too, where Jeffrey had been elected Dean
of the Faculty of Advocates and was soon to become Lord Advocate. For Jeffrey (who was in due course to become a Lord of Session in Edinburgh) to be elected at such a period of party tension

to the leadership of the Scots Bar was an achievement as great as Sydney's becoming—with all his political disadvantages— a dignitary even of Bristol: a Deanery and a Canonry between the two principal projectors of the *Edinburgh Review* was a considerable achievement, showing a major shift in the political climate. Greater promotions were to be looked for: 'I shall not be easy till he is fairly on the Bench,' Sydney remarked to Murray: 'His robes, God knows, will cost him little; one buck rabbit will clothe him to the heels.'* 'Philosopher Malthus', whom Sydney teased repeatedly about his theories, was another of the 1831 visitors. 'I got an agreeable party for him of unmarried people,' Holland House was told: 'There was only one lady who had had a child, and for her I apologised. . ., but he is a very good natured man, and if there are no appearances of approaching fertility is civil to every lady.'*

The Somerset rectory was different from Foston in one important respect: the dispersal of the family meant that Sydney and his wife were frequently alone. Wyndham was showing a taste for field sports, and his next sister Emily, happily married to Nathaniel Hibbert, was busy producing a family of her own. 'You are a little girl in pocket,' Sydney wrote charmingly to his daughter after his first grandchild arrived following a difficult birth; 'and if you are ever as proud of her as I am of you, you will think your sufferings amply recompensed.' (He added in reference to a winter dinner he had given for the local community that 'the farmers were just as tipsy as farmers ought to be when dining with the parson.')* An even more important addition to the family was the acquisition of the widower Dr Henry Holland as a son-in-law in January 1834. Sydney humorously lamented the loss of his elder daughter Saba to the rising physician, and told Lady Grey that he would like to borrow her Georgiana as a substitute, adding 'but as I am afraid she would soon be reclaimed, I shall advertise—perhaps as follows—

Wanted for adoption a daughter. She must be good natured, cheerful, musical and not ill looking, fit for town or country, fond of books and not Evangelical. Any person who may accord with this description will find all the necessary explanation by applying &c.*

It was reported that Dr Holland had fallen in love with Saba when he had surprised her at Combe Florey while she was mixing rhubarb and magnesia in the rectory dispensary—'beauty, benevolence and pharmacy combined could not fail to charm'. Holland's own children were soon part of the Combe Florey family at holiday time: 'all our grand children natural and adopted are here screaming and perspiring intensely', Sydney reported to Lord Morpeth in August 1835.* Sydney was fond of his son-in-law, already a well-known London practitioner at the time of the marriage. 'The Doctor one day or another will be knighted, and Saba will be *Lady Holland*,' he wrote gleefully to her ladyship at Holland House. 'She must then fit herself up with Luttrells, Rogerses, John Russells, etc. Sydney Smiths she has.'* Henry Holland was indeed knighted in good time for there to be plenty of badinage about the other Lady Holland's rival establishment. 'Think dear Lady Carlisle of the audacity of Saba in giving a dinner to Lady Holland,' Sydney wrote in 1835: 'The day was gay and agreeable, and Lady Holland was pleased—the dinner good. Saba was very much alarmed all the morning but Dr Holland gently elevated her by bark and camphor draughts up to the proper pitch.'*

As in Yorkshire, the prospect of more frequent visits to London was invigorating. He was not prepared to vegetate at Combe Florey, even though he wrote of himself when proposing a week's visit to Holland House in 1830 that 'I am grown very old, silent and stupid, but you must overlook that, for the memory of old times'.* That was a visit which probably included a Fox family wedding ('a marriage, a great scene of blubbering, and Amen')* and was the first of a new series of visits to the Hollands from Somerset. As his reputation spread, however, he received invitations from all sides and he was accustomed to dine promiscuously, taking care to advise friends like John Murray: 'Do not imagine I am going to rat. I am a thoroughly honest, and I will say liberal, person, but have never given way to that puritanical feeling of the Whigs against dining with Tories.

> Tory and Whig in turn shall be my host,
> I taste no politics in boiled and roast.'*

Having eventually achieved ecclesiastical position in London, duty sometimes took him to town when the company was far from smart. 'London is very empty but by no means disagreeable,' he told Lady Grey in November 1834. 'I find plenty of friends and feel an affection for cousins, which somehow or another disappears in the more brilliant seasons of the year'*— a reminder of a favourite joke, to his cousin Longman the publisher, that 'my house is full of country cousins. I wish they were once removed.'*

As in Yorkshire, too, he was able to send his annual tributary cheeses, of good political pedigree as well as excellent make. A Cheddar was sent to Lady Grey in 1831 with the assurance that it was made by a reforming farmer, and three years later the annual order to Martha Davis, the Quaker cheesemonger in Taunton, was accompanied by a few words of political teasing to her and her shop-boy. 'Lord Melbourne's speech ... is excellent, and I recommend it to thee and the Friends. Oh Martha! what are talents without prudence and discretion? Look at friend Brougham—Nature has taken more pains with him than the best dairyman with the best cheese in thy shop; and what is he now? Martha, I hope the fall of Brougham will be a warning to Peter, and that he will not wax proud as he becomes wiser in cheese and butter, but keep his heart down as he rises before men.'*

Politics were a continuing preoccupation during his early years in Somerset. The question of Catholic emancipation in its concluding phases had to be finally settled before he could turn his attention fully to that of Parliamentary Reform. There was a certain amount of local fun when Sir Thomas Lethbridge, the county Member, who had been vehemently opposed to emancipation, joined the Duke of Wellington in the capitulation on the question in March 1829. (Sydney remarked that Lethbridge 'cannot keep the friendship of the Pope and that of the county of Somerset at the same time', but was prepared to support him as it was right to encourage such 'apostates'.*) By then, however, the whole matter had been worked over far too often. 'Men are tired to death with the Catholic question,' Sydney had written in February 1829 to Wilmot Horton, who had proposed some belated refinements of argument. '[They] are upon the eve of getting rid of it, and will take no more trouble about it.'* A few months later he was able to write to Archdeacon Wrangham in Yorkshire: 'Thank God there is an end to it, and an end at the same time to a great part of the power of fools—and knaves the movers of fools.'*

In the following year this mood of rather exhausted irritation with the whole question had passed, and he was able to enjoy a quiet personal satisfaction in a result for which he had striven anonymously in the *Review*, pseudonymously in *Peter Plymley's Letters*, and personally in tiny minorities at angry clerical meetings in the country. Satisfaction, too, at the news that a Roman Catholic, Philip Howard of Corby Castle, had been elected MP for Carlisle. Sydney wrote to congratulate Howard's father in August 1830: 'It is a pure pleasure to me to see honourable men of an ancient family restored to their birthright. I rejoice in the temple which has been reared to Toleration; and I am proud that I worked as a bricklayer's labourer at it—without pay, and with the enmity and abuse of those who were unfavourable to its construction.'*

A second political issue dear to his heart was by now coming into prominence, although at nearly 60 he felt rather too old for another major campaign. Jeffrey's becoming Lord Advocate for Scotland was an honour which presaged stirring times; as Sydney wrote to John Murray about it at the beginning of 1830, 'I can hardly picture to myself the rage and consternation of the Scotch Tories at this change, and at the liberality which is bursting out in every part of Scotland, where no lava and volcanic matter were suspected'. However, he added that 'I love liberty, but hope it can be so managed that I shall have soft beds, good dinners, fine linen, etc.' for the rest of my life. I am too old to fight or to suffer.'* Towards the end of the year the Duke of Wellington's firm declaration against Lord Grey's proposals for parliamentary reform brought the issue to a head, and (much to Sydney's delight) Lord Grey to the leadership of the ministry. 'I never felt more sincere pleasure than from Lord Grey's appointment,' he wrote to Lady Grey: 'After such long toil, such labour, privation, and misrepresentation, that a man should be placed where providence intended him to be, that honesty and virtue should at last meet with its reward is a pleasure which rarely occurs in human life, and one which I confess I had not promised myself.'*

He was well aware of the precariousness of the political balance, and of the volatile nature of the urban and rural poor, some of whom had been incited to rick-burning by the inflammatory propaganda of 'Captain Swing'. He attempted to counteract 'Swing's' handbills by letters to the *Taunton Courier* which were intended for distribution to labourers, warning them of the fate which awaited them. 'I am a sincere friend to the poor,' he concluded, 'and I think every man should live by his labour: but it cuts me to the very heart to see the honest husbandman perishing by that worst of all machines—the gallows, under the guidance of that most fatal of all leaders—Swing!'* Sydney wrote to Caroline Fox that 'They have had an excellent effect. There is one from Miss Swing threatening to destroy crimping-irons for caps and washing machines, and patent tea-kettles; vowing vengeance also on the new bodkin which makes two holes instead of one. Justices' wives are agitated and female constables have been sworn in.'*

Just before the introduction of the Reform Bill, he wrote to Lady Grey conforting her anxiety—'When I am very nervous I always do sums in arithmetic, and drink camphor julep'. He was holding himself in readiness to help, giving a message to Grey that 'If I can at any time be of any use in writing anything to support the good cause I am ready at a moment's warning, and will come up to town—but there are so many better men than me, that this can hardly be the case.'* As soon as the Bill was introduced—'I call it a magnificent measure, and am heartily glad it is understood to be his *individually*', Sydney commented to Lady Grey*—he began to give it vigorous public support in Somersetshire.

He spoke at a Reform meeting at Taunton on 9 March 1831, maintaining that the Bill was 'the greatest measure which has ever been before Parliament in my time'. The cumulative agitation of the entire country for a measure too long neglected now made the passing of Reform inevitable. Much of his speech was devoted to the question of the vested interests of the 'pocket borough' proprietors, whose arguments he disposed of nicely, ending up by dismissing a suggestion that they might be compensated for their loss, by a neat parallel:

When I was a young man, the place in England I remember as most notorious for highwaymen and their exploits was Finchley Common, near the metropolis; but Finchley Common, gentlemen, in the progress of improvement, came to be enclosed, and the highwaymen lost by these means the opportunity of exercising their gallant vocation. I remember a friend of mine proposed to draw up for them a petition to the House of Commons for compensation, which ran in this manner—'We, your loyal highwaymen of Finchley Common....' Gentlemen, I must leave the application to you.*

The following day he reported encouragingly to Lady Grey that 'I delivered a glowing harangue at Taunton in favour of it; justice compels me to say that there were only five coats in the room; the rest were jackets and smock-frocks. They were delighted with me, and said they should like to bring me in as Member.'*

Parliament was dissolved in late April, after the Bill (safely through its second reading) foundered in Committee. Sydney heard the news while on holiday at Sidmouth, and reported to Lady Grey that he had had no sleep as a result—'a meeting of freeholders at the Inn at Sidmouth, much speaking and frequent sound of Lord Grey's name thro' the wall; I had a great mind (being a Devonshire freeholder) to have appeared suddenly in night cap and dressing gown and to have made a Speech.' His intervention was this time made pseudonymously, but transparently so. 'I have left off writing myself but I have persuaded a friend of mine a Mr Dyson to publish his speech,' he informed Lady Grey, begging her discretion about the authorship. 'It is a mite to the public stock of liberal principles, and not worth caution or trouble, but my plan has always been to contribute my *mite*, and in my own particular way.'* 'Dyson' adjured the freeholders to 'Stick to the Bill—it is your Magna Carta and your Runnymede', developing many of the arguments in Sydney's first Taunton speech, in favour of the Grey ministry and against the old borough system, the abuses of which he depicted thus:

The eldest son of my Lord is just come from Eton—he knows a good deal about Æneas and Dido, Apollo, and Daphne—and that is all; and to this boy his father gives a six-hundredth part of the power of making laws, as he would give him a horse or a double-barrelled gun.... A neighbouring country gentleman, Mr Plumpkin, hunts with my Lord—opens him a gate or two, while the hounds are running—dines with my Lord—agrees with my Lord—wishes he could rival the South Down sheep of my Lord—and upon Plumpkin is conferred a portion of the government.... such people, in whose nomination I have no more agency than I have in the nomination of the toll-keepers of the Bosphorus, are to make laws for me and my family—to put their hands in my purse, and to sway the future destinies of this country.*

'Work well!' he exclaimed derisively in answer to the assertion that the present system was a good one. Mr Dundas had said that there was no eagerness for Reform in Edinburgh: 'Five minutes before Moses struck the rock, this gentleman would have said that there was no eagerness for water'. As with most of Sydney's political pronouncements, the immediate argument has a more general application. 'There are two methods of making alterations,' he maintained: 'the one is to despise the applicants, to begin with refusing every concession, then to relax by making concessions which are always too late, by offering in 1831 what is then too late, but would have been cheerfully accepted in 1830.... The other method is, to see at a distance that the thing must be done, and to do it effectually, *and at once*; to take it out of the hands of the common people, and to carry the measure in a manly liberal manner, so as to satisfy the great majority.'*

While 'Dyson's' speech was being circulated, Sydney met Lord John Russell, who was passing through Exeter while the Smiths were in Devon. His promotion of Reform in the Commons made him the hero of the hour, but Sydney found he had to make apologies for his diminutive friend: 'The people along the road were very much disappointed by his smallness,' he told Lady Holland. 'I told them he was much larger before the Bill was thrown out, but was reduced by excessive anxiety about the people. This brought tears into their eyes.'*

The Bill passed its next second reading in July, and throughout the hot summer continued grinding through its legislative channel. Sydney wrote to Lady Grey early in August: 'The passing of the bill in this weather—and against such opposition will be honourably remembered, and all is virtue, and courage . . . you may depend upon it that any attempt of the Lords to throw it out will be the signal for the most energetic resistance from one end of the kingdom to the other.'* The prospect of opposition in the Lords was anticipated, and Sydney wrote to Lord Grey urging him to recommend the creation of enough peers to secure the passage of the measure (adding, however, that 'you can only advise Kings, not compel them').* The Lords rejected the Bill on 8 October, to a widespread and dangerous public outcry. Sydney continued to send information, advice, and good-humoured encouragement to Lord and Lady Grey, and was soon given an opportunity to make the most famous of his political speeches— blowing his penny trumpet in a little market town, as he referred to such occasions—at a Reform meeting at Taunton on 11 October. His main intervention was brief but telling, and the heart of it was an apologue which soon became famous:

As for the possibility of the House of Lords preventing ere long a reform of Parliament, I hold it to be the most absurd notion that ever entered into human imagination. I do not mean to be disrespectful, but the attempt of the Lords to stop the progress of reform reminds me very forcibly of the great storm of Sidmouth, and of the conduct of the excellent Mrs Partington on that occasion. In the winter of 1824, there set in a great flood upon that town—the tide rose to an incredible height—the waves rushed in upon the houses, and every thing was threatened with destruction. In the midst of this sublime and terrible storm, Dame Partington, who lived upon the beach, was seen at the door of her house with mop and pattens, trundling her mop, squeezing out the sea-water, and vigorously pushing away the Atlantic Ocean. The Atlantic was roused. Mrs Partington's spirit was up; but I need not tell you that the contest was unequal. The Atlantic Ocean beat Mrs Partington. She was excellent with a slop or a puddle, but she should not have meddled with a tempest. Gentlemen, be at your ease— be quiet and steady. You will beat Mrs Partington.*

The *Taunton Courier* reported that 'fervent and reiterated applause attended the delivery of various parts of this address'. Mr Bickham Escott then attempted to speak in favour of the rejection, but was hissed down until Sydney courteously pleaded with the audience for a hearing for the intrepid minority, 'seeing, as they did, that he stood alone in such an assembly'.* Business then continued until unanimous resolutions were settled. In a matter of days 'Dame Partington and the Ocean' had found its way—after having been copied into *The Times*—into the print-sellers', with Wellington as the old countrywoman.* It marks the end of Sydney's political activity, although he sent Lady Grey several further letters discussing the question of possibly creating peers to secure the passage of the Bill, ending with a note of sincere congratulation as soon as the measure reached the statute book in June 1832.

Other controversial questions, such as the possibility of providing for the Catholic clergy of Ireland out of the revenues of the Protestant Church, were soon raised, but without the old enthusiasm. Sydney was glad to be able to entertain the victorious Lord John Russell, and to think of his butler charging the people a penny a peep for a glimpse of the great man through the shutters ('I wonder what he will charge for Lord Grey if he should come here', he asked Lady Grey).* But like many reformers the results of 1832 had run his stock of zeal rather low. He had the satisfaction of having worked hard and effectively; and, almost incidentally, he had at last acquired an adequate reward on the ecclesiastical ladder.

Whig parliamentary successes and the settlement of the Catholic question led Sydney to look for further promotion in the Church. The Bristol canonry with a convenient and agreeable Somerset living left him decently placed but inadequately rewarded. Although he was to find before long that he had not been forgotten by his friends, his first letter of the period to solicit preferment (surviving in a copy sent to Lord Grey) is addressed to the Duke of Wellington at the end of April 1830. 'In the fluctuations of life,' Sydney began philosophically, 'every man must be content to be sometimes up and sometimes down, but it is a sad life to be always down.' He based his application, naturally enough, on the Catholic campaign:

I have for twenty years been the uncompromising advocate of that question which you have so lately and so honourably settled. I have published a great deal upon the subject, and in all meetings of the clergy and on every public occasion which fairly presented itself, have been its strenuous, and often its solitary defender.

The misrepresentations, abuse and obloquy to which I have in consequence subjected myself, I need not state to your Grace. If the splendour of your life could not guard you, you may easily conceive too what a country clergyman must have been exposed.

It is not, I think, presumptuous to say, I might have advanced my fortunes, if I had defended error with half as much earnestness as I have contended for truth and justice. May I now ask you for some preferment in the Church?*

Not surprisingly, perhaps, this request met with no recorded response, but rapidly changing political alignments kept him in a state of perpetual expectation. In May 1830 he wrote to his wife that 'All kinds of intrigues are going on about the change of ministry, and all kinds of hopes and fears afloat. Nothing is more improbable than that I should be made a Bishop, and if I ever had the opportunity I am now (when far removed) decidedly of opinion that it would be the greatest act of folly and absurdity to accept it—to live with foolish people, do foolish and formal things all day, to hold my tongue or to twist it into conversation unnatural to me!!!!'* Four exclamation marks perhaps reveal a sense of *volo episcopari* beneath the denials, but there is enough truth in the remoteness of any offer and the dislike of pomp to dispel an impression of sour grapes. Whig prospects, however, were good enough to encourage patience, and a summer at Combe Florey eased any sense of neglect: 'I thank God for my comfortable situation in my old age,' Sydney wrote to Lady Holland in July 1831, 'above my deserts, and beyond my former hopes'.* A few months earlier, with a weather eye on the higher dignities, he had told Murray that 'I think Lord Grey will give me some preferment if he stays in long enough, but the upper parsons live vindictively, and evince their opposition to a Whig ministry by an improved health. The Bishop of Ely has the rancour to recover after three paralytic strokes, and the Dean of Lichfield to be vigorous at 82—and yet these are the men who are called Christians.'*

Lord Grey himself was anxious to promote Sydney. 'Now I shall be able to do something for Sydney Smith', he had said to his son-in-law John Bulteel on becoming Prime Minister.* Grey, like Sydney, had his eye on the health of elderly clergymen, and went so far as to promise Sydney Dr Andrew Bell's prebend at Westminster; but Bell recovered unexpectedly from a severe stroke, and the disappointed beneficiary had to write to Lady Grey that 'I hear that Dr Bell has been applying for my living of Combe Florey in case anything happens to me'.* But less than a month after the Westminster prebendary revived, a better place fell to the Government, and on 10 September 1831 Lord Grey wrote to Sydney: 'You are much obliged to Dr Bell, for not dying as he had promised. By the promotion of the Bishop of Chichester to the See of Worcester, a Canon Residentiary of St Pauls becomes vacant. A snug thing, let me tell you, being worth full 2000 per annum ... I do not think it likely that you can be *dis-*appointed a second time by the old Bishop coming to life again.'* Sydney was installed by the end of the month, writing to thank Mrs Meynell for her congratulations with the pleasant reflections that 'It is, I believe, a very good thing, and puts me at my ease for life. I asked for nothing—never did anything shabby to procure preferment.'*

His prebendal house was at Amen Corner ('an awkward name on a card, and an awkward annunciation to the coachman on leaving any fashionable mansion'),* but he decided not to occupy it during the three months of official residence at the Cathedral. The formalities of his appointment were concluded by a visit at Court, where he went, 'horrible to relate! with strings to my shoes instead of buckles—not from Jacobinism, but ignorance. I saw two or three Tory lords looking at me with dismay, was informed by the Clerk of the Closet of my sin, and gathering my sacerdotal petticoats about me (like a lady conscious of thick ankles), I escaped further observation.'* Sydney soon became an important figure in the administration of the Cathedral, and although (as we shall see) it was some time before he gave up all hope of higher preferment, he was to serve St. Paul's well as priest and adminis-trator until the end of his life.

In spite of Sydney's misgivings about the address, Amen Corner was apparently a pleasant residence. In 1839 Sydney's colleague R.H. Barham (author of *The Ingoldsby Legends*) wrote to his sister: 'What do you think of Mr Sydney Smith having offered me his residentiary house to live in, together with a garden at the back, which . . . is magnificent for London, containing three polyanthus roots, a real tree, a brown box border, a muff-coloured jessamine, a shrub which is either a dwarf acacia or an overgrown gooseberry bush, eight broken bottles, and a tortoise-shell tom-cat asleep in the sunniest corner . . . with a varied and extensive prospect of the back of the Oxford Arms, and a fine hanging wood (the New Drop at Newgate) in the distance; all being situate in the midst of a delightful neighbourhood, and well worth the attention of any capitalist wishing to make an investment.'* The light tone of Barham's letter shows that the two canons had much in common, although one was Tory to the other's Whig. They became friends and it was to Barham that Sydney wrote in November 1841 acknowledging a gift of game: 'If there is a pure and elevated pleasure in this world it is a roast pheasant with bread sauce. Barn door fowls for dissenters but for the real Churchman, the thirty-nines times articled clerk—the pheasant, the pheasant.'*

Social pleasantries with his colleagues undoubtedly made the three separate months of canonical duty each year much more enjoyable. He kept his residences regularly, and became a popular preacher in the Cathedral, in his customarily brief and energetic manner. He did his humourous best to deter friends from attending: 'To go to St Paul's is certain death,' he wrote in November 1839: 'The thermometer is several degrees below zero—my sentences are frozen as they come out of my mouth and are thawed in the course of the sermon, making strange noises and unexpected assertions in various parts of the Church.'* Cards were provided so that the virgers could find good seats for his friends: 'The Virgers have the strictest orders not to accept money just as the footmen have in all serious families not to kiss the maids. That these orders are equally well carried out neither you nor I have the smallest doubt.'*

He warned Mrs Grote not to flatter herself 'with the delusive hope of a slumber: I preach violently, and there is a strong smell of sulphur in my sermons'.* but there is ample testimony to his discourses being plain and effective, without too much display. Greville reported on an evening sermon in 1834 that Sydney was 'very good; manner impressive, voice sonorous and agreeable, *rather* familiar but not offensively so, language simple and un-adorned, sermon clever and illustrative'.* A few months later, Sydney's American friend George Ticknor noted in his Journal that a St Paul's sermon was 'an admirable moral essay, to prove that righteousness has the promise of the life that now is. It was written with great condensation of thought and purity of style, and sometimes with brilliancy of phrase and expression, and it was delivered with great power and emphasis. It was by far the best sermon I ever heard in Great Britain . . . and both the manner and the matter would have been striking anywhere.'*

So considerable a pulpit talent was employed in delivering what Sydney described to Lord John Russell as 'a sermon of admirable advice to Victoria', preached at St Paul's soon after her accession in 1837.* It is a plain discourse enjoining on the young sovereign her responsibilities for securing education, peace, and religion, and concluding:

The patriot Queen, whom I am painting, reverences the National Church—frequents its worship, and regulates her faith by its precepts; but she withstands the encroachments, and keeps down the ambition natural to establishments, and by rendering the privileges of the Church compatible with the civil freedom of all sects, confers strength upon, and adds duration to, that wise and magnificent institution. And then this youthful Monarch, profoundly but wisely religious, disdaining hypocrisy, and far above the childish horrors of false piety, casts herself upon God, and seeks from the Gospel of his blessed Son a path for her steps, and a comfort for her soul. Here is a picture which warms every English heart, and would bring all this congregation upon their bended knees before Almighty God to pray it may be realised. What limits to the glory and happiness of the native land, if the Creator should in his mercy have placed in the heart of this royal woman the rudiments of wisdom and mercy; and if, giving them time to expand, and to bless our children's children with her goodness, He should grant to her a long sojourning upon earth, and leave her to reign over us till she is well stricken in years! What glory! what happiness! what joy! what bounty of God! I of course can only expect to see the beginning of such a splendid period; but when I do see it, I shall exclaim with the pious Simeon,—'Lord, now lettest thou thy servant depart in peace, for mine eyes have seen thy salvation.'*

That is a fair specimen of Sydney's sermon style at its most sonorous, but we can only imagine the diction and pulpit manner which his hearers found so affecting. Some six years of the new reign would show him just how far his hopes for a soverign of quiet domestic piety and religious feeling were to be fulfilled; longevity was of course to magnify the influence enormously. One might read into such sentiments the feeling of a Georgian clergyman for a nascent Victorian age; Sydney's own view, expressed to Mrs Villiers when acknowledging her good opinion of his sermon, was more straightforward. 'I hope the subject was a proper one, and that it was honestly treated,' he said, 'but sufficient for the day is the sermon thereof.'* To closer friends he was disposed to be less respectful about his new sovereign. 'Victoria has had a very fine day for her visit to the City,' he reported to Mrs Austin: 'it disgusts me to see a million of people busying themselves about the foolish ceremonies of a dumpy little girl of eighteen—America for ever.'* One should not read too much republican feeling into such opinions sent to divert radical friends, but he certainly had but little esteem for 'little Victoria' on her accession, and on Melbourne's position at Court he commented 'how lucky to have got the first hold of Victoria'.*

Although even by the time of Grey's ministry he had (in spite of some humorous aspirations to the Bishopric of Worcester) begun to feel that he was at sixty no longer energetic enough to fulfil his ideal of episcopacy, the acquisition of his 'snug' canonry did not diminish his desire for further preferment. For some years he was divided between the *volo* and *nolo* of episcopal appointment. 'Perhaps he may offer to make me a Bishop,' he mused of Lord Grey in 1833, 'but I doubt very much if I would accept it. My present parsonage is most beautiful, and I shall never be so well off as I am—but after all the temptation may not come—if it does I hope I shall not be such a fool as to yield to it.'* But only a year later he expressed himself on the matter, with a long outgrown outspokenness, to Lord Holland (a rather unusual fount of religious patronage, but well placed in the ministry to press Sydney's case). He had felt slighted by Holland's having mentioned casually that Samuel Butler rather then Joseph Allen should have been made Bishop of Bristol. As Holland had long felt that his friend should be on the episcopal bench, Sydney felt himself entitled to ask 'whether I am to consider myself as entirely laid upon the shelf, and passed over by that party for whom I have all my life hazarded so much abuse and misrepresentation.'* His usual ambivalence about elevation came into his rather pathetic appeal: 'It is not that I care for being a Bishop. If the See of Bristol had been offered to me nothing would have induced me to take it—there is scarcely any Bishopric I *would* take; but I think I do not deserve the disgrace from my party of being passed over and the dignity never offered to me.'* The 'slight' mattered more than the 'sacrifice', but it was clearly the thought that this Bristol appointment might be the last for which he was eligible that led to Sydney's urgent plea to a man who had often said to him that he would get drunk on the day Sydney was made a Bishop. His case, as he put it to Lady Holland, did not consist in asking Lord Holland 'why he had not made me a Bishop, but why he thought I ought not to be one'.* The distinction was, however, a narrow one so far as the Hollands were concerned; fortunately Sydney did not press the matter too far, recalling as he did with tactful gratitude 'the favour and patronage of Holland House' of which he was so proud.

He declared in this correspondence of 1834 that he considered the failure at Bristol as being 'an end of the Mitre for ever', but the question continued to agitate him. In April 1835 he once again took the matter up with Lord Holland: 'My own opinion of myself is that I should make a very good Bishop, that I should be a firm defender of liberal opinions, and I hope I am too much a man of honour to take an office without fashioning my manners and conversation so as not to bring it into disrepute.'* There he defends himself against one of the possible objections to his appointment, that of levity and the risk of impropriety. Next, he recognized that he had missed the boat when Grey was Prime Minister, as no proper vacancies had occurred at the beginning of the administration; he did Grey the credit of thinking that he would have been brought forward to fill a suitable place. Finally, in naming Grey's successor he pointed to another major obstacle, for Sydney and Melbourne were never on close terms. 'Lord Melbourne always thinks *that* man best qualified for office whom he has seen and known the least,' Sydney remarked to Holland, rather galled that recent appointments included men not hitherto conspicuous for their opinions: 'Liberals of the eleventh hour abound,' he continued 'and there are some of the first hour of whose work in the toil and heat of the day I have no recollection.'* But to add to these external objections, that he might be too dangerous, too forthright, too high-spirited, and that he was unsympathetic to the Prime Minister, he could honestly add one other: 'that I have entirely lost all wish to be a Bishop; the thought is erased from my mind, and in the very improbable event of a Bishopric being offered to me I would steadily refuse it; in this I am *perfectly honest and sincere*.'* 'Nolo E——', he exclaimed to Wilmot-Horton at the end of 1835 by way of confirmation: 'I dread the pomp, trifles, garments, ruinous expense and vigilant decorum of the episcopal life—and this is lucky as I have not the smallest reason for believing that anyone has the most remote intention of putting the mitre on my head which would unquestionably shake it off if ever so imposed.'*

Such remained his settled opinion to the end of his life. Melbourne, however, seems to have had a change of heart, once telling a friend (who later passed it on to Sydney's daughter) that there was nothing he more deeply regretted, in looking back over his past career, than not having made Sydney Smith a bishop.* Such kind words came too late for Sydney's career, but in 1840 he had written to Lady Holland that 'I have long since got rid of all ambition and wish for distinctions, and am much happier for it.'* Patronage merely remained a subject for mild joking. 'The Chancellor's rout prevented me from coming', Sydney once wrote to Charles Babbage, apologizing for missing a party. 'A clergyman always attends first to those who have any preferment to give away—and though I am so full of preferment that I can hold no more the old habit prevails.'*

Sydney diverted some of his energy in pursuit of patronage to securing a place in the civil service for his only surviving son; in this he had greater initial success but ultimately much disappointment.

Wyndham Smith, Sydney's younger son, proved to be an unworthy substitute for the admirable Douglas. In 1831 he was sent to Trinity College, Cambridge, and Sydney was soon shown by personal experience the truth of his frequent assertion that 'the only consequences of a University education are the growth of vice and the waste of money'.* In 1834 Sydney told Lady Grey that 'St Paul behaved extremely well to me last year, and well it was he did so for I have had some thumping bills from Cambridge.... great alterations are promised, and I believe sincerely intended'.* Less than a year later, detection in a minor gambling offence, backed presumably by other evidence of bad character, led Dr Wordsworth, the Master of Trinity, to order Wyndham's expulsion. Sydney wrote immediately to the Master arguing rather pathetically and at length against the severity of the punishment: sending Wyndham down 'would amount to his entire ruin', and the possibility of his being moved to another college required a formal *bene decessit* from Trinity. A transfer to Caius was arranged, and Wordsworth replied tersely but without conviction that he hoped the young man's '*future* conduct' would not discredit the generosity of Caius in taking in such an obviously difficult case. Little is recorded of Wyndham's later university career, but his father was still paying off Cambridge

1. John Henning,
portrait medallion, 1805

2. Edwin Landseer, portrait sketch, 1840s

DAME PARTINGTON and the OCEAN (OF REFORM)

Published by Thos McLean, 26 Haymarket, Octr 75.th 1831

3. 'HB' (John Doyle). 'Dame Partington', 1831. See p. 159

B. Sketches, Nº 655.

"DIVES AND LAZARUS"

4. 'HB' (John Doyle). 'Dives and Lazarus', 1840. See p. 180

5. H. P. Briggs, portrait, 1840

debts at the end of 1837.* In soliciting a place for him in a Government office, Sydney remarked that Wyndham had 'some natural shrewdness with only a moderate attachment to Greek and Roman learning', but sought a position which would not require him to take a Treasury examination ('not that the young man is incompetent but nervous, and might fail from agitation rather than from deficiency').* It had been particularly disappointing for one so learned in the techniques of Church preferment to have an only son whose inclinations turned out to be far from clerical. 'I had intended my son for the Church,' Sydney wrote to Lord Palmerston (having previously tried Melbourne), 'but he thinks the Church is falling and will not go into it. I had for the purpose of giving him a good Living kept myself at the head of the preferment list at St Paul's—and the good things I had in store for him must now go to some one else.'*

Melbourne ('to stay my stomach', as Sydney put it) appointed Wyndham to a minor clerkship in the Audit Office,* but the father continued to badger Lord John Russell and others for a better situation. 'The only good the Ministry can do me,' he wrote to Lord John, 'is to give my son some emolument in some public office.... This is all I wish and want in this world, and this would be a receipt in full for that mitre to which a long life of depression for liberal principles bravely avowed had doomed me at the age of 63.'* A further application to Lord Melbourne was answered by the private secretary suggesting a very lowly Customs appointment, which produced the hurt and disgusted retort 'As to the Land Waiter's place I have too much real confidence in the proper feeling of Lord Melbourne and yourself to suppose for a moment that you are treating me with derision, and have therefore only to say plainly, that my situation in life places me above the necessity of accepting such an offer, and *ought* perhaps to have guaranteed me from the pain of receiving it.'* It was Lord John who eventually found a place for Wyndham, Sydney acknowledging the patronage with the assurance that 'I am sure he will attend steadily to the duties of his office and I think he will turn out to be a very shrewd person with a good share of mother wit and worldly cleverness.'* Wyndham, however, served for no more than two years, and was discharged from the Home Office for misconduct.* As his nickname 'The Assassin' (acquired after killing a bull-dog during his college days) might suggest, his interests lay elsewhere. Wyndham became a well-known racing man, unreliable (once a defaulter over the Derby), and a worry to his father throughout his life. A heavy charge, too, with £4,000 of debts cleared in 1842, and in 1843 separation and exile to Southampton on £500 a year.* He has a precarious footnote in literature as Spavin, a racing man about the clubs, in Thackeray's *Book of Snobs*: poor consolation to a father who had been much humiliated by having to beg on his son's behalf, who was later to make a substantial bequest to him conditional on living apart from his mother and on continued good behaviour.

Soon after his installation, the Dean and Chapter began to entrust their new canon with the conduct of much of the practical business of the Cathedral. Chapter minutes time after time show tasks being deputed to him and carried out efficiently. It was Sydney who laid the foundations of the movement for reforming the administration of St Paul's, which was to lead to the Cathedral being one of the glories of the metropolis later in the century— Hale, Milman, and Gregory were to follow on the same lines. Dean Milman told Saba that 'I find traces of him in every particular of Chapter affairs; and on every occasion where his hand appears, I find stronger reasons for respecting his sound judgement, knowledge of business, and activity of mind; above all, the perfect fidelity of his stewardship. ... His management of the affairs of St Paul's (for at one time he seems to have been *the* manager) only commenced too late and terminated too soon.'*

Sydney's superintendence covered all aspects, not just the building and finances. The musical arrangements and provision of choristers had long been a matter of contention, but he helped to solve some of the difficulties, writing for example to the Organist, William Hawes, with his usual common sense when an application was made in 1844 to have the number of boys increased: 'I think the Choir of St Paul's as good as any in England. We have gone on with it for two hundred years; why not be content? You talk of competing with other cathedrals, but cathedrals are not to consider themselves rival opera houses. We shall come by and by to act anthems. It is enough if your music is decent, and does not put us to shame. It is a matter of perfect indifference to me whether Westminster bawls louder than St Paul's. We are there to pray, and the singing is a very subordinate consideration.'* Common sense led also to adequate fire-fighting equipment being installed, and indeed to the Cathedral being insured. 'I beg leave to remind you,' he once wrote to the Dean of Ely, 'that though considered by many people as a Radical, I was the first person to insure cathedrals in this country. I forget the name of my antipodes predecessor who burnt down the library at Alexandria.'* The Cathedral library, too, was much improved during the period of his canonry.

He looked carefully over both divisions of the Cathedral income—the Chapter common fund which provided for general expenses and the Fabric Fund administered by trustees for the maintenance of the building. Sydney's management of Fabric Fund expenditure and his relations with C.R. Cockerell, the Surveyor, show him at his best as a diligent and efficient businessman, looking into the accounts in a way which might have pleased even his father. This supervision eventually won Cockerell's respect, although Sydney's early letters to the Surveyor are curt in manner and suspicious in tone. The first of a long series reminds Cockerell of the Dean and Chapter's wish to 'husband our feeble resources as much as possible', and other letters of his first summer residence, in 1832, show Sydney's insistence on the careful preservation of records of work carried out, and the thorough auditing of all accounts. Attention to detail was very minute—'I trust no more will be done with the dog-spikes in the stonework till I have seen you and conversed with you on the subject'—but was, to begin with, quite essential.* As Cockerell remarked to Lady Bell in 1851: 'he investigated with the greatest minuteness all transactions which were placed under his superintendence, and that with a severity of discipline neither called for nor agreeable. His early communications, therefore, with myself, and I may say with all the officers of the Chapter, were extremely unpleasant; but when satisfied by his methods of investigation, and by a "little collision", as he termed it, that all was honest and right, nothing could be more candid or kind than his subsequent treatment; and our early dislike was at length converted into unalloyed confidence and regard.'*

The 'little collision' seems to have been spread over several years. In July 1832 Sydney gave an oral message through his servant, which was evidently passed on to Cockerell as forcefully as it may have been intended. The recipient reported having received 'a message of a very unusual nature ... which I take for granted was not by your order'.* 'What I said to my servant,' Sydney explained, 'was to say that I was particularly vexed or sorry (I forget which) at not having received an answer as I was going out of town. If I did not respect you and all other gentlemen too much to leave such a message as you allude to, you may depend upon it I respect myself too much to do so.'* This elegancy settled matters for a while, and Sydney and Cockerell met to discuss the new accounting methods. A similar row flared up in 1838 when Sydney had cause to feel that 'knowing the time and trouble I have given up to the Cathedral I think it is but fair that the paid architect of the Cathedral should render me some assistance when I request his advice'*. His rebuke to Cockerell is one of balanced dignity.

I wish to go on with you quietly, civilly, and good naturedly as I do with Hodgson and Sellon and other officers of the establishment. I honour your genius and your talents but then I must require in my turn, civility and common attention.... From me you will always experience that respect which your situation as a gentleman and your great Eminence in your profession have a right to command. When your health will permit I hope and believe I shall receive in return from you that professional attention which my zeal for the Cathedral really deserves. What is past is of course forgotten.*

The correspondence shows Sydney's sound grasp of the details of the building and of the comparative prices of respectable tradesmen. 'Your idea of respectability seems to be that no tradesman can be respectable who does not charge high prices', he remarked to Cockerell. 'Without entering into any reasoning about the matter, one safe and only rule should be to get the work done as cheaply as we can, consistently with it being done well, and if any man of whose respectability there is the usual presumptive evidence will undertake our work at reduced prices, we ought to employ him.'*

Nothing was too small for his close attention in the Cathedral: glaziers' prices, stink traps in the Chapter House, fire precautions with slate cisterns in the Gallery, a stove for the library (properly heated for the first time). When the Surveyor's painter estimated double the price quoted by Sydney's man, Sydney proposed that 'both aisles shall be done—the one by your man the other by mine; this will enable us to make a better acquaintance with them both and to see what they are made of.'* Cockerell came to respect Sydney's personal intrepidity in the Cathedral, as well as his skill with the accounts: 'An unpractised head and a podagrous [gouty] disposition of limbs might well have excused the survey of those pinnacles and heights of our cathedral, which are to all both awful and fatiguing; but nothing daunted him; and once, when I suggested a fear that his portly person might stick fast in a narrow opening of the western towers, which we were surveying, he reassured me by declaring, that, "if there were six inches of space, there would be room enough for him".*

He paid much attention to the monuments, and wrote to Milman (then a canon of Westminster) in July 1838: 'Pray tell me the sort of person you employ for cleaning the monuments. Is it the curate, or a statuary, or is it a mere mason's labourer? Or does it (as in the case of a Scotchman caught and washed for the first time) require acid? I propose to establish a cleaning fund and to compel every dead hero to pay something towards keeping himself clean.'*

The Fabric Fund itself required careful supervision. It derived from the invested residue of the original rebuilding fund established after the Great Fire, managed by Trustees who insisted that the Chapter's spending on the fabric should be kept within the limits of income. There was of course occasional over-expenditure. In 1832 a debit incurred by repairs to the Chapter House led to Sydney's taking part in official correspondence between the Dean and the Trustees. Phrases such as the Chapter's rejection of an attempt 'to fling the burthen upon individuals'— of financing Chapter House repairs by reducing dividend from the common fund—have the authentic ring of Sydney militant.

Legal and administrative problems brought Sydney into close touch with Christopher Hodgson, the Chapter Clerk, who constantly held that 'Mr Sydney Smith was one of the most strictly honest men he ever met in business.'* There seems to have been little of the friction Sydney experienced with Cockerell; he recommended Hodgson to Archdeacon Hale as 'the perfection of good sense upon such subjects'.* When kept in the country by ill-health in August 1841, Sydney wrote to Hodgson, alluding to his current antipathies: 'I am building an ark for fear of a flood—there shall be no Minor Canons in it nor Vicars Choral, but there shall be a place for the Chapter Clerk.'* He was a worthy lieutenant during Sydney's administration.

Much of Sydney's energy was disinterested—he could not benefit from the Fabric Fund which he did so much to enhance, as it was quite separate from the divisible income of the Chapter. But the annual distribution of the capitular dividends had its charms as well, as Sydney wrote to Lady Ashburton, declining an invitation for the day in question: 'On one day of the year the Canons of St Paul's divide a little money—an inadequate recompense for all the troubles and anxieties they undergo— ...

when we all dine together, endeavouring to forget for a few moments, by the aid of meat and wine, the sorrows and persecutions of the Church.'* In the previous year, his colleague James Tate wrote to a friend that 'much of my happiness in this place, much also of our collective prosperity as to finance, ... depends on our brother canon, Sydney Smith'*.

Soon after his appointment, Sydney had written to Lady Morley that 'I find too (sweet discovery!) that I give a dinner every Sunday, for three months in the year, to six clergymen and six singing-men, at one o'clock'.* The custom of feeding the minor canons and vicars-choral between services was long-standing, and Sydney found it increasingly burdensome. During his spring residence in 1839 Sydney tried to have the privilege commuted, and wrote to the Warden of the College of Minor Canons that 'the hour of dining is so inconvenient and so little accommodated to the state of the times that it would be better perhaps for all parties that a money payment should be substituted.'* His proposal of a commutation of £10 to the Minor Canons and Vicars Choral was refused. When he returned in July, he wrote in greater detail to the Warden:

The Sunday dinners between the services are extremely inconvenient. My eyes are failing very fast, as is my general health. I find great difficulty in reading my sermon in the bad light of St Paul's and I want the time immediately before the service to impress the sermon on my memory. I am (as you all know) a very temperate man, but it is almost impossible as master of the house to sit down among my guests without eating and drinking to a certain extent, and to do so at the very unusual hour of half past one and to preach after it invariably gives me a bad headache.*

Postponing the meal until after the second service would remove its original function and turn it into a mere party: 'and if the manners of the age are not favourable to parties on a Sunday, it would be unwise in a body of clergymen not to respect public opinion on such subjects'.* Sydney felt that absenting himself from the meals would turn his residence into a mere tavern, and again proposed a monthly payment of £4 for each Sunday, calculated from his careful record of the expense. He recalled the pleasure of having entertained 'so many gentlemanlike and agreeable men' at his table, which reflected the Minor Canons' own sense of the privilege of dining at the Residentiaries' board—the basis of their refusal to accept a cash substitute.*

Nor did the College yield when Sydney's tone became

sharper—'I am afraid the Minor Canons have mistaken courteous language for hesitation as to my own rights . . .'* They even refused his suggestion of their dining four times a year in his own house at his invitation, which would have been 'in all respects preferable to our hasty dinners on Sunday'.* The custom had become a privilege and was now interpreted as a right, so Sydney's attempts to commute it—made with the support of the Chapter—were bound to fail. It was not until 1843 that the Sunday dinner was abolished, when the Chapter added £15 to the annual stipends of the recipients.*

In 1837 Sydney was once more engaged in ecclesiastical controversy with Lord John Russell, as the Home Office tried to insist that the Cathedral should be opened free of charge as a national monument. The Dean and Chapter had long been accustomed to making a charge of twopence (which went to pay the virgers) for visitors outside the hours of Service. They felt that the charge was an essential deterrent, to limit casual and defer rowdy sightseers to preserve standards of decent behaviour. Sydney engaged in a long correspondence with the Home Secretary, pointing out the dangers of St Paul's becoming 'a rendezvous for the worst characters of both sexes in the Metropolis'.* The experiment of free opening had been tried, but with very disagreeable results, enough to show the danger that 'the Church would become as it has been in times past, a place of assignation for all the worst characters male and female of the Metropolis; it would be a Royal Exchange for wickedness as the other Royal Exchange is for commerce. . . . The mischief and indecorum which takes place in St Paul's is very notorious; the Cathedral is constantly and shamefully polluted with ordure . . . the right of entry must be restricted or St Paul's must be opened as a Gallery of Sculpture and shut as a place of worship. Our duty is to consider the interests of religion as paramount to the interests of art.' Sydney's detailed replies to the Home Secretary give a horrifying and unexaggerated picture of popular irreligion in contemporary London.

Extraordinary policing was impracticable, and the Home Office withdrew their suggestion with bad grace. But similar questions were asked four years later by a Select Committee on National Monuments and Works of Art, before which Sydney appeared as a highly competent witness.* The admission charges were eventually abolished at the time of the Great Exhibition in 1851, and a general improvement in public behaviour helped to prevent any further general indecorum.

St Paul's provided Sydney with a certain amount of patronage in the Church. He used it wisely, having over the years become learned in the dispensation of ecclesistical favour. His wife recalled that he rewarded his old and faithful servant David Leaf with one of the virgerships, worth £300 a year.* The Chapter took presentation to vacant livings in turn, the presenter going to the bottom of the list if he took up the option. Several prosperous livings came Sydney's way, but he was never seriously tempted to accept one for himself. Early in 1840 he had written to Lord Grey that 'I may be driven by adverse circumstances to take a living from St Paul's, but I think it is not likely',* but he was referring only to the state of the Church. He tried instead to benefit Grey's sons. In 1839 Francis Grey had been offered the good living of Barnes,* which he declined. Sydney was relieved: 'I think if Francis had taken Barnes he would have been ruined by luncheons; an Howard and a Grey united would have been suffocated at Barnes by their numerous connexions.'* Sunbury-on-Thames was also offered to Grey, who declined before Sydney offered it (not very enthusiastically) to his nephew Cecil with the warning that something better might turn up before Sydney rose again to the top of the list.*

His next magnanimous piece of patronage was at Edmonton, following the death of James Tate in 1843. Sydney first offered the living to John Grey, who refused it, thereby avoiding (as Sydney remarked to Lady Grey) 'the very unpleasant task of getting dilapidations from Tate's ruined family'.* The Tate family had been left in poverty through the misconduct of others,* and were expecting to be turned out of the parsonage. It was generally thought that Sydney would take the living himself, as it was so near London. His solution was to present Tate's son and curate to his late father's cure. Sydney announced his decision melodramatically to the assembled Tate family, with the inevitable result, as he reported to his wife:

They all burst into tears. It flung me also into a great agitation of tears, and I wept and groaned for a long time. Then I rose, and said I thought it was very likely to end in their keeping a buggy, at which we all laughed as violently. The poor old lady, who was sleeping in a garret because she could not bear to enter into the room lately inhabited by her husband, sent for me and kissed me, sobbing with a thousand emotions ... I never passed so remarkable a morning, nor was more deeply impressed with the sufferings of human life, and never felt more thoroughly the happiness of doing good.*

'It has raised them all up from the dust', Sydney told Lady Grey.* His action was universally praised. The parishioners of Edmonton sent him an address conveying their thanks. Sydney replied with corresponding dignity, emphasizing the worthiness of their young new pastor and his respect for the memory of his predecessor.* Bishop Blomfield wrote approving of Sydney's kind and generous intentions; he replied telling the Bishop something of the family scene. 'The transition from despair to joy was awful, I shall never forget it. Virtue they say is its own reward, but there was an auxiliary premium for in a moment I was smothered with the kisses of the four ugly women and the sick mother.'* It is a pity that the end of the story is less than happy. 'You have seen more than enough of my giving the living of Edmonton to a curate,' he told Mrs Grote two months later. 'The first thing the unscriptural curate does, is to turn out his fellow-curate, the son of him who was vicar before his father ... The Bishop, the Dean and Chapter, and I have expostulated; he perseveres in his harshness and cruelty.'* Although it was tarnished so soon by the conduct of his nominee, Sydney's disinterested goodwill at Edmonton is very affecting.

Towards the end of Sydney's time at St Paul's, William Hale (a residentiary canon from 1840 and Archdeacon of London from 1842) began to take an active interest in the administration of the Cathedral. Sydney wrote to him often, asking him to 'excuse my frequent epistles but as it has pleased divine providence to send us a sensible man, I lean upon him.'* Hale was a clear-headed and vigorous reformer, rather over-anxious to tackle longstanding problems such as the admission of the choristers or the distribution of 'Cupola money'—the admission fees to the Whispering Gallery—to the minor canons. He even hoped to effect one major domestic improvement: 'You are a romantic Canon to talk about warming St Paul's,' Sydney wrote to him at Christmas 1840; 'The only real way of doing it is to warm the County of Middlesex, to which our revenues are hardly adequate.'* Heating *was* gradually introduced, partly by stopping gaps and glazing openings, but it was a slow process, requiring knowledge and tact, as Sydney urged on his new colleague. 'I need not say to a person of your sense and prudence that it will be better to wait a little and become acquainted with the Cathedral thoroughly before you plan any great alteration.'* Hale, however, continued to act rather too zealously for Sydney's liking and in 1844 received yet another sensible rebuke: 'I have no doubt of the goodness of your motives but your zeal will wear off a little by time and experience. You will find that the way to go through the world is with one eye open and the other shut, unless you mean to lead a life of endless contention and litigation—and I am very sure you are too good natured a person to have any such meaning."*

Although Hale was taking an increasingly large part in the administration of Chapter business in Sydney's last years, it is clear that Sydney was powerful and determined to the end. It was, for example, his duty to arrange the disposition of seats in the Cathedral Yard at the time of the Queen's visit to the City in October 1844, allotting particular places to the various livery companies. One of the Company clerks remarked to him, ' "Perhaps, Mr Smith, all these details had better be left to us. We will form a little committee of our own and spare you all further trouble in the arrangement. Too many cooks, you know, spoil the broth." ' ' "Very true, Sir," ' was the reply, ' "but let me set you right in one particular: here there is but one cook—myself; you are only scullion, and will be good enough to take your directions from me." '*

It was not only in domestic management that St Paul's Cathedral found its new canon a willing and energetic worker. Sydney's position in the Cathedral gave him a special interest in the defence of its endowments and privileges, and prompted his final major pamphleteering campaign. After the Reform Bill was passed into law, Sydney underwent a change in attitude not unfamiliar in one of his age, or indeed to one of his earlier radical enthusiasms. His later writings show him increasingly as a defender of institutions rather than as an advocate of political or ecclesiastical change. It is therefore not without its amusing side that Sydney's latterly conservative tendencies should have been most strikingly demonstrated when the reforming spirit he had done so much to encourage turned its attention to the Church of England. The Church, and particularly the upper clergy, had been notoriously unpopular during the Reform agitation: 'it was not safe for a clergyman to appear in the streets,' Sydney later reminisced, 'I bought a blue coat, and did not despair in time of looking like a Layman.'*

Something had to be done, and Sydney himself did not deny the necessity for reform: but the Ecclesiastical Commission permanently founded in 1836 for the management of Church business was not to his liking. Many of its recommendations threatened the establishments, revenues, endowments, and patronage of cathedrals; most of its active personnel were bishops whose own income and patronage would not be abated by the Commission's work. Such an imbalance cried out for a spirited defence, and Sydney proved more than willing to supply it. The episcopal bench continued to fill him with a humorous fascination. A couple of years previously, when the Archbishop of York was reported as staying with the Archbishop of Canterbury, Sydney had remarked to Lady Carlisle 'What a pleasing reflection is that of the Archbishops dwelling together. What an accumulation of power, what a luxury of sanctity—the Right Revd Pelion on the Right Revd Ossa—Gog and Magog. What an Halo of Holiness must surmount them.'*

The fact that his own diocesan, Charles James Blomfield, Bishop of London, was the strenuous and efficient spirit behind the Commission (he was called 'an ecclesiastical Peel' by his enemies, and had much in common with the statesman who had instigated it)* was an additional stimulus to Sydney. His own bishop, bent on impoverishing the Cathedral but not reducing the massive episcopal revenues, gave just the right relish of personality that Sydney needed to prepare a defence in his old manner; it scarcely needed a polite request from Thomas Singleton, Archdeacon of Northumberland, for his views of the Commission to elicit from Sydney a trio of essays in characteristic style.

The preliminary commissions of inquiry which had recommended the setting-up of a permanent executive body had also advocated major reforms in the cathedrals, especially appropriating their surplus revenues to increase the income of the parochial clergy. The number of canonries was to be reduced to four in each cathedral, and their other dignities restricted; but as St Paul's had only three canonries, a fourth was to be created—at episcopal nomination—to bring it in line with the others. The patronage assigned to individual dignities (such as that which Sydney had been able to exercise in favour of Tate's family) was to be transferred to the bishop. Canonical incomes were to be reduced to £1,000, deans cut to £2,000. It was a busy programme of reform and, in spite of the protection of existing rights, a threatening one for the future of St Paul's. Bishop Blomfield, acting with his usual energy, had pressed it forward strongly, probably disregarding the danger he faced from an opposition able skilfully to use against him the facts of his own enhanced privileges and retained income.

Sydney's first *Letter to Archdeacon Singleton* (a tract of 72 octavo pages) was published early in 1837. It opens with a quietly stated attack on the episcopally biased constitution of the Commission; Sydney had long ago developed his techniques for dealing with bishops in the *Edinburgh Review*. While he admitted the urgent need for reform, he found that the lords spiritual had attempted to do too much at once in agitated response to extremist attacks on the Church. 'I would not', he added, 'have operated so largely on an old and (I fear) a decaying building.'* Rich prebendal estates were to be confiscated to form part of a fund for the augmentation of stipends, but Sydney asked whether it would not have been better, instead of just confiscating these sinecures, to have annexed them to demanding and underpaid parishes so that the prebendaries could earn their stipends. Merely forming a fund to augment lesser stipends would do nothing useful, for, as Sydney pointed out, the entire income of the Church of England from all sources, evenly divided between all its clergy, 'would not give to each Clergyman an income equal to that which is enjoyed by the upper domestic of a great nobleman'.* A mean stipend equal to that of a peer's butler was no temptation to effort. Sydney turned therefore to an elaboration of the system of prizes and blanks, the professional lottery that he had discussed before.

It seems a paradoxical statement, but the fact is, that the respectability of the Church as well as of the Bar, is almost entirely preserved by the unequal division of their revenues. A Bar of one hundred lawyers travel the Northern Circuit, enlightening provincial ignorance, curing local partialities, diffusing knowledge, and dispensing justice in their route; it is quite certain that all they gain is not equal to all that they spend; if the profits were equally divided there would not be six and eightpence for each person, and there would be no Bar at all. At present, the success of the leader animates them all—each man hopes to be a Scarlett or a Brougham—and takes out his ticket in a lottery by which the mass must infallibly lose, trusting (as mankind are so apt to do) to his good fortune, and believing that the prize is reserved for him, disappointment and defeat for others. So it is with the Clergy; the whole income of the Church, if equally divided, would be about £250 for each minister. Who would go into the Church and spend £1200 or £1500 upon his education, if such were the highest remuneration he could ever look to? At present, men are tempted into the Church by the prizes of the Church, which enables them to live in decency, supporting themselves, not with the money of the public, but with their own money, which, but for this temptation, would have been carried into some retail trade. The offices of the Church would then fall down to men little less coarse and ignorant than agricultural labourers—the clergyman of the parish would soon be seen in the squire's kitchen; and all this would take place in a country where poverty is infamous.*

Such an argument, Sydney knew, could be regarded as being 'mammonish', but Sydney felt that it was more in touch with the realities of 1837 than a proposal that could only damage the Church by reducing standards of clerical education and encourage the growth of a low, fanatical clergy:

You will have a set of ranting, raving Pastors, who will wage war against all the innocent pleasures of life, vie with each other in extravagance of zeal, and plague your heart out with their nonsense and absurdity; cribbage must be played in caverns, and sixpenny whist take refuge in the howling wilderness. In this way low men doomed to hopeless poverty, and galled by contempt, will endeavour to force themselves into station, and significance.*

The *First Letter* contains much cogent criticism of the technicalities of patronage, and legal argument on the issue that cathedral property could only be confiscated at the expense of oaths solemnly taken to defend it. Again and again Sydney returns to the episcopal bench and the ways in which the Commission's proposals would benefit the bishops. There is a delightful characterization of episcopal presumption and the need to guard against it:

A good and honest Bishop (I thank God there are many who deserve that character!) ought to suspect himself, and carefully to watch his own heart. He is all of a sudden elevated from being a tutor, dining at an early hour with his pupil (and occasionally, it is believed, on cold meat), to be a spiritual Lord; he is dressed in a magnificent dress, decorated with a title, flattered by Chaplains, and surrounded by little people looking up for the things which he has to give away; and this often happens to a man who has had no opportunities of seeing the world, whose parents were in very humble life, and who has given up all his thoughts to the Frogs of Aristophanes and the Targum of Onkelos. How is it possible that such a man should not lose his head?*

As in his Taunton speech on reform where the widow Partington provided an ideal humorous example to give point to his serious arguments, Sydney leavens the Singleton *Letter* with a fictitious extract from a Dutch chronicle of the Synod of Dort, an annal in which (with the addition of a technical footnote for verisimilitude) the bishops feast off the canons' dinner, to be praised by the townspeople for their charity. It was an analogy that received popular recognition from the caricaturists.

Sydney did not direct his attention to the whole bench—some bishops were aged, feeble, or absent from the Commission. It was of course one man who was firmly in his sights:

the Bishop of London is passionately fond of labour, and has certainly no aversion to power, is of quick temper, great ability, thoroughly versant in ecclesiastical law, and always in London. He will become the Commission, and when the Church of England is mentioned, it will only mean *Charles James, of London*, who will enjoy a greater power than has ever been possessed by any Churchman since the days of Laud, and will become the *Church of England here upon earth.**

As one might expect, Sydney was very far from having that 'dropping-down-deadness of manner'* that he maintained the bishops liked best in their clergy. He attacked them, and attacked hard, anticipating several of the arguments that might be used against him. He was at pains to point out that he had no personal or pecuniary interest in the matters he was discussing. He was well aware too, that he would be 'laughed at as a rich and overgrown Churchman'—

be it so. I have been laughed at a hundred times in my life, and care little or nothing about it. If I am well provided for now—I have had my full share of blanks in the lottery as well as the prizes. Till thirty years of age I never received a farthing from the Church, then £50 per annum for two years—then nothing for ten years—then £500 per annum, increased for two or three years to £800, till, in my grand climacteric I was made Canon of St Paul's; and before that period, I had built a Parsonage-house with farm offices for a large farm, which cost me £4000, and had reclaimed another from ruins at the expense of £2000. A Lawyer, or a Physician in good practice, would smile at this picture of great Ecclesiastical wealth; and yet I am considered as a perfect monster of Ecclesiastical prosperity.*

And as for the argument that such protests were indecent, themselves endangering the Church:

We are told, if you agitate these questions among yourselves, you will have the democratic Philistines come down upon you, and sweep you all away together. Be it so; I am quite ready to be swept away when the time comes. Everybody has their favourite death: some delight in apoplexy, and others prefer marasmus. I would infinitely rather be crushed by democrats, than, under the plea of the public good, be mildly and blandly absorbed by Bishops.*

Sydney's first *Letter* met with considerable literary *réclame*, which it still deserves although its detailed arguments perhaps require a burden of explanation too heavy for its passing into general literary recognition. His colleague James Tate urged a friend to buy the pamphlet: 'Twelve pennyworth of sterling stuff you will get for your money: and especially you will be gratified to find that time, which has "thinned his flowing hair", has not chilled the flow of his language, the current of his reasoning, or the tide of his imaginative wit. More passages than one are worthy of Peter Plymley in his brightest days.'* The political success of the Singleton *Letters* was much less. It failed to convince the Whigs, in spite of his declaration of Whig sympathy:

As for my friends the Whigs, I neither wish to offend them nor anybody else. I consider myself to be as good a Whig as any amongst them. I was a Whig before many of them were born—and while some of them were Tories and Waverers. I have always turned out to fight their battles, and when I saw no other Clergyman turn out but myself—and this in time before liberality was well recompensed ...*

One Whig in particular remained unconvinced—Lord John Russell. Sydney wrote to him in February 1837 with the affection of longstanding friendship, and a genuine admiration of his political career:

You say you are not convinced by my pamphlet. I am afraid that I am a very arrogant person. But I do assure you that, in the fondest moments of self-conceit, the idea of convincing a Russell that he was wrong never came across my mind. Euclid (dear John) would have had a bad chance with you if you had happened to form an opinion that the interior angles of a triangle were not equal to two right angles, the more poor Euclid demonstrated, the more you would not have been convinced.
Influenza, indigestion, and loss of patronage to the Bishops.
I shall have great pleasure in dinning with you on Sunday. I thought you had known me better than to imagine I really took such things to heart. I will fight you to the last drop of my ink; dine with you to the last drop of your claret; and entertain for you, *bibendo et scribendo*, sincere affection and respect.*

Russellian infallibility was a theme to which Sydney returned in his *Second Letter*, and a bantering Whiggery was one which he had previously explained, in another letter to Lord John two years previously, before Sydney's views on Church reform had reached the printer:

I must correct a mistake into which you have fallen my dear John respecting me. I am not a lover of abuses, and have no passion for them ... I am a sincere friend to the Reform of the English, and to the circumspection of the Irish, Protestant Church, and I have said so at public meetings and in print three or four times. What you mistake for a love of abuses is first a love of talking nonsense and joking upon all subjects; secondly a much greater apprehension of political changes than you seem to entertain, a conviction that the best understandings often cannot see the consequences of measures; that the game, though it must be played, is one of great difficulty and danger. You must not forget of me that I began attacking abuses between thirty and forty years ago when it was safer almost to be a felon than a reformer, and you must not mistake my afternoon nonsense for my serious and morning opinions.*

Sydney's *Second Letter to Archdeacon Singleton* is like its predecessor much taken up with the abolition of prebends and the management of capitular property, estates which are likely under sound ecclesiastical management to be of greater good to the public than under an unpredictable succession of squires. He returned to his favourite theme of lottery, suggesting that a 'parliament of Curates' would reject the small increase that the Commission proposed, in favour of the chance to draw a great prize in a system which now attracted so wide a social range into the service of the Church:

the great emoluments of the Church are flung open to the lowest ranks of the community. Butchers, bakers, publicans, schoolmasters, are perpetually seeing their children elevated to the mitre. Let a respectable baker drive through the city from the west end of the town, and let him cast an eye on the battlements of Northumberland House, has his little muffin-faced son the smallest chance of getting in among the Percies, enjoying a share of their luxuries and splendour, and of chasing the deer with hound and horn upon the Cheviot Hills? But let him drive his alum-steeped loves a little farther, till he reaches St Paul's Churchyard, and all his thoughts are changed when he sees that beautiful fabric; it is not impossible that his little penny roll may be introduced into that splendid oven. Young Crumpet is sent to school— takes to his books—spends the best years of his life, as all eminent Englishmen do, in making Latin verses—knows that the *crum* in crumpet is long, and the *pet* short—goes to the University—gets a prize for an essay on the Dispersion of the Jews—takes orders—becomes a Bishop's chaplain—has a young nobleman for his pupil—publishes a useless classic, and a serious call to the unconverted—and then goes through the Elysian transitions of Prebendary, Dean, Prelate, and the long train of purple, profit, and power.*

Alliteration usually shows Sydney on top of his form, and in his second letter he is able to deal some sprightly blows at the Bishop of Lincoln, who had ill-advisedly published a pamphlet on the subject. ('His Lordship is certainly not a man full of felicities and facilities, imitating none and inimitable of any; nor does he work with infinite agitation of wit.')* The burden of the Bishop's argument was that the cathedrals would have to give up their property because the bishops' incomes had already been reduced. But had they been reduced enough, Sydney asked (rhetorically, since he was in favour of so tempting a reward in the lottery):

Could not all the Episcopal functions be carried on well and effectually with half of these incomes? Is it necessary that the Archbishop of Canterbury should give feasts to Aristocratic London; and that the domestics of the Prelacy should stand with swords and bag-wigs round pig, and turkey, and venison, to defend, as it were, the Orthodox gastronome from the fierce Unitarian, the fell Baptist, and the famished children of Dissent?*

And, finally, Lord John Russell comes in for some humorous salvoes extending into public print Sydney's private teasing:

There is not a better man in England than Lord John Russell; but his worst failure is, that he is utterly ignorant of all moral fear; there is nothing he would not undertake, I believe he would perform the operation for the stone—build St Peter's—or assume (with or without ten minutes' notice) the command of the Channel Fleet; and no one would discover by his manner that the patient had died—the Church tumbled down—and the Channel Fleet been knocked to atoms.*

Naturally enough, there were suggestions that Sydney had gone too far in writing this of a man well known to be his personal friend, even though a note confirmed that it was not Lord John's absence of feelings but his control of them that was being written about. Lord Carlisle protested at this invasion of private life, and Lady Carlisle, following in a family tradition that had taken Sydney to task for similar outspokenness years before, remonstrated with him. She was assured that Lord John himself had told Sydney that he had found nothing to complain of. 'I fully appreciate that spirit of kindness, and deep feeling of propriety which would induce a person of your quiet and retiring disposition to criticise a scribbling Caliban like me,' Sydney added to his short explanation, 'but I make an honest reply, and leave it with you to weigh what it is worth. I have done with this subject except under gross provocation.'*

The first two *Letters* had stirred up so much pamphlet controversy, so many episcopal Charges had been devoted to the subject, that Sydney was obliged, though weary of the whole business, to write a *Third Letter*, and a further forty pages appeared in 1839. 'In spite of many Bishops' charges, I am unbroken', he declared, and he remained firm in his opinion 'that the mutilation of Deans and Chapters is a rash, foolish, and imprudent measure'.* Much of this final pamphlet consists of a commentary on special issues, some of them raised in a Charge by Bishop Blomfield, that 'holy innovator', who is treated with an egregious courtesy throughout. Much less deferential is his treatment of Bishop Monk of Gloucester, who had written on the subject. Learning of Monk's attack, Sydney had promised Lady Grey a reply that would 'repay him with five per cent compound interest. "Oh Simon, Simon, I have somewhat to say unto thee".'* Repaid Bishop Monk was, and in good measure:

You must have read an attack upon me by the Bishop of Gloucester, in the course of which he says, that I have not been appointed to my situation as Canon of St Paul's for my piety and learning, but because I am a scoffer and a jester. Is not this rather strong for a Bishop, and does it not appear to you, Mr. Archdeacon, as rather too close an imitation of that language which is used in the apostolic occupation of trafficking in fish? Whether I have been appointed for my piety or not must depend upon what this poor man means by piety. He means by that word, of course, a defence of all the tyrannical and oppressive abuses of the Church which have been swept away within the last fifteen or twenty years of my life; the Corporation and Test Acts; the Penal Laws against the Catholics; the Compulsory Marriages of Dissenters, and all those disabling and disqualifying laws which were the disgrace of our Church, and which he has always looked up to as the consummation of human wisdom. If piety consisted in the defence of these—if it was impious to struggle for their abrogation, I have indeed led an ungodly life.*

It had been an odd campaign for Sydney, showing his consistently-held attitudes but reviving many of the literary techniques that he had perfected in his youth but rarely used since. The Archdeacon Singleton letters have the impudent quality of *Peter Plymley* rather than recalling the Reform and Emancipation speeches and writings. His anger had been roused, and an evacuation was called for. 'My attack on the Bishops, or rather I should say my defence of the Prebendaries, appears at Longman's on the 15th,' he had written to Lady Ashburton in January 1837: 'I hope you will not think it too severe, but the truth is I wrote it to save my life. I should have died of bile and rage, but for this remedy.'* Sydney's public campaign had been conducted at the same time as a prolonged private correspondence with Blomfield, in which all the main issues of fragmentation of livings, pluralities, and non-residence are dealt with in detail.

To Blomfield himself Sydney remained courteous but uncompromising in tone. February 1837 saw him writing to his diocesan that 'I hope there was no incivility in my last letter. I certainly did not mean that there should be any; your situation in life perhaps accustoms you to a tone of submission and inferiority from your correspondents, which neither you nor any man living, shall ever experience from me.'* Sydney was not merely, as he put it, 'fighting with the bishops at Ephesus' over the Commission,* but with the cabinet as well. Lord John Russell was treated to a detailed discussion of every point of the debate, but even he must have tired of this unremitting clerical onslaught; there is a reference in Sydney's correspondence to the statesman having 'tabooed' his letters.* But their general correspondence appears to have continued on affectionate terms: 'As for little John, I love him though I chastise him', Sydney had written to Lady Holland in September 1838.*

There were of course suggestions that Sydney had gone too far, that he had turned and attacked his friends. In February 1838 Lady Holland had written that 'Sydney Smith is going to publish another attack upon the Church Commission. To be sure the *mischief is done* by his former publication; but he is shutting the door closer to a Bishopric as the Archbishop would strongly resist any disposition in his favour from the Ministry. But with all his wit and talents, he is woefully deficient in tacte, or as dear Lauderdale calls it, *tack*.'* He could counter such opinions with assertions of ecclesiastical urgency, political consistency, and continuing personal attachment, but it was felt that Sydney's zeal as a reformer had shown its limits; some thought that his extreme attitudes damaged his cause. Although he proved a vigorous assailant with a sharpness necessary to give the right effect to his arguments, he won only minor points, some of which are chronicled in the footnotes of the successive editions that literary reputation called for. Blomfield was ruthless, and most of the plans of the Commissioners were put through, despite Sydney's having drafted and secured the reading of a recapitulatory petition to the House of Lords in July 1840. Discussion dragged on, however, and Blomfield, who had made references to Sydney in a Lords speech on the spiritual desolation of the metropolis, was given a final thrust in a very long letter Sydney sent to *The Times* in September 1840. 'I have found it necessary to give the Bishop of London a valedictory flagellation,' he reported to Lady Carlisle, alluding to the earlier remonstrations he had received from her and her husband:

I know you and my excellent Earl Carlisle disapprove of these things—but you must excuse all the immense differences of temper, training, situation, habits, which make Sydney Smith one sort of person, and the Lord of the Castle another—and both right in their way. If he (the Bishop) had not published his speech, I would not have written a word, but there is too much boasting in it, and too much cant—and then to call me his facetious friend is down-right impertinence.*

Sydney's *Times* letter is a good one, going once again over old ground, but dealing with the imputation of facetiousness in characteristic manner:

You call me in the speech your facetious friend, and I hasten with gratitude in this letter to denominate you my solemn friend; but you and I must not run into commonplace errors; you must not think me necessarily foolish because I am facetious, nor will I consider you necessarily wise because you are grave: but whether foolish or facetious, or what not, I admire and respect you too much not to deplore this passage in your speech; and, in spite of all your horror of being counselled by one of your own canons, I advise you manfully to publish another edition of your speech, and to expunge with the most ample apology this indecent aggression upon the venerable instructors of mankind.*

It was not in Sydney's forgiving and sociable nature to allow even such hard-hitting debate as he had enjoyed with Blomfield to interfere with the routines of civilized life. A little while after the *Times* letter, he wrote to Christopher Hodgson, the Chapter Clerk of St Paul's, asking him to act as an intermediary to restore his intercourse with the Bishop to a more suitable footing:

I don't like writing to the Bishop of London—it is making a fuss, and looks as if I regretted the part I had taken in Church Reform, which I certainly do not. But I should be much annoyed, if the Bishop were to consider me as a perpetual grumbler against him and his measures—

I really am not: I like the Bishop and his conversation—the battle is ended and I have no other quarrel with him and the Archbishop but that they neither of them ever ask me to dinner.

You see a good deal of the Bishop and, as you have always exhorted me to be a good boy, take an opportunity when you are paying some large fine to set him right as to my real disposition towards him and exhort him as he has gained the Victory to forgive a few hard knocks.*

CHAPTER VI

※

IT was entirely appropriate that Sydney should have considered his relationship with Bishop Blomfield as having a social as well as an ecclesiastical side, for the Smith's position in London society was very firmly established by his appointment to St Paul's. Instead of being a regular visitor he became a seasonal resident of the area which he singled out for special merit: 'I believe the parallelogram between Oxford Street, Piccadilly, Regent Street and Hyde Park, encloses more intelligence and human ability, to say nothing of wealth and beauty, than the world has ever collected in such a space before.'* The Smiths began to go out together into society, with a string of routs or receptions, breakfasts or dinners to give or attend throughout the periods of residence at the Cathedral. Sydney remained an assiduous diner-out, and was inclined to lament it when old friends ceased to issue invitations. He complained to Richard York that Beilby Thompson (Lord Wenlock) and his wife 'have lost that highest of all accomplishments, the habit of giving dinners, an art which I am sure (for the benefit of your friends) you will continue to excel in, as long as you live: any falling off in this particular would I am afraid impair our friendship.

> Talk not of those who in the Senate shine
> Give me the man with whom the jovial dine
> And break the ling'ring day with wit and wine.'*

Sydney and his wife gave their share of dinners, but also became well known for their routs, usually on Thursday evenings. They were jolly occasions, as may well be imagined, but Sydney chose to tempt some of his guests by the promise of a much frowzier affair. He wrote to Georgiana Harcourt, the Archbishop of York's daughter, that

188

Our rout generally consists of half a dozen highly respectable old Women, the same number of greasy philosophers, the ladies Harley (the only little bit of nobility we can raise), and Mr Henry (late Colonel) Vernon Harcourt who represents the amorous part of the community. There are also half a dozen young ladies unquestionably the plainest in Europe and indeed I might extend my geographical limits for the purposes of this comparison. All this is out of your line— think of the wilderness of a drawing room where in the whole horizon there is not a duchess or a countess to be seen!!!!!*

Such was Sydney's highly individual recipe for what he chose to call 'that scene of simplicity, truth, and nature—a London rout.'*

In 1835, tired of taking furnished houses, Sydney bought 33 Charles Street, Berkeley Square ('about as big as one of your travelling trunks', he told Lady Carlisle), and four years later he and his wife moved to a larger property at 56 Green Street, off Grosvenor Square, which was to be their London house for the rest of his life. It was there that Sydney, following the current fashion, gave his breakfast-parties. As with the routs, he chose to suggest that he could scarcely invite those who were socially most in demand. He described to the much-sought-after Monckton Milnes the fellow guests he might expect to find at the Green Street breakfast table in 1841: 'all very common persons, I am ashamed to say, who see with their eyes, hear with their ears, and trust to the olfactory nerves to distinguish filth from fragrance'.* Milnes was a *habitué* of Sydney's breakfasts, which were of course quite substantial mid-morning meals and, under their host's management, humorous and intelligent gatherings of the notable. 'Real philosophers' were promised to those invited— 'no assertion admitted without reasoning and strict proof'.* 'I have a breakfast of philosophers tomorrow at ten punctually,' he wrote to Thomas Moore: 'muffins and metaphysics, crumpets and contradiction. Will you come?'*

The whole range of London social entertainments was open to him, and he took full advantage of them while he was fit enough to do so. Only musical entertainments, as before, proved to be beyond him. 'Never hear Mendelshome or Troublesome or whatever may be his name play on the pianoforte, it is intolerable nonsense', he warned Georgiana Harcourt.* It was therefore rather unusual to see him declining an invitation from Lord John Russell because he was already booked by Adelaide Kemble, but the explanation is simple. 'I am engaged to dine with Mrs Sartoris the singing woman,' he replied, 'not that I have any pleasure in the voice of singing men or singing women—but as Adam said when they found him in breeches, "the woman asked me and I did eat".* There were late evening parties so numerous that a large portion of his later correspondence consists of a juggling of social engagements. 'Davenport lectured me last night for not attending your party,' Sydney wrote to Mrs Davenport in June 1835:

My excuse arranges itself under the following heads. First: All evening parties are contracts of imperfect obligation, and are so considered by the practice of the world—'I am at home' the Mistress of the house says, '*if it suits you to come*'. Second Argument: I am an old gentleman and often (though not ill) indisposed, and heartily tired before the hour of evening parties, and must be allowed full liberty on that point by all who honour me with their notice. Third Argument: In the only instance when you have been so kind as to ask me I was fully engaged long before I received your invitation. I think the united force of these arguments (which I consider as Hallam proof) will procure me a verdict of acquittal, and exculpate me from a suspicion of disrespect to you—of little importance, but decisive against my character for good feeling and just discernment if I could be guilty of it.*

It was at the dinner table itself that Sydney Smith excelled, insisting on general conversation clearly spoken. He told his daughter that

Most London dinners evaporate in whispers to one's next-door neighbour. I make it a rule never to speak a word to mine, but fire across the table; though I broke it once when I heard a lady who sat next me, in a low, sweet voice, say, 'No gravy, Sir.' I had never seen her before, but I turned suddenly round and said, 'Madam, I have been looking for a person who disliked gravy all my life; let us swear eternal friendship.' She looked astonished, but took the oath, and what is better kept it. 'You laugh, Miss—; but what more usual foundation for friendship, let me ask, than similarity of tastes?'*

All this metropolitan social life, when Sydney consolidated his position as one of the great lions of his time, much increased the circle of the Smiths' acquaintance. But acquaintance much of it necessarily was, as Mrs Sydney once remarked in her quietly crushing way when reporting an agreeable visit to Combe Florey by a London friend in 1841: 'We have long known Mr Pierrepont as people know each other at a London dinner party which is not at all.'* Life in London did, however, allow Sydney to continue real friendships long established, and to make new ones. Macaulay, known since his visit to Foston from the York Assizes, whom Sydney continued to regard as 'a book in breeches' notable for his 'occasional flashes of silence', remained on the best of terms, both at table—and for teasing. Not long before Macaulay became Secretary for War, Sydney remarked that he 'had resolved to lead a literary life but cannot withstand the temptation—like ladies who resolve upon celibacy if they have no offers'.* And when Macaulay gave up office in 1841, the comment was made to Lady Grey that he was believed 'unaffectedly glad' to have done so: 'Literature is his vocation. Nothing would do him more good than a course of the waters of Lethe; if he could forget half of what he reads he would be less suffocating than he is; he breakfasted with me this morning and three other very clever men much disposed to talk, but it was not Macaulay's disposition that they should say a word—I might as well have had three mutes from a funeral.'* Macaulay's verbal spate is well attested, and is indeed best known from Sydney's many short sallies ('Macaulay is in prime talk and ... upon the whole it is a loud season with him'*), but he was later anxious to acquit himself of any discourtesy. After her father's death he wrote to Saba that 'in one thing ... he was unjust to me. He fancied that I did not listen to him; and I was not so tasteless and senseless as to be inattentive when he talked.'* This may well be so; but it is Sydney's impression of the notorious 'waterspouts of talk'* that remains most vividly in the mind.

Charles Dickens was a new friend from Sydney's later life in London. Sydney had been quite an early admirer, and had urged Paulet Mildmay: 'Read Boz's Sketches if you have not already read them—I think them written with great power and that the soul of Hogarth has migrated into the body of Mr Dickens. I had long heard of them but was deterred by the vulgarity of the name.'* Any remaining doubts were removed by the time *Nicholas Nickleby* was coming out, when Sydney wrote to Sir George Philips that 'Nickleby is very good. I stood out against Mr Dickens as long as I could, but he has conquered me.'* Their curiosity was mutual, as Dickens had written to William Longman in April 1839 that 'I wish you would tell Mr Sydney Smith that of all the men I heard of and never saw, I have the greatest curiosity to see and the greatest interest to know him.'* By that summer they had established their friendship, and just as Sydney had written to Constable from Yorkshire to acknowledge critically each of the Waverley novels as they came out, he was now to send Dickens regular comments on newly published works. 'You have many attributes—but I love your humour most' is a natural enough reaction.* Thus in January 1843, soon after *Martin Chuzzlewit* started, Sydney wrote appreciatively to Dickens of the first number that 'Pecksniff and his daughters, and Pinch, are admirable—quite first-rate painting, such as no one but yourself can execute.'* A few months later, when Chuffey made his appearance, he was described as 'admirable. I never read a finer piece of writing; it is deeply pathetic and affecting. Your last number is excellent. Don't give yourself the trouble to answer my impertinent eulogies, only excuse them.'*

Sydney's attitude was not uniformly eulogistic, however, and when the later numbers of *Chuzzlewit* contained passages on 'Yankeedoodledom' which could be taken as ungrateful to the hosts who had made such a lion of Dickens in America, Sydney remarked to Lady Carlisle that 'I am very sorry for the turn Dickens's novel has taken. It seems as if he had gone over to America on purpose to raise a sum of money by exposing their ridicules. This is a bad trade, and I am heartily sorry such a man as Dickens has condescended to carry it on.'* It was perhaps as well that older friends could keep a critical eye on the development of a young man in danger of having his head turned by success. Thus when Dickens was being fêted in America at the beginning of 1842, Sydney wrote, possibly to Thomas Carlyle: 'pray tell Dickens from me to remember that he is still but a man—and that however elated by his American Deification he must return to the Anthropic State and that he will find us (you and me) good friends but bad Idolaters'.* Such an attitude preserved respect on both sides—devotion indeed, on Dickens's, who was to cherish the memory of Sydney Smith, after whom he named his seventh son.

Richard Monckton Milnes was another younger friend on whose rapid progress in society Sydney kept rather a wary eye. He was in his late twenties when his considerable political abilities, which were to see him made first Lord Houghton, and his even greater social talents, very quickly became apparent to London society. 'I wish you many long and hot dinners with lords and ladies, wits and poets',* Sydney had ended a letter to him in June 1838; Milnes was to have his fill of the hospitality of both groups, and regular invitations to breakfast or dinner with the Smiths were to do not a little to further his meteoric rise in the smartest society. Milnes was much attracted by Sydney, and recorded in his notebooks many *mots* that have become the common coin of authentic Smith quotations. Sydney however was sometimes decidedly sharp with the young man; once when he made someone the impudent proposal that he should be taken uninvited to Gore House to be introduced to Lady Blessington, whom he was anxious to know, Sydney was reported as suggesting that he should be taken in as 'the cool of the evening'.* Remarks like this struck home. Some were published in society papers, and Milnes was enough stung to remonstrate angrily with Sydney—with whom he had by then stayed at Combe Florey— about their authorship. The other offending phrases are known from Sydney's disclaimer: 'The names "the cool of the evening", "London Assurance", "Inigo Jones" are, *I give you my word*, not mine. They are of no sort of importance, they are safety valves, and if you could by paying sixpence get rid of them, you had better keep your money.'*

Monckton Milnes had been both premature and over-demonstrative in his angry letter to Sydney, who replied with a kindly dignity and much worldly wisdom: 'beginning your career in London so oddly, how can you expect not to be laughed at and commented upon—but people are beginning to understand that (though you were in rather too great an hurry about it) you have only put yourself in the place you were entitled to. There is no person who has said more good of you than I have done, or borne witness to your wit, genius, and good nature and talents for society. Ask Lady Holland if this is not so. . . . I can only say if you choose to be sulky with me for what I have nothing on earth to do with, so be it—but I had rather live in good humour with you and everybody else.'* Milnes's reply to this calculatedly moderate answer has (perhaps fortunately) not survived. Only a couple of days later Sydney had to acknowledge a further on-slaught; he did it with what Milnes's biographer James Pope-Hennessy calls 'a masterpiece of urbanity and common sense':*

Never lose your good temper, which is one of your best qualities, and which has carried you safely through your *startling eccentricities*. If you turn cross and touchy, you are a lost man. . . . You do me but justice in acknowledging that I have spoken much good of you. I have laughed at you for those follies which I have told you of to your face; but nobody has more loudly and more constantly asserted that you were a very agreeable, clever man, with a very good heart, unimpeachable in all the relations of life, and that you *amply deserved* to be *retained* in the place to which you have too hastily elevated yourself by manners unknown to our cold and phlegmatic people.

I thank you for what you say of my good-humour. Lord Dudley when I took leave of him, said to me 'You have been laughing at me for the last seven years, and you never said anything that I wished unsaid'—this pleased me.*

There spoke all the experience of one who had in his time been ill at ease at Holland House, who had considered the deportment of a young man in society in his *Sketches of Moral Philosophy*,* and who had been genuinely preparing to pass on the honours of the metropolis to the coming generation. 'Modest Milnes has just left us,' he had reported to Lady Ashburton in August 1840: 'I feel bashful—it is a catching quality. What a pity as in his instance to see the splendour of genius struggling through the fog of diffidence.'* But by September 1843 he could tell Georgiana Harcourt that 'I am retiring from business as a diner-out, but I recommend to your attention as a rising wit, Mr Milnes, whose misfortune I believe it is not to be known to you.'*

London social life had gradually become rather wearing even for one so naturally gregarious. Sydney latterly began to relish more keenly the pleasures of smaller dinners with old friends. In 1840 he wrote to Lady Georgiana Grey debating with her 'whether it is or is not a crime to dine out in Passion Week. In my eyes', was his conclusion, 'it is none to eat and drink temperately with good people—if this is the Northumberland doctrine also I will if you please dine with you on Monday 13th.'* Much earlier than this he was pleading old age and tiredness as an excuse for not attending late evening parties, and there were sometimes occasions when he felt it necessary to make special requests of his dinner hostesses. 'I drink a good deal after dinner—but not Wine,' Lady Canning was told in 1836. 'Might I ask for a decanter of lemonade? I must either ask for this beforehand, or bring it, which seems foolish, or go without it, which seems hard.'* Increasing prudence at table prolonged his social career in 'the parallelogram', but in 1842, three years before his death, he had to write to Charles Babbage that 'We are always desirous of coming to your agreeable parties but we are ancient and ailing people, disglued, unscrewed, and tumbling to pieces and we are often forced to go to bed when we would be lemonading. Such has been the case for the two last Saturdays. I hope you will give us an opportunity of showing our improvements if we can.'*

It was during his years at St Paul's that Sydney's reputation as a conversational wit became generally established. Previously he had mainly been known in the Holland House circle, but now, 'tasting no politics in boiled and roast', he became much more widely appreciated. Whether at a great soirée or an intellectual breakfast, the effect was the same, and society memoirs contain frequent references to his style and effect. Many of his sayings passed into general currency, but often when they have been specifically recorded they require so much explanation of their circumstances as to deaden them. There is, however, from an early period ample testimony to his manner. 'I never heard anything more entertaining than Sydney Smith,' Charles Greville reported after a very agreeable breakfast at Rogers's in 1831, 'such burst of merriment, and so dramatic.'* The style had been commended by Maria Edgeworth's sister Harriet in a letter from London in 1822: 'Sydney Smith is delightful, he is much more of a converser than I had expected. I had thought he had been a teller of stories and a joker but I had not known that he could follow so well whatever subject you choose to converse upon— a style of conversation which delights Maria particularly—his jokes never have the least appearance of preparation and his loud hearty laugh is never at the past, but for the coming, jest.'* Such spontaneity and naturalness of manner were agreeably at odds with the tradition of dining that Frances Lady Shelley reported as prevailing before the days when 'dinners were not, as now, a jumble of pairs like the animals entering the Ark':

Dinners were then arranged with care and thought, so as to secure the most agreeable conversation. This lent an especial charm to those select gatherings.

Tommy Moore, Luttrell, Rogers and Sydney Smith were the regular 'diners out'. They were invited especially to give the *ton*, and to lead the conversation, whose brilliancy had often been prepared with as much care as a fine lady bestows upon her Court dress. The conversation was seldom impromptu—like the talk of my lively and most agreeable husband—yet everyone accepted its charm without scrutinising too closely the manner of its 'get-up'.

During my early life the dazzling brilliancy of table talk shone brightly. Then came a change: people wished to hear their own voices, and dinner-table wit sank away for ever!*

A formal tradition of this kind ensured that the individual styles of the main practitioners were valued—Samuel Rogers's asperities, Henry Luttrell's puns (which Oliver Elton described as 'the toll taken of Laughter by Fashion in that day')* and the sprightliness of Sydney Smith's fancy. And in Sydney's case at least, Lady Shelley's remarks on the getting-up of conversation should not lead us to infer a careful rehearsing of impromptus like a character of Max Beerbohm's; it was enough that the stage should have been set by an atmosphere of keen expectancy, sufficient to stimulate the talker to do his best. It was risky for hostesses to mix any of the principal lions: 'too much quince with the apple tart', as Abraham Hayward once put it to Lady Chatterton when with some trepidation she invited both Sydney and Macaulay to a party that fortunately proved large enough to absorb them both—and Milnes, Hallam, Babbage, Rogers, and others to boot.*

The constantly high standard that was expected of the wit himself often led to disappointments in his hearers. Mrs Brookfield wrote to her husband in 1843 that she had been at a rout in Wilton Crescent where she had listened to Sydney talking to Mrs Sartoris (the 'singing woman'): 'What a hideous, odd-looking man Sydney Smith is! With a mouth like an oyster, and three double chins. I did not hear him say anything strikingly amusing.'* A few years earlier, Henry Crabb Robinson had met Sydney at Miss Rogers's, and remarked in his diary, 'His manner that of a person who knows that a joke is expected. He assumes a look of gaiety but he said nothing worth quoting.'* These observations by disappointed chroniclers should not be taken as indicating failing powers; perhaps more important (as we shall see) may be the fact that a change in society meant that Sydney's style was becoming dated at the end of his life. The knowledge that there was a general expectation that 'something worth quoting' ought to be said, though stimulating in its way, must have placed a considerable strain even on Sydney's virtuosity, for his characteristic style was less one of making the elaborated *mots* cherished by diarists than of a continuous barrage of fanciful banter, playfully elaborating on points picked up from general conversation, in which the actual 'sayings' may often have been more apparent than real.

Charles Greville acutely pointed to the problem in a long obituary passage discussing Sydney in his diary:

It is almost impossible to overrate his wit, humour, and drollery, or their effect in society. Innumerable comical sayings and jokes of his are or have been current, but their repetition gives but an imperfect idea of the flavour and zest of the original. His appearance, voice and manner added immensely to the effect, and the bursting and uproarious merriment with which he poured forth his good things never failed to communicate itself to his audience, who were always in fits of laughter.

If there was a fault in it, it was that it was too amusing. People so entirely expected to be made to die of laughing, and he was so aware of this, that there never seemed to be any question of conversation while he was of the party, or at least no more than just to afford Sydney pegs to hang his jokes on. This is the misfortune of all great professed wits, and I have very little doubt that Sydney often felt oppressed with the weight of his comical obligations, and came on to the stage like a great actor, forced to exert himself, but not always in the vein to play his part. It is well known that he was subject at home to frequent fits of depression, but I believe in his own house in the country he could often be a very agreeable companion, on a lower and less ambitious level, though his talk never could be otherwise than seasoned with his rich vein of humour and wit, for the current, though it did not always flow with the same force, was never dry.*

Greville's analysis, based though it is on hearsay for its domestic information, rings true. He was a skilled observer, and shows some of the difficulties of interpreting the witticisms recorded in contemporary memoirs, both in particular instances and for the general tone of Sydney's wit. And in addition to the social context, the textual, literary evidence for some of Sydney's reported *mots* must be examined closely before they can be certified accurate, or even be definitely ascribed to him. A salutary example is the retort which Greville recorded in 1838: 'Landseer asked Sydney Smith to sit to him for his picture, and he replied "Is thy servant a *Dog* that he should do this thing?".'* The remark has the authentic ring of Sydney, but it appears not to have been originally his. John Gibson Lockhart retrieved it for himself in a letter written over ten years later: 'The *mot* is universally given to Sydney Smith, but Edwin Landseer swears he never did, nor could have asked so ugly a fellow to sit, and thinks it unfair that I should have been robbed of my joke in favour of so weighty a joke-smith. If it was mine, I had quite forgot the fact and adopted the general creed on this weighty point.'* (In 1842, indeed, Lockhart had passed it on to Haydon as Sydney's own, provoking a remark from the painter that 'Lockhart told me a bit of blasphemy of Sydney Smith, which is beyond bearing. He really ought to be dismissed the Church.')* 'Here is a good illustration of the value of evidence', Lockhart commented, objecting only to the allegation of Sydney's ugliness ('I always admired his countenance as the most splendid combination of sense and sensuality').* Perhaps the best explanation of the whole incident is found in Mrs Brookfield's diary in 1859; Landseer told her that Sydney himself had told it to him as a saying of Lockhart's, 'adding playfully, "I think I shall take it".'*

Haydon's sour accusations of blasphemy in the adoption of biblical words (2 Kings 8:13) in the Landseer jest can be matched by other comments which show that some of his religious allusions were distinctly out of fashion by the 1840s. They had long been part of his stock-in-trade. When Rogers asked him how he liked the candles in his dining-room being placed in high wall sconces to show off the pictures, Sydney had replied 'Not at all; above there is a blaze of light, and below nothing but darkness and gnashing of teeth'.* Barham's son remarked primly that 'in the adoption ... of the phraseology commonly employed upon solemn subjects he is, perhaps, almost too dexterous, occasionally trembling on the very verge of propriety'.* This is not the later Victorian reaction that was to rediscover and shudder at Sydney's contemptuous remarks on Methodists and missionaries in the early numbers of the *Edinburgh* (one modern commentator sees the reviews on Baptist missionaries as the 'indelible blot' on Sydney's fame, only to be read with 'indignant fury').* It was an adjustment in conversational proprieties which no longer allowed Sydney to get away with saying he had told Selwyn, as first bishop of New Zealand, to be sure to have a cold clergyman on the sideboard to meet the tastes of his native guests.* In 1843 Mrs Stanley of Alderley reported to Lady Stanley that she had dined at Lady Holland's, where she had found 'Sydney Smith disgusting—he was ever the first to scoff at things of good repute, described how the whole Church was in expectancy ready to make a rush upon China—a Bishop of Hong Kong in the bakehouse.... He was dull upon the whole, being full of an imaginary wit and having none of his own.'* Sydney's more robust Georgian style was unlikely to preserve its appreciative following when different standards were coming to be generally applied.

As well as presenting problems in attribution and taste, some of Sydney's sayings may be in need of textual adjustment. There is a good case for amending even the well-known 'My idea of heaven is eating *pâté de foie* to the sound of trumpets'; it is certain that Sydney used similar words, more doubtful that he used them about himself. Probably the joke was used more than once, just as he preached a good sermon several times. The remark as written displays some textual difficulties; '——s idea of heaven' was Saba's suggestion to the editor of Rogers's *Table Talk* in which it first appeared,* and it seems to have been made not merely to protect the reputation of a clergyman from having made humorous speculations about the hereafter. The remark is surely best applied to Sydney's friend and fellow-wit, one of the best-known gourmets of the period, the very man whom Sydney had described as having a 'soup-and-pattie look'.* When this friend was thought to be dying, Sydney wrote to Lady Davy that he was 'going gently down-hill, trusting that the cookery in another planet may be at least as good as in this; but not without apprehensions that for misconduct here he may be sentenced to a thousand years of tough mutton, or condemned to a little eternity of family dinners'.* It must surely have been *Henry Luttrell's* idea of heaven that was eating those pâtés.

Such explications are inimical to the proper appreciation of Sydney's wit, which is a quick and joyous thing that loses all its vitality when a ponderous *stemma* has to be erected for every joke. Fortunately his letters, which exist in considerable quantities, particularly for the later years of his life, preserve in their lightness of touch something of Sydney's conversational style. One recent critic has remarked that Sydney's openness and lack of any (permanent) sense of frustration means that he never quite reaches the 'ranks of the great letter-writers. It is not from a player on the human scene so confident and so fulfilled that the half-lights and nuances of a great letter-writer are to be expected', Ian Jack has commented.* But letters so fresh and vitally humorous make it possible to appreciate him without the discussions of attribution or descriptions of social setting that might otherwise have been needed to explain his phenomenal success in the salons of London in the 1830s and 1840s.

'All lives out of London are mistakes,' Sydney wrote to Mrs Austin in the winter of 1836, 'more or less grievous, but mistakes.'* But at whatever cost of melancholy and isolation, Sydney always recognized his duty to 'hasten home and feed my starving flock'* and returned to the country at the end of his periods of residence at St Paul's, always hoping for a series of visitors to give him relief from the boredom which increasingly came to oppress him. 'The summer and the country dear Georgiana have no charms for me,' he told Miss Harcourt, 'I look forward anxiously to the return of bad weather, coal fires, and good society in a crowded city. I am afraid you are not exempt from the delusions of flowers, green turf and birds. They all afford slight gratification not worth one hour of rational conversation; and rational conversation in sufficient quantities is only to be had from the congregation of a million people in one spot.'* And yet he could sometimes derive quiet enjoyment from his home in the country, even though there were no children at home and fewer visitors to divert him. Those who went and recorded their impressions leave an attractive picture of the Somerset rectory. His American friend Edward Everett, visiting the Smiths early in 1844, reported that

The house at Combe Florey is a plain two storey cottage; and would be thought an unpretending residence in any country town in the neighbourhood of Boston—within however it is excessively comfortable. This is not so difficult a thing to obtain in the south of England as in Massachusetts. I could hardly fancy it winter. A very respectable Magnolia Grandiflora was trained against the chimney—the garden walls were covered with roses in full bloom...

We passed Friday and Saturday in driving round the neighborhood and visiting the neighbors, some of whom dined with us each day. It is Mr Smith's practice to invite all the neighboring gentry once a year to dine; while to the poorer classes he makes himself a great benefactor, by keeping in his house a well furnished apothecary's shop from which he dispenses medicine gratuitously ... in grave cases he writes up to Esculapius Holland for counsel; so he calls his son-in-law. I ought before now to have spoken of Mrs Smith, as a most amiable and intelligent lady, highly cultivated by reading, and a long life spent in the society of the most distinguished persons of both sexes in Great Britain and of the foreigners who throng London....

On Sunday we all went to the village church; Mr Smith preached on the parable of the publican and the pharisee, a sound, practical, useful sermon:— in the afternoon he read the Evening Service and after church was over catechised the children—a queer squad to be sure, speaking a dialect hardly intelligible.*

So the old tradition of practical parochial activity was continued from Yorkshire days, particularly in basic medication of the parishioners. Saba tells the story of her father stomach-pumping a manservant who had eaten rat poison by accident, and Mrs Marcet that of Sydney leaving his breakfast table to baptise a new-born child thought to be dying. 'Why,' he said on returning, 'I first gave it a dose of castor-oil, and then I christened it; so now the poor child is ready for either world.'*

Lady Holland's *Memoir* also shows how the tradition of domestic brightness, so notable at Foston, also prevailed in Somerset. The oblong library and breakfast room was 'surrounded on three sides with books, and ended in a bay-window opening into the garden: not brown, dark, dull-looking volumes, but all in the brightest bindings; for he carried his system of furnishing for gaiety even to the dress of his books'. When his servant was told to 'glorify the room', 'this meant that the three Venetian windows of the bay were to be flung open, displaying the garden on every side, and letting in a blaze of sunshine and flowers'.*

Yet even with so fortunate a situation, Sydney became more and more depressed by life in the country, which he wrote of as 'a sort of healthy grave'.* Running a country parish in his earlier, Yorkshire, way required more physical energy than he could muster, and in his mid-sixties Sydney felt his age. 'Mrs Sydney and I have been leading a Derby and Joan life for these two months, without children,' he wrote to Lady Grey in February 1836. 'This kind of life might have done very well for Adam and Eve in Paradise, where the weather was fine, and the beasts as numerous as in the Zoological Gardens, and the plants equal to anything in the Gardens about London; but I like a greater variety.'* When Sir George Philips tried to cheer him, he refused to be jollied: 'You say I have many comic ideas rising in my mind; this may be true; but the champagne bottle is no better for holding the champagne.' He referred uncharacteristically to Carlin, the eighteenth-century Parisian harlequin who was liable to fits of depression, adding not very reassuringly that 'I don't mean to say I am prone to melancholy; but I acknowledge my weakness enough to confess that I want the aid of society, and dislike a solitary life'.*

Unlike York, the country around Taunton provided few rural sociabilities for him, and although Bowood and Saltram were within visiting distance he lacked a house like Castle Howard with its family in the immediate neighbourhood. By 1840 visiting was becoming difficult. He had to apologize to Mrs Paulet Mildmay for being ill with lumbago at her house (though since returning calomel and a very hot bath had made him 'as upright as the conduct of Aristides'): 'the melancholy fact is,' he added, 'I am getting too old to pay visits, and it will soon become my duty to keep my miseries and infirmities to myself'.* It was to her husband that he had reported on a meeting of the British Association in Bristol four years earlier:

I thought you had been paying a visit to the wise men of Bristol. Their occupations appear to be of the greatest importance. On Monday they dissected a frog; on Tuesday they galvanized a goose; on Wednesday they dissected a little pig, and showed that wonderful arrangement of the muscles of the throat by which that animal is enabled to squeak of grunt at pleasure. On Thursday they tried to go up in a balloon: but the balloon would not stir. The causes of the failure were, however, pointed out in a most satisfactory manner. On Friday a new and philosophical mode of making butter was brought forward, and several pats of butter exhibited. On Saturday they all set off on the outside of coaches, believing they had conferred the utmost benefits on the human race. You and I and Mrs Mildmay know better.*

Increasing wealth made it possible for Sydney to contemplate foreign travel once again. In October 1835, Sydney (believing that 'I think every wife has a right to insist upon seeing Paris')* went to France with his wife and Emily and Nathaniel Hibbert. In retrospect he reported to Sir Robert Wilmot Horton that 'we saw all the cockney sights, and dined at all the usual restaurants, and vomited as usual into the channel which divides Albion from Gallia. Rivers are said to run blood after an engagement: the Channel is discoloured, I am sure, in a less elegant and less pernicious way by English tourists going and coming.'* The passage was disagreeable, to be sure ('I rolled on the deck not wholly unlike a porpoise and quite as wet'),* but the standards of Dessein's hotel at Calais were a revelation. 'To compare it with any hotel in England is a violation of common sense in breakfasting and dining. Such butter was never spread in England, no English hen could lay such eggs, no English servant could brew such coffee. The waiter and the chambermaid were as well bred as Lord and Lady Carlisle, and the Boots in manner was not inferior to Edward Ellice.'* Their French sightseeing was conventional enough—they were particularly pleased with Rouen and they saw much of Paris, including the Opera: 'I Puritani was dreadfully tiresome, and unintelligible in its plan. I hope it is the last opera I shall ever go to.'* Though introductions could doubtless have been procured, they went little into society. 'I have seen Madame de Lieven once or twice,' Sydney reported to Lady Grey, 'but I never attempt to speak to her or to go within six yards of her. I am aware of her abilities and the charms of her conversation and manner to those whom it is worth her while to cultivate: but to us others she is as it were the Goddess Juno, or some near relation to Jove.'* Gastronomically the trip was a great success. 'How shall I be able to live upon the raw limbs of meat to which I am destined?' he asked Richard York after he returned; 'Where shall I find those delicious stews, that thoroughly subjugated meat which opposes no resistance to the teeth and still preverves all its gravies for the palate? It fills me with despair and remorse to think how badly I have been fed—and how my time has been misspent and waisted [*sic*] on bread sauce and melted butter.' Soups were poor, bread too crusty, but as for the salads: 'their delightful oil and their pleasant vinegar—almost wine, like a lady who has just lost her character'*. The French visit enlarged his experience of the table and his capacity for culinary epigrams, for he remarked to Lady Holland the next year after reading Beauvilliers' *L'Art de cuisinier*, 'I find as I suggested that garlic is power; not in its despotic shape, but exercised with the greatest discretion.'*

A short trip to the Low Countries in May 1837—Sydney's last foreign journey—was rather less successful. He found that 'Holland and the Netherlands are not fit countries for the habitation of man. They are usurped from the kingdom of frogs, and are the proper domicile of aquatic reptiles.'* Mrs Sydney was an assiduous tourist, reading guidebooks and histories, but her husband felt that 'the aujourdhui of life is enough for me'.* 'I have seen between 7 and 800 large women without clothes painted by Rubens—till I positively refuse Mrs Smith to see any more',* he wrote to Lady Carlisle from Rotterdam, on a trip which was to include much hospitality in Belgium from their friend the diplomatist Sylvain Van der Weyer and a royal dinner at Laeken. Alluding to one of his best-known *mots* he reported to Caroline Fox that 'I dined with the King at Brussels, eating pâte de foie gras while the trumpets were sounding'.* They finished their journey on the Rhine, preferring the scenery near Coblenz to the flatness of Holland: 'The Rhine is like an army tailor,' he wrote, 'it gains immensely by contracting.'*

Foreign travel was, however, a rare interruption of the routines of residence in London and Somerset, and increasingly he needed frequent diversion at Combe Florey. It took the company of visitors, whether family or friends, to reconcile him to Somerset, and 'a good run of the road', which he had so relished in Yorkshire, cheered him immensely, although he now troubled himself less about enticing them. 'If any body thinks it worth while to turn aside to the valley of flowers I am most happy to see them, but I have ceased to lay plots and to toil for my visitors', he explained to Lady Holland in 1836: 'I save myself by this much disappointment.'* This made for a quiet enjoyment in which visitors felt happy and welcome. A whole string of learned ladies visited the rectory in 1838—the Berry sisters and their friend Lady Charlotte Lindsay among them. 'When they talk altogether it is just like the clamour of sea birds', he told Paulet Mildmay, fearing they would be impregnated by a male penguin when they went to the coast.* Mrs Grote and Mrs Marcet were also there that summer, when Sydney warned Lady Grey that she must 'overlook a little pedantry and a tinge of the stocking blue when I see you again'.* But by December the winter low spirits had descended again. 'I have been dining out two or three times in the country—a state of some suffering, but it reminds you of the value of your own Society, and prevents a great deal of anger and heart-burning which the seclusion of any individual produces among his neighbours.' 'You,' he wrote to Mrs Austin, 'who are revelling in the luxuries of Mayfair, may spare a moment of commiseration for diners-out in West Somersetshire.'*

Lady Holland, in widowhood, once threatened a visit but gave it up, reprieving the local poultry,* and newer friends like Monckton Milnes were given good warning of what Sydney himself took to be a not very exhilarating prospect. 'It is but fair to add that nothing can be more melancholy than Combe Florey,' Sydney had warned him in 1840, 'that we have no other neighbours than the parsonism of the country, and that in the country I hibernate and live by licking my paws. Having stated these distressing truths and assuring you that (as you like to lay out your life to the best advantage) it is not worth your while to come, I have only to add that we shall be very glad to see you.'* Milnes, needless to say, was happy to accept. To the end of Sydney's life the contrast continued between the resignation of 'I ennuie myself in the country'* and the high spirits generated by a handful of lively visitors. 'You and I are both inn-keepers,' he wrote in 1843 to Georgiana Harcourt at Bishopthorpe, echoing his old sentiments about Foston, 'and are occupied from one end of the week to the other in looking after company. I think we ought to have soldiers billetted upon us. My sign is "The Rector's Head", yours "The Mitre". My Devonshire curate and his wife are just come, and are drinking in the tap.'*

The extension of the railroad, which gradually approached Taunton in the closing years of Sydney's life, was eagerly welcomed as an asset to country living by one who had long suffered from 'the endless succession of inns, waiters and veal cutlets in the old method'.* By 1841 the journey took him only nine hours door to door;* soon the rail was within five miles and Bath was reachable in two hours, London in six; every accident seemed to lead to an improvement in standards, Sydney told Lord Murray, and all that was then needed was 'an overturn which would kill a bishop, or, at least, a dean'.* The shortened travelling times were particularly welcome to Mrs Sydney as her health deteriorated.

The new mode of travel allowed Sydney to keep in good fettle his controversial powers, which might well by the age of seventy have been thought exhausted by the prolonged efforts of the Singleton period. In 1842 Sydney was moved by news of a railway accident in Paris to write to the *Morning Chronicle* attacking the directors of the Great Western Railway as officious monopolists for insisting, unlike other British companies, on locking their passengers into the carriages of moving trains. Their ostensible reason was to prevent drunkards or suicides from climbing out, but Sydney suspected economy and mere cussedness. The three main letters of the series (included in his *Collected Works*) are rather heavy in manner, drawing too much on Sydney's usual alliteration and humorous sesquipedality; but equally characteristically they develop the argument from humorously selected details ('the early Scotchman scratches himself in the morning mists of the North, and has his porridge in Piccadilly before the setting sun') into general points concerning the administration of a virtual monopoly ('The first person of rank who is killed will put everything in order, and produce a code of the most careful rules').* The Great Western gave in—perhaps wisely, considering Sydney was meditating another letter in which he would have described the board of directors gazing with satisfaction on a burnt train-load of captive passengers, including 'a stewed Duke ... Two Bishops done in their own Gravy ... Two Scotchmen dead but raw, sulphuric acid perceptible'.* Sir Robert Peel, who had been incautious enough 'to attribute all my interference with the arbitrary proceedings of rail roads to personal fear', was given a good-humoured reply in the *Chronicle*: 'I thought only of you, and for you, as many Whig gentlemen will bear me testimony who rebuked me for my anxiety.'* Sydney's rejoinder was all the more effective for being genuinely respectful of its addressee. Sydney's three fairly short letters to the newspapers show that his vigour was as unchanged as his manner, and they produced the desired result very effectively.

After the Reform agitation, Sydney's political activities had been very much circumscribed. For a little while he continued to send detailed advice through Lady Grey, for example urging the necessity of making governmental provision for the Roman Catholic clergy of Ireland out of the revenues of the Protestant Church there: 'It will divide the Cabinet, and agitate the country, but you must face the danger, and conquer or be conquered by it. It cannot be delayed, there is no alternative between this and a bloody war and reconquest of Ireland.'* Such suggestions gradually became fewer, and by December 1832 Sydney was devoting himself to more appropriate activities. At the time of the elections then, he wrote to Mrs Meynell that 'I am delighted to find the elections have gone so well. The blackguards and democrats have been defeated almost universally, and I hope Meynell is less alarmed, though I am afraid he will never forgive me Mrs Partington; in return I have taken no part in the county election, and am behaving quite like a dignitary of the Church; that is, I am confining myself to digestion.'*

He remained an interested observer, however, and political events are frequently referred to in his correspondence. Sir Robert Wilmot Horton received an interesting commentary in letters sent to him during his governorship of Ceylon. In January 1835 Sydney wrote:

Never was astonishment equal to that produced by the dismissal of the Whigs. I thought it better at first to ascertain whether the common laws of nature were suspended—and to put this to the test I sowed a little mustard and cress seed and waited in breathless anxiety the event. It came up. I looked through the window and saw the male sparrow rendering the same devoted attention to his female—and by little and little I perceived that as far as the outward world was concerned, the dismissal of Lord Melbourne had not produced much effect. Brougham threatened to destroy the solar system—but it was soon found when the seal was taken away he was Nobody and those creations are turning round each other as before

Brougham is by this time quite forgotten, he has run away to Italy—to give them a specimen of the beautiful ...*

The former Lord Chancellor, it seemed by August, was 'laid on the shelf for ever—it seems to me about as difficult to keep Brougham on the shelf as it would be to keep a pound of quicksilver on the shelf however there he is—and there he seems likely to remain'.* Early in the following year, Sydney gave Horton an impression of his general mood of mistrust and mild disillusionment:

I agree with the Whigs in all they are doing and have only that mistrust which belongs to the subject of politics—and is inseparable from it. I see no probability of the Tories returning for any time to power—public opinion is increasing in favour of the Whigs who are in my opinion acting wisely though boldly, nor do I see any great mistake they have committed.*

Local politics also provided some amusement. When the Somerset member retired after seventeen years in the Commons, Sydney wrote to Paulet Mildmay that 'It is proposed to present Charles Kemyss Tynte with a piece of plate *for his eminent services in Parliament.* I cannot hear what piece of plate it is but I believe it is a silver toothpick. The inscription is to be omitted for want of latitude, and longitude in the metallic memorial.'*

Sydney's final political intervention was the pamphlet on *Ballot* that he published early in 1839. It had been written the previous autumn, when Sydney reported to Philips that 'I have done it to employ my leisure. No politics in it, but a *bona fide* discussion. I am an anti-ballotist. It will be carried however, write I never so wisely.'* I have taken the Conservative or falling side which may probably under the consulship of Roebuck cost me my head,' he wrote to Richard York after it came out.* It was not, however, entirely surprising that he should have taken the side he did, as the issue of secret voting by ballot formed one of a group of proposals—shorter parliaments and wider suffrage were also among them—which made up a programme that Radicals such as Grote and Roebuck were pressing as an immediate and (in the eyes of the Whigs) premature development from the Reform Act.

Sydney's tract is cogently argued, without too whimsical a humour, and is full of the rhetorical questions that give it more of the tone of political oratory than his other publications. There are humorous touches, to be sure: a footnote on Grote shrewdly described him as 'a very worthy, honest, and able man; and if the world were a chess-board, would be an important politician', and a favourite but too easy theme is returned to when Sydney places records intimidation by mob violence as against presumed intimidation by aristocratic influence:

Did not the mob of Bristol occasion more ruin, wretchedness, death, and alarm than all the ejection of tenants, and combinations against shopkeepers, from the beginning of the century? and did not the Scotch philosophers tear off the clothes of the Tories in Mintoshire? or at least such clothes as the customs of the country admit of being worn?—and did not they, without any reflection at all upon the customs of the country, wash the Tory voters in the river?*

Such comical touches apart, Sydney is in *Ballot* engaged in one of his favourite occupations, the pursuit of Fallacy. In addition to showing the exaggeration of charges of bribery, corruption, and undue agricultural and commercial influence, he attempts to show that such evils would not necessarily be diminished by secret voting; concealment would be *dis*advantageous in reducing the guidance local worthies give to the unsure in compelling those who glory in their cause to act furtively, and in admitting the probability of much local duplicity and deception. And as for universal suffrage:

there is no act or folly or madness which it may not in the beginning produce. There would be the greatest risk that the monarchy, as at present constituted, the funded debt, the established church, titles, and hereditary peerage, would give way before it. Many really honest men may wish for these changes; I know, or at least believe, that wheat and barley would grow if there was no Archbishop of Canterbury, and domestic fowls would breed if our Viscount Melbourne was again called Mr Lamb; but they have stronger nerves than I who would venture to bring these changes about. . . . The people seem to be hurrying on through all the well known steps to anarchy; they must be stopped at some pass or another: the first is the best and the most easily defended. . . . Most earnestly and conscientiously wishing their good, I say, NO BALLOT.*

The pamphlet was popular and successful, and met with approbation in quarters where Sydney hoped it might find favour. He was able to write to the Earl of Durham in March 1839 that 'Lady Grey writes me word that my pamphlet on the ballot made Lord Grey laugh heartily, which is to me the pleasantest thing I have heard about it. When I come out with my universal suffrage, I hope to put him in convulsions.'*

Ballot was produced just in time to find its way into the third volume of Sydney's *Works*, published in 1839 with a fourth following in 1840 to complete the canon of his principal writings and set the seal on his literary reputation. A few short additions were to be made later (notably on American subjects) but the substantial record of work could now be fully displayed. In the *Works* he even included *Peter Plymley's Letters*, whose authorship he had so frequently denied in the past, and the collection was given a retrospective preface recounting the early history of the *Edinburgh Review* and the growth of its influence, and ending with a few kicks at the bishops and the Ecclesiastical Commission. Presenting a copy to Mrs Crowe in January 1840, Sydney remarked that 'I printed my reviews to show, if I could, that I had not passed my life merely in making jokes; but that I had made use of what little powers of pleasantry I might be endowed with, to discountenance bad, and to encourage liberal and wise, principles. The publication has been successful. The Liberal journals praise me to the skies; the Tories are silent, grateful for my attack upon the ballot.'* He was much gratified by the reception ('I honestly confess that the praise and approbation of wise men is to me a very great pleasure'), but even this honest pleasure was exceeded when in 1843 Jeffrey gathered his own *Review* articles in four volumes and dedicated them in flattering terms to his old friend Sydney Smith, 'the original projector of the *Edinburgh Review*, long its brightest ornament and always my true and indulgent friend'.

Sydney had a large number of American friends, and delighted in the company of natives of a country which he had frequently praised, in correspondence and in the *Review*, for its practical demonstration of unpompous egalitarianism, religious amity, common sense, and progressiveness; everything there except the continuing tolerance of slavery greatly appealed to him, and he showed his respect in his friendships. In 1838 he had written to the young Charles Sumner that 'I have a great admiration of America, and have met with a great number of agreeable, enlightened Americans. There is something in the honesty, simplicity and manliness of your countrymen which pleases me very much.'* Edward Everett, when American ambassador in London, reported that 'Though it was not till Lord Grey came into power and made him a canon of St Pauls (£2000) that his income was ample, I suppose as many Americans have been entertained at his house as at any in London.'* A variety of public men, such as George Ticknor, Samuel Gridley Howe, and Daniel Webster (whom Sydney described as 'much like a steam-engine in trousers')* left appreciative accounts of Sydney's hospitality and wit. Ticknor recorded some of his host's opinions as well as his witticisms, and it is to him that we owe Sydney's views of the aristocracy or one of his accounts of the foundation of the *Edinburgh Review*. Everett, during his ambassadorship, endured press accusations of neglect of duty by having stayed a month with Sydney at Combe Florey; it was in fact only two days, but it is clear from his detailed letters about it that he would willingly have stayed longer.

At the time of Everett's visit, Sydney was not in good odour with parts of the American press. Although remaining an ardent 'philoyankeeist',* his *Edinburgh Review* work had previously given him some experience of the chauvinism of American journalists. His second article on America in the *Review*, published in 1820, had contained his well-known remarks on the cultural immaturity and literary pretension of the new nation—'in the four quarters of the globe, who reads an American book? or goes to an American play? or looks at an American picture or statue?' The reaction to his remarks was so strong that Sydney had to refer to American sensitivity in an 1824 *Edinburgh* article: 'We really thought at one time they would have fitted out an armament against the Edinburgh and Quarterly Reviews, and burnt down Mr Murray's and Mr Constable's shops, as we did the American Capitol.'* Sydney, this time under his own name rather than the *Review*'s, was to come in for a second round of attacks. In the early 1840s some American states had financed extensive programmes of public works by issuing bonds, but Pennsylvania was one of those which defaulted from repayment in a period of general economic recession. Sydney had a small holding of Pennsylvania bonds (about £1,000 worth, according to Everett) but he had managed to dispose of them at 60 per cent.* He was not by no means the only British sufferer; Wordsworth also lost by the repudiation and wrote his bitter sonnet 'To the Pennsylvanians' on the subject.

It was the principle, rather than the actual loss which he could by then easily accommodate, which enraged him, and he began a final pamphleteering campaign, writing with brevity but continuing forcefulness. At first he prepared a 'Humble Petition to Congress', which was also printed in the London *Morning Chronicle* in May 1843 and received widespread publicity in the United States. It was a formal document which with appropriate dignity drew attention to the wrong, and confessed a personal disillusionment and regret at 'that immense power which the bad faith of America has given to aristocratical opinions, and to the enemies of free institutions, in the old world'.* Aimed at public opinion rather than legislative remedy, it certainly had the desired effect, being widely reprinted; most newspapers gave no commentary, although one in Boston attacked Sydney's manner as 'impudence, bombast and impertinence', a New York one his clerical probity as a speculator: Ticknor answered them both resoundingly.* There were other attacks which had by November provoked Sydney into writing a *Morning Chronicle* letter in his old style, in a cause generally agreed to be just, and put forward with trenchant wit. Payment was still being withheld: 'In every grammar-school of the old world *ad Græcas Calendas* is translated—the American dividends.' He provided a brief analysis of the state accounts, showing that a small taxation would raise the necessary funds to service the debt. Perhaps retaliation was called for:

I never meet a Pennsylvanian at a London dinner without feeling a disposition to seize and divide him; to allot his beaver to one sufferer and his coat to another; to appropriate his pocket-handkerchief to the orphan, and to comfort the widow with his silver watch, Broadway rings, and the London Guide, which he always carries in his pockets. How such a man can set himself down at an English table without feeling that he owes two or three pounds to every man in company I am at a loss to conceive: he has no more right to eat with honest men than a leper has to eat with clean men. If he have a particle of honour in his composition he should shut himself up and say, 'I cannot mingle with you, I belong to a degraded people—I must hide myself— I am a plunderer from Pennsylvania'.*

The Bostonian Ticknor felt personally insulted by this onslaught, complaining to a correspondent that 'Sydney was foolish to treat us all as pickpockets', and that he had damaged his cause by too strident a tone.*

Sydney, however, was gleeful, telling Lady Grey that his letter 'is generally found fault with as being too favourable, and to this I plead guilty, but I find I get more mild as I get older and more unwilling to be severe; but if they do not (as men of business phrase it) book up by Christmas, I shall set at them in good earnest'.* In fact his second letter (also in the *Morning Chronicle*) came out on 22 November, defending himself against the charge of having 'a morbid hatred of America', and unexpectedly moderate in tone with more of elegance than abusiveness ('It may be very true that rich and educated men in Pennsylvania wish to pay the debt, and that the real objectors are the Dutch and German agriculturists, who cannot be made to understand the effect of character upon clover'). He drew his contribution to a close with:

And now, having eased my soul of its indignation, and sold my stock at 40 per cent discount, I sulkily retire from the subject, with a fixed intention of lending no more money to free and enlightened republics, but of employing my money henceforth in buying up Abyssinian bonds, and purchasing into the Turkish Fours, or the Tunis three-and-a-half per cent funds.*

'My bomb has fallen very successfully in America, and the list of killed and wounded is extensive,' he told Mrs Grote in mid-December: 'I have several quires of paper sent me every day, calling me monster, thief, atheist, deist, etc.' 'All the papers combine in abusing me', another friend was told,* but there were groceries as well as grousing, and admirers sent him gifts of American cheese and apples. He only achieved the highest point of notoriety eponymously. In August 1844 he wrote to Miss Berry that

I must tell you of the honour paid to me at New York. There arrived there at the beginning of the month a Sydney Smith, whose name was in due form announced in the papers; forthwith a meeting and a debate whether or not he should be tarred and feathered, carried in the negative; proposed and carried, by an immense majority, that he should be invited to a public dinner: in short, an uproar *à la mode de Dickens*! The arriver turned out to be a young man, a cooper. My correspondent at New York encloses me an invitation to myself to pay him a visit, and to accompany him in a tour to Niagara. So, though you think so little of me in May Fair, I am a great personage in the other quarter of the world.*

And to Captain Morgan, who had sent him the tribute of apples, he reaffirmed his attachment to America in his letter of acknowledgement: 'I am much obliged to you by your present of Apples, which I consider as apples of concord not discord. I have no longer any pecuniary interest that your countrymen should pay their debts, but as a sincere friend to America I earnestly hope they may do so.'*

Early in February 1843 Sydney's brother Courtney had died of an apoplexy, with fortunate results, as the beneficiary explained to Lady Grey: 'For the last eighteen years he has avoided his family and has lived almost entirely estranged from them. I cannot pretend to feel grief for his loss. He had left behind him two testamentary papers unsigned and unwitnessed and I believe quite invalid. If they are set aside as I believe they will, and I have little doubt of it, I shall benefit to the amount of about

£30,000 or more, which will come just in time to gild the nails of my coffin.'* Courtney, who had shared his father's unpleasant characteristics to such a degree that he escaped much of the cantankerousness and abuse Robert Smith thrust at his other offspring, had been an Indian administrator, skilled in languages and business, but arrogant to his superiors and sometimes reprimanded by them for his 'sauciness'.* In 1817 the Marquess of Hastings had been forced to request, on reinstating Courtney after a scrape, that he should observe towards the Superior Court 'that politeness of tone which is really indispensible in the conduct of public affairs'.* Such ingrained habits of opposition were not crushed by reprimand, and in 1827 Sydney wrote to Lady Holland: 'You see my younger brother Courtney is turned out of office in India, for refusing the surety of the E. Indian Company. Truly the Smiths are a stiff-necked generation and yet they have all got rich but me. Courtney they say has £150,000—and keeps only a cat. The last letter I had from him which was in 1782 he confessed that his money was gathering very fast.'*

Three kinsmen were eligible to benefit from the intestate property—Bobus, the younger Cecil, and Sydney himself. Whether Courtney would have approved of the last sharing in his estate is doubtful, as one of the invalidated documents apparently contained some 'inculpative remarks' on his brother.* Cecil at first suppressed them from his uncle, provoking the rebuke that 'I am sure your motives were very amiable but the better way would have been to have told me at once of the testamentary abuse of the amiable defunct'.* Attorneys were appointed, the matter came before Doctors Commons, and by 15 March 1843 Sydney could report to Cecil, after voluminous preparatory correspondence, that 'we won in a canter'.* Courtney was found to have been keeping more than a cat; for years he had been warmly attached to Miss Henrietta Lee of the Covent Garden Theatre, who had been named in both his unsatisfactory documents. Sydney proposed an *ex gratia* payment to her by the family representatives, brushing aside the objections of his clergyman nephew with a robust 'It is too late to lift up the petticoats of Miss Lee ... but we have nothing to do with her virtue—he has made two wills in her favour and there will be a cry if something is not done for her.'* By the end of March all was settled amicably; Sydney could now reckon himself a very rich man, and told Lady Grey that 'I am gradually stepping into my fortune and find it not unpleasant.'*

In time to gild the nails of his coffin this unexpected fraternal legacy had been, and the funereal hint in Sydney's announcement was not inappropriate from one whose later letters show him moving quietly into an acceptance of old age and death. Lord Holland's death in 1840 was a severe blow to him, for in spite of their exchanges over Sydney's aspirations to a bishopric in 1834, their affection had been strong throughout. Sydney could console himself a little with continued joking about Holland's demanding widow, but he had a genuine sympathy for her in her desolation. Lord Grey's health gave Sydney cause for concern in 1843, and there was Lord Carlisle to worry about too. As for himself, when he had turned sixty, the illnesses of old age began gradually to take their toll of an ample frame and generally robust consitution. For many years gout was to be his principal afflic- tion, and he frequently found himself 'hardly ... able to walk across the room, nor to put on a Christian shoe'.* Regular dosages of colchicum kept the gout in check, though somewhat uncertainly: 'I had last week an attack of gout,' he wrote to Lady Morgan (Sydney Owenson) in 1842, 'which is receding from me (as a bailiff from the house of an half-pay captain) dissatisfied, and terrified by the powers of colchicum.'* Eating little and drink- ing only water also helped to stave off attacks, and he frequently meditated on the moral qualities of sound diet: 'I am convinced digestion is the great secret of life; and that character, talents, virtues and qualities are powerfully affected by beef, mutton, pie- crust, and rich soups. I have often thought I could feed or starve men into many virtues and vices, and affect them more power- fully with my instruments of cookery than Timotheus could do formerly with his lyre.'*

Stoutness was the other concomitant of rich diet, and Sydney (never thin) became fat and gross. He came to feel his weight as he also felt his age, and in 1840 wrote from London to Richard York that 'I dine out eight or nine times every week. If people will talk across the table it is agreeable but I hate whispering to the lady next to me—when I have asked her whether she has lately been to the opera, I am knocked up entirely and don't know what else to say—and I know she hates me for being a large fat parson and for not [being] slim and elegant. One of the greatest evils of old age is the advance of the stomach over the rest of the body. It looks like the accumulation of thousands of dinners and luncheons. It looks like a pregnant woman in a cloth waistcoat and as if I were near my time and might reasonably look for twins.'

Undeterred by the dietetic threat, he concluded by remarking: 'I am very glad, my dear York, that toasted cheese is brought in now after dinner—I have done with fashions and look for realities.'*

Sydney, himself now past seventy, began to see his declining years as leading to a release from aches and pains, and liked to look forward to a sort of celestial rout. 'We shall all meet again in another planet,' he told Lady Holland, 'cured of all our defects. Rogers will be less irritable; Macaulay more silent; Hallam will assent; Jeffrey will speak slower; Bobus will be just as he is; I shall be more respectful to the upper clergy.'*

In a little over a year, however, Bobus Smith's health was failing and his increasing blindness was alarming Sydney, although he could in December 1843 report that his brother 'bears up against the evils of age heroically'.* Such decay was ominous. Even though the brothers were considered closer by society, which relished Bobus's conversational wit almost as much as Sydney's, than they were intimate in personal life, natural affinity gave Sydney cause for worry. Even closer to him, Mrs Sydney's health, which had for several years needed careful watching and occasional seaside visits, was also getting worse. Fortunately a fine and happy summer at Combe Florey assisted her recovery. 'I set off in despair of reaching home,' Sydney wrote to Georgiana Harcourt, 'but, on the contrary, Mrs Sydney got better every scream of the railroad, and is now considerably improved.'* Even Sydney was forced to admit the beauty of the countryside after London, during his last summer at Combe Florey. An uncertain harvest turned into a good one, Mrs Sydney recovered after her London illness, and Sydney reckoned himself in tolerable condition.* Even though his health had improved, Sydney was not entirely reconciled to the soft Somerset weather and replied to Lady Grey's comments on the climate of Northumberland that 'I dare say it has its evils but nothing so bad as the enervating character of this. It would unstring the limbs of a giant, and demoralise the soul of Cato. We have just sent off a cargo of London people who have been staying here three weeks. They say that all their principles and virtues are gone.'*

The Londoners were a musical family called Kingston who had fallen on hard times; Sydney, 'finding them all ill, and singing flat', had brought them down to Combe Florey for a long holiday.* A graver visitation had been threatened. 'Lady Holland talks seriously of coming to Combe Florey which alarms me not a little,'

Sydney reported to Lady Grey early in July 1844.* He hoped that her well-known fear of the railroad and the threat of a long tunnel might deliver him from so demanding a visitor. A few weeks later he wrote to Lady Carlisle that

a thousand rumours reach me, and my firm belief is, she will come. I have spoken to the sheriff, and mentioned it to the magistrates. They have agreed to address her, and she is to be escorted from the station by the Yeomanry. The Clergy are rather backward, but I think that after a little bashfulness they will wait upon her. Brunel, assisted by the ablest philosophers, is to accompany her upon the railroad—and they have been so good as to say that the steam shall be generated from soft water, with a slight infusion of camomile flowers.*

But the visit never took place, Sydney later remarking to Lady Holland that 'I should feel compunction to bring you to so dull a place. You must be tired to death of me, and at this distance from London it is impossible to be sure of any agreeable addition, and you have been so used to fine intellects that common understandings not only do not nourish you, but they make you ill. I have seen you often turn pale at commonplace observations.'* Quizzing her ladyship was to remain one of his main occupations.

Jeffrey, too, long the subject of gentle derision, came in for further joking during an illness in August; Sydney envisaged him being cared for by a committee who would 'report to his loves—consisting of several scores of young ladies, and others more advanced in years. It is a science by itself the management of the little man.'* The politics of 1844 must have seemed as traditional to him as the objects of his humour; O'Connell's trial and the success of his appeal to the Lords that summer continued the Irish debate, and the current crux of the Catholic question in Ireland raised issues which Sydney—even though he was scarcely up to further controversial writing—considered too straightforward for pamphlet discussion. 'I am thinking of writing a pamphlet to urge to necessity of paying the Catholic Clergy,' he had written to Lady Grey, 'but the ideas are all so trite and the arguments so plain and easy that I gape at the thought of such a production. Lord Grey can have no doubt of the wisdom of paying the Catholic Clergy.'*

Early in October he had an alarming attack of giddiness, which the local practitioner thought due to stomach trouble. After a fortnight's recuperation ('eating nothing that I like and doing nothing that I wish')* he returned to London to put himself under his son-in-law's care. For a while he made good progress, and reported to Lady Carlisle that 'I am in a regular train of promotion. From gruel, vermicelli, and sago, I was promoted to panada—from thence to minced meat, and (such is the effect of good conduct) I was elevated to a mutton-chop. My breathlessness and giddiness are gone, chased away by the gout. If you hear any tidings of 17 or 18 lbs of human flesh, they belong to me— I look as if a curate had been taken out of me.'* Friends and acquaintances frequently enquired after him, among them Sir Robert Peel, to whom Sydney wrote when in his dietary progression he had reached 'that most detestable of all human diet, "light and innocent puddings" '.* Lady Holland frequently came to ask about his progress—and to be teased. As Sydney put it to Lady Grey, 'One comfort during my illness has been the delight and amusement it has been to Lady Holland. I took a malignant pleasure in misstating symptoms and became so preposterous in some of my replies to her hourly cross questioning that she became quite impatient for an early determination having staked her credit up on it.'*

He was able for a while to take an interest in affairs at Combe Florey, where his nephew Cecil was keeping an eye on the parish for him, and also on Chapter business at St Paul's. One of his very last letters was to propose to Dean and Chapter that, during a member's illness in London, a proxy vote would be valid; it was, as one might expect, a piece of patronage business which lay behind the suggestion.* But he was scarcely up to serious work, and declined rapidly in the new year, dying peacefully at 56 Green Street on 22 February 1845.

In the previous summer Sydney had written to a Frenchman who sought some biographical details for an article he was writing for the *Revue des deux mondes*: 'I am seventy-four years of age; and being Canon of St Paul's in London, and a rector of a parish in the country, my time is divided equally between town and country. I am living amongst the best society in the metropolis, and at ease in my circumstances; in tolerable health, a mild Whig, a tolerating Churchman, and much given to talking, laughing, and noise. I dine with the rich in London, and physic the poor in the country, passing from the sauces of Dives to the sores of Lazarus. I am, upon the whole, a happy man, have found the world an entertaining world, and am thankful to Providence for the part allotted to me in it.'*

A passage like that was typical of him, even down to a very ordinary pun with biblical connotations. It shows something of his delight in London society and of his sense of the duties of simple pastoral work in the country, and above all of a contentment which was characteristic at least of his later years. Towards the end of his life he had looked back on his literary career when writing a Preface for his *Works* and found much to satisfy him. 'I see very little in my Reviews to alter or repent of,' he had written of his *Edinburgh* articles, 'I always endeavoured to fight against evil; and what I thought evil then, I think evil now.'* Thinking back to the repressive Toryism of the earliest years of the century, he took pleasure in breathing a freer atmosphere and in feeling, with justice, that his work for the quarterly magazine he had helped to found had contributed to the more liberal attitudes of early Victorian Britain. It was a satisfying achievement, which helped to compensate for years of apparent neglect in ecclesiastical preferment, where a decent canonry had perhaps never really matched his greater expectations in middle life. His writings have endured in spite of their ephemeral nature: review-essays and controversial pamphlets are not usually the most enduring of literary forms.

To his friends and contemporaries he left something more precious than his essays and his letters—the freshness and gaiety of a fine spirit, recollected in the thousands of good things in his conversation and his boisterous presence on the social scene. Lord Dudley, one of Sydney's regular butts, once wrote of the pleasure of being a victim; it was done 'so good-humouredly and inoffensively, as well as with so much drollery, that it is impossible even for the object of his attack not to laugh and be pleased'.* That was no mean achievement. It struck Bulwer Lytton in the same way, and he annotated his family album in which Sydney's letters were mounted: 'Sydney Smith, unexcelled in our time for the kind of humour which has drollery for its form and strong sense for its substance. His conversation was still more racy than his writings. His spirit was as joyous as Nature on a sunny day.'*

REFERENCES

✻

MANUSCRIPT SOURCES

Manuscript material is cited from the following sources, and grateful acknowledgement is made to all the owners and curators concerned for their permission to use documents in their keeping. (In the list which follows, the cue-titles used for the more frequently quoted sources precede where necessary their alphabetically-arranged entries.)

Mr D.R. Bentham, Loughborough, Leicestershire.
Bodleian Library, Oxford.
British Library, London.
Brotherton Library, University of Leeds.
Buckinghamshire Record Office, Aylesbury.
Castle Howard: Mr George Howard, Castle Howard, Yorkshire.
Chatsworth: The Duke of Devonshire, Chatsworth, Derbyshire.
Mrs C.E. Colvin, Oxford.
Dr J.C. Corson, Lilliesleaf, Roxburghshire.
Derby Public Library.
Durham University, Department of Palaeography and Diplomatic.
Fondren Library, Rice University, Houston, Texas.
Free Library of Philadelphia, Pennsylvania.
Mr P.R. Glazebrook, Cambridge.
The Earl of Halifax, Garrowby, York.
Hampshire Record Office, Winchester.
The late Viscount Harcourt, Stanton Harcourt, Oxfordshire.
Harvard: Houghton Library, Harvard University, Cambridge, Massachusetts.
Haverford College Library, Haverford, Pennsylvania.
Hertfordshire Record Office, Hertford.
Mr D.C.L. Holland, Haywards Heath, Sussex.
Hunt: Henry E. Huntington Library, San Marino, California.
IOL: India Office Library, London.
Keele University Library, Staffordshire.
Mr Walter Leuba, Pittsburgh, Pennsylvania.

Massachusetts Historical Society, Boston.
National Library of Scotland, Edinburgh.
National Library of Wales, Aberystwyth.
NCO: New College Library, Oxford.
NYRO: North Yorkshire Record Office, Northallerton.
Osborn: James M. and Marie-Louise Osborn Collection, Yale University Library, New Haven, Connecticut.
Mr W. Hugh Peal, New York.
Pierpont Morgan Library, New York.
Public Record Office, London.
Ray: Mr Gordon N. Ray, New York.
Rochester University Library, Rochester, New York.
Royal Institution of Cornwall, Launceston.
Royal Library, Windsor Castle, Berkshire.
St Aldwyn: Earl St Aldwyn, Williamstrip, Gloucestershire.
St Paul's Cathedral Library, London.
Society of Antiquaries of London.
Trinity College Library, Cambridge.
University College Library, London.
University of California Library, Los Angeles.
Mr L.P. Wenham, York.
Mr C.E. Wrangham, Catterick, Yorks.
Yale: Beinecke Rare Books and MSS Library, Yale University, New Haven, Connecticut.
York: Mr Christopher York, Long Marston, York.
York Diocesan Archives, St Anthony's Hall, York.

PRINTED SOURCES

The following five cue-titles are used for the works most frequently cited in the list of references following:

Mem.: *A Memoir of the Reverend Sydney Smith.* By his daughter, [Saba] Lady Holland. Fourth edition, London 1855.

NCS: *The Letters of Sydney Smith,* ed. Nowell C. Smith. Oxford 1953. (Two volumes continuously paginated and numbered. Letters for which an acceptable text is available in this edition are cited below by addressee and (simplified) date, and by their serial number in Nowell Smith's edition. Texts for which important new manuscript variants have been discovered to adjust the printed text are cited by their NCS number with particulars of the location of the original documents.)

Reid: Stuart J. Reid, *The Life and Times of Sydney Smith.* Fourth edition, London 1896.

Sketches: *Elementary Sketches of Moral Philosophy, delivered at the Royal Institution, in the Years 1804, 1805, and 1806.* By the late Rev. Sydney Smith. Second edition, London 1850.

Works: The Works of Reverend Sydney Smith. London 1839–40. (This four-volume edition has been used, but in a very few cases the two-volume edition of 1859 has been explicitly cited for its supplementary contents.)

NOTES

2	thumbs	*Mem.* 293.
	design	*Mem.* 1.
	coal-heavers	*Mem.* 2.
	accounts	Robert Smith to William Burrows, 26 Apr. 1781: MS IOL.
	ruined	To same from same, 17 Jan. 1781: MS IOL.
3	stocks	To M. H. Beach, 1801: NCS 60.
	1827	*Mem.* 2.
	India	Courtney's name was spelled with disconcerting variation by his family; I have used what appears to have been his own preference.
4	world	*Mem.* 5.
	Stonham	*Mem.* 6; 'Narrative for my Grandchildren' by Catharine Amelia Smith (MS D. C. L. Holland).
	away	*Mem.* 6.
5	vice	Ibid.
	life	*Works,* iii. 80.
	education	*Works,* i. 258–9.
6	shorts	*Works,* i. 228, 222, 225–6 (from *Edinburgh Review,* 1809).
	men	*Works,* i. 260–1 (from *ER,* 1810).
	force	E. C. Mack, *Public Schools and British Opinion, 1780 to 1860* (London, 1038), 156.
	fortifications	*Mem.* 8–9.
7	Winchester	*Mem.* 9.
	kings	*Works,* i. 227, 226 (*ER,* 1809).
	with it	'Calumnies against Oxford', xvi (1810), 184.
	ambition	*Mem.* 10.
8	1796	To M. H. Beach, 2 Apr. 1795; NCS 4.
	air	To Robert Smith, spring 1798: MS Hunt.
	dry	To M. H. Beach, 26 July 1794: NCS 1.
	wilderness	Ibid.
9	indeed	'A list of the Netheravon poor', 1793; MS (transcript) Ray.
	through	To——, 10 Dec. 1794: MS Ray.
	roasting	To Mrs Beach, winter 1794–5: NCS 4.
	master	To M. H. Beach, 25 May 1795: NCS 5.

10	need	To Mrs Beach, 11 Jan. 1796: NCS 6.
	antipathy	Ibid.
	me	To Robert Smith, 26 June 1796: MS Hunt.
11	talents	To same, 9 July 1796: MS Hunt.
	polite	To same, 25 Nov. 1797: MS Hunt.
	arranged	To same, 10 Dec. 1794: MS Hunt.
12	Improvement	To M. H. Beach, 23 Aug. 1797: NCS 10.
	each	To Robert Smith, 5 Nov. 1797: MS Hunt.
	Weimar	To same, 29 Dec. 1797: MS Hunt.
	negotiated	Ibid.; and to M. H. Beach, 19 Jan. 1798 (NCS 13).
	advantage	To Robert Smith, 25 Nov. 1797: MS Hunt.
	me	To M. H. Beach, 1 Dec. 1797: NCS 11.
13	Smith	See John Sparrow, 'Jane Austen and Sydney Smith' (1954), in his *Independent Essays* (London, 1963), 88–96.
	June	To Robert Smith, spring 1798, 31 May 1798: MSS Hunt.
	overpaid	To same, 29 Dec. 1797: MS Hunt.
14	you	To same, 31 May 1798: MS Hunt.
	eye	To Mrs Beach, 16 June 1798: NCS 18.
15	delicacy	To J. G. Clarke, 5 Dec. 1798: MS British Library (one of a group in *London Mercury*, 1930, 512–17).
	tread	To M. H. Beach, 30 June 1798: NCS 19.
16	obligation	To same, 12 Aug. 1798: MS Nat. Lib. of Wales.
	attention	To Mrs Beach, 15 July 1798: NCS 20.
	village	To same, 4 Nov. 1798: NCS 26.
	Parish	To J. G. Clarke, 27 Oct. 1799: MS British Library.
	efficacious	To Mrs Beach, 23 Sept. 1798: NCS 23.
17	die	To J. G. Clarke, 5 Feb. 1799: MS British Library.
18	them	To Mrs Beach, 15 July 1798: NCS 20.
	forty	To same, 26 Aug. 1798: NCS 21.
	you	To same, Nov. 1798: NCS 28.
	them	To same, 3 Aug. 1798: MS Nat. Lib. of Wales.
	other	To Leonard Horner, 26 Aug. 1842: Leonard Horner, *Memoirs and Correspondence of Francis Horner* (2nd edn., London, 1853), 463–4.
19	dispositions	Ibid. 91.
	novelties	Ibid. 173.
	approval	Henry Cockburn, *Life of Lord Jeffrey* (2nd edn., Edinburgh, 1852) ii. 107.
	philosopher	To Francis Jeffrey, June 1801: NCS 58.
20	lost	*Mem.* 31–2.
	myself	To Francis Jeffrey, 1 Aug. 1801: NCS 59.
	satisfaction	To Mrs Hicks Beach, 3 Aug. 1798: MS Nat. Lib. of Wales.
	succeeded	To M. H. Beach, 30 June 1798: NCS 19.
	them	To same, 16 Jan. 1799: NCS 30.
21	first	To Mrs Beach, 4 Mar. 1799: NCS 33.
	Comrade	To Michael Hicks Beach (junior), summer 1799: NCS 38.

	apology	To M. H. Beach, 22 Sept. 1799: *NCS* 41.
	me	Michael Hicks Beach to his father, 3 Oct. 1799: MS Lord St. Aldwyn.
22	incident	To M. H. Beach, 2 Oct. 1799: *NCS* 43.
	tea	Michael to his father, 26 Nov. 1799, 14 Mar. 1800: MSS Lord St. Aldwyn.
	South	To Mrs Beach, 3 Mar. 1800: *NCS* 50.
23	my life	To Robert Smith, 1798: MS Hunt.
	heart	Ibid.
24	living	'Narrative': MS D. C. L. Holland.
	husband's life	To J. G. Clarke, 27 Oct. 1799: MS British Library.
	meannesses	Catharine Pybus to Robert Smith, 6 Dec. 1798: MS IOL.
	conspicuous	Martha Pybus to same, 3 Jan. 1799: MS IOL.
	ourselves	Catharine Pybus to same, 4 Mar. 1800: MS IOL.
	fortune	*Mem.* 50.
25	years	To Robert Smith, June 1800: MS Hunt.
	management	'Narrative': MS D. C. L. Holland.
	do	To Robert Smith, Feb. 1801: MS Hunt.
	God	To same, 28 Mar. 1803: MS Hunt.
	this	To same, 1798: MS Hunt.
26	lot	To J. G. Clarke, 27 Oct. 1799: MS British Library.
	tutorship	To Mrs Beach, 11 Apr. 1800: *NCS* 52; MS Lord St. Aldwyn.
	myself	To M. H. Beach, 24 June 1800: *NCS* 54.
27	letters	Note by Mrs Beach's daughter, Mrs St. John, in her transcription of Sydney's correspondence with her family: MS Ray.
	ways	To Mrs Beach, autumn 1800: trs. Ray.
	behaviour	From same, autumn 1800: ibid.
	reply	To same, autumn 1800: ibid.
	1799	To J. G. Clarke, 5 Feb. 1799: MS British Library.
28	sleep	To Mrs Beach, 20 Jan. 1800: *NCS* 49.
	it	To same, 12 Nov. 1799: *NCS* 45.
	years	Henry Cockburn, *Journal* (Edinburgh, 1874), ii. 244–5.
	father	To Robert Smith, 28 Mar. 1800: MS Hunt.
	day	John Leyden to Richard Heber, 24 Apr. 1800: MS (transcript) Nat. Lib. of Scotland.
	causes	*Mem.* 81.
29	Methodists	*Mem.* 83–5, revised from *Sermons* (2nd edn., London, 1801), xix-xxv.
	blames	*Mem.* 89.
	quotation	See Samuel. F. Pickering, 'The Reviews of Sydney Smith's Sermons of 1800 and 1801 and the Founding of the "Edinburgh Review"', *Anglican Theological Review* (1972–3), 205–19.
	subject	Ibid. 212n.
30	receive	To Mrs Beach, 9 Nov. 1800: trs. Ray.
	exorbitant	To same, 3 Dec. 1800: trs. Ray.

	point	From same, Dec. 1800: trs. Ray.
	inspire	To same, 28 Dec. 1800: trs. Ray.
31	dictate	To same, 2 Feb. 1801: trs. Ray.
	hopes	Robert Smith to Mrs Beach, 7 Feb. 1801: trs. Ray.
	intentions	To Robert Smith, Feb. 1801: MS Hunt.
32	be	To Mrs Beach, 21 Feb. 1801: trs. Ray.
	appearance	To Robert Smith, 25 Oct. 1801: MS NCO.
	fortune	Ibid.
	brilliant	To Robert Smith, 7 Nov. 1801: MS Hunt.
	him	To M. H. Beach, 10 Nov. 1801: trs. Ray.
	man	To Mrs Beach, 25 Jan. 1802: trs. Ray.
33	1801	To same, 13 Dec. 1801: NCS 61.
	life	To same, 25 Jan. 1802: trs. Ray.
	master	To same, 26 Mar. 1802: trs. Ray.
	proud	To M. H. Beach, 31 May 1802: trs. Ray.
	pain	To Robert Smith, 7 Nov. 1801: MS Hunt.
34	to it	To same, 24 Nov. 1801: MS Hunt.
	wife	To same, 25 Dec. 1801: MS Hunt.
35	journal	*Works*, i. v-vi.
36	name	To James Mackintosh, 13 Jan. 1802: MS Keele Univ. Lib.; see *TLS*, 9 Apr. 1970, 388.
	metaphysicians	To Francis Jeffrey, June 1801: NCS 58.
37	opinion	*The Letters of Sir Walter Scott* [VII], *1821–1823*, ed. H. J. C. Grierson (London, 1934), 379.
	tremble	To Francis Jeffrey, 22 July 1802: NCS 67.
38	world	*Works*, i. 1–2.
	gratification	Ibid. 30.
39	church	To Francis Jeffrey, Aug. 1802: NCS 68; MS NCO.
	offer	To Archibald Constable, Apr–May 1803; NCS 75.
40	reference	To Mrs Beach, Feb. 1802: trs. Ray; see Psalm 72, v. 10.
	correspondence	To same, 26 Mar. 1802: NCS 62.
	wives	To Caroline Fox, 14 June 1802: NCS 63.
	together	To Mrs Beach, July 1802: NCS 64.
	discretion	To same, July 1802: trs. Ray.
	caprice	To same, autumn 1802: trs. Ray.
41	twenty-five	To same, Jan. 1803: trs. Ray.
	fear it	To same, 12 Jan. 1803. trs. Ray.
	best	To same, 14 Feb. 1803: trs. Ray.
	incredulity	To same, 9 May 1803: trs. Ray.
42	root	To Francis Jeffrey, 1 Aug. 1801: NCS 59.
	possible	Henry Cockburn, *Life of Lord Jeffrey* (Edinburgh, 1852), ii. 79.
	Edinburgh	To Francis Jeffrey, 12 Aug. 1803: NCS 78.
43	town	*Mem.* 108; Reid 99.
	well	To Francis Jeffrey, 28 Oct. 1803: NCS 86.
44	wrote	To same, Dec. 1803: NCS 88.
	delivery	To same, 16 Feb. 1805: NCS 96.
	joined in	R. J. Mackintosh, *Memoirs of the Life of Sir James Mackintosh* (London, 1835), ii. 190–1.

	acquaintance	To Francis Jeffrey, Sept. 1803 and 16 Feb. 1808: NCS 83, 125.
	Brougham	To same, 16 Feb. 1805: NCS 96.
45	administered	To same, 21 Dec. 1806: NCS 112.
	company	To Francis Jeffrey, 3 Apr. 1806: MS J. C. Corson.
	drink	To same, 20 Jan. 1806: NCS 106.
	anatomy	To same, 16 Feb. 1805: NCS 96.
	admirers	To same, 28 Oct. 1803: NCS 86.
46	ease	To same, 25 Feb. 1807: NCS 113.
	yourself	To same, Apr.–May 1804: NCS 91.
	respect	To same, 12 June 1805: NCS 100.
	place	Cockburn, *Jeffrey*, i. 155.
	friends	To Francis Jeffrey, 16 Feb. 1808: NCS 125.
47	Recorder	To James Mackintosh, 1 Dec. 1804: MS Nat. Lib. of Scotland.
	last	To same, 20 Feb. 1805: ibid.
	adhered to	To Lady Holland, 10 Jan. 1809: NCS 147.
48	Lady H.	To James Mackintosh, 1 Oct. 1805: NCS 103.
	amusement	To Lady Grey, 1 Feb. 1836: NCS 710.
	dreadful	To Lord Holland: see NCS, p. 70n.
49	himself	To Francis Jeffrey, 12 June 1805: NCS 100.
	heeded	Princess Marie Liechtenstein, *Holland House* (London, 1874), i. 157.
	coxcomb	To Lord Holland, summer 1806: NCS 107.
	already	*Lord Granville Leveson Gower, Private Correspondence 1781 to 1821*, ed. Castalia Countess Granville (London, 1916), ii. 313.
50	Sydney	Derek Hudson, *Holland House in Kensington* (London, 1967), 59.
	confidence	*Mem*. 124.
	water	To Lady Holland, 10 Jan. 1809: NCS 147.
	London	To Robert Smith, 1798: MS Hunt.
	him	To Mrs Beach, Nov. 1803: NCS 90; trs. Ray.
51	anywhere	T. F. Dibdin, *Reminiscences of a Literary Life* (London, 1836), 751.
	man	*The Diary of Benjamin Robert Haydon*, ed. W. B. Pope (Cambridge, Mass., 1960), i. 33.
	comprehension	*Letters to 'Ivy' from the First Earl of Dudley*, ed. S. H. Romilly (London, 1905), 24.
	conversation	*The Diary of Francis Lady Shelley*, ed. Richard Edgcumbe (London, 1912), i. 15.
	violent	Augustus Hare, *The Story of My Life* (London, 1900), iii. 316–17.
52	first	*The Diaries of Sylvester Douglas, Lord Glenbervie*, ed. Francis Bickley (London, 1928), ii. 66.
	offence	*Mem*. 139–40.
	passion	*Mem*. 140–1.
	you	To Josiah Wedgwood, 6 July 1805: MS Keele Univ. Lib.
53	parish	To Gerrard Andrewes, Dec. 1805: NCS 108, 109.

	half	From same, 17 Dec. 1805: MS (transcript) D. C. L. Holland.
	fanatic	To same, Dec. 1805: NCS 110.
	interest	From same, 21 Dec. 1805: NCS 110 dated from MS (transcript) D. C. L. Holland.
	history	To James Mackintosh, 1 Dec. 1804: MS Nat. Lib. of Scotland.
54	difficulty	To Francis Jeffrey, 16 Feb. 1805: NCS 96.
	sensible	Leonard Horner, *Memoirs of Francis Horner* (1853), 295–6.
	season	Remark to Monckton Milnes, quoted Reid, 125, thence NCS, p. 101n.
	laughing	*Mem.* 128–9.
	audience	Dibdin, *Reminiscences*, 228.
55	without	*Mem.* 131, 133.
	end	To Francis Jeffrey, Apr. 1805: NCS 98.
	plain	*The Letter-Bag of Lady Elizabeth Spencer-Stanhope, 1806–73*, ed. A. M. W. Stirling (London, 1913), i. 4.
56	studies	*The Farington Diary*, ed. James Greig (iii, London, 1924) 237.
	with	*Letter-Bag*, i. 143.
	fevers	To Henry Reeve, 29 Oct. 1805: NCS 105.
	nothing	To Lady Holland, May 1805: NCS 99.
	gone	To William Whewell, 8 Apr. 1843: NCS 915; MS Trinity College, Cambridge.
57	philosophy	*Sketches*, 3.
	proceed	Ibid. 17.
	categories	Ibid. 54.
58	death	Ibid. 163.
	pigs	Ibid. 195–6.
	other	Ibid. 111.
59	laughter	Ibid. 145.
	behind	Caroline Smith to Robert Smith, 1803: MS IOL.
60	you	To Robert Smith, 15 Apr. 1803: MS Hunt.
	there	To M. H. Beach, 26 Apr. 1803: NCS 74.
61	for a divorce	Cecil Smith to Robert Smith, 22 Jan. and 22 Feb. 1803: MSS IOL.
	joke about	To Caroline Fox, Apr. 1803: NCS 73.
	on a divorce	To same, 29 July 1803: NCS 76.
	woman	Cecil Smith to Robert Smith, 9 Apr. 1803: MS IOL.
	matter	See same to same, 7 June 1804: MS IOL.
	does	To Maria Smith 12/16 Nov. 1804: MS Hunt.
	again	Ibid.
62	impertinent	To Robert Smith, late 1804: MS Hunt.
	blame	To Maria Smith, 12/16 Nov. 1804: MS Hunt.
	entitled	To Robert Smith, late 1804: MS Hunt.
63	information	Cecil Smith to Robert Smith, 9 Sept. 1805: MS IOL.
	me	To Maria Smith, 1805: MS Hunt.
	children	To Francis Jeffrey, Apr. 1805: NCS 98.
64	record	*Mem.* 123.

	mine	To Robert Smith, 31 Dec. 1805: MS Hunt.
	man	Drafted on Sydney to Maria Smith, 9 Jan. 1807: MS Hunt.
65	offence	To Maria Smith, 11 Jan. 1807: MS Hunt.
	task	To same, 19 Jan. 1807: MS Hunt.
	saw	To same, 11 Feb. 1807: MS Hunt.
	anger	Catharine Smith to same, 11 Jan. 1807: MS Hunt.
	strained	To Lady Holland, 9 Dec. 1807: NCS 122.
	suspended	To Maria Smith, 13 Jan. 1807: MS Hunt.
66	civil	To same, 14 Feb. 1807: MS Hunt.
	before	To same, 23 Jan. 1807: MS Hunt.
	Company	To same, 24 Dec. 1807: MS Ray.
	1809	To Francis Jeffrey, Apr. 1810: NCS 181.
67	devour	To same, 28 Oct. and 30 Nov. 1803: NCS 86, 87.
	livelihood	To same, 13 Nov. 1804: NCS 95.
	right	To Caroline Fox, spring 1804: NCS 92.
	review	To Francis Jeffrey, summer 1804: NCS 94.
68	so	To same, 29 Oct. 1805: NCS 104.
	in it	To same, Jan. 1808: NCS 124.
	hurt	*The Letters of Sir Walter Scott* [II], *1808–1811*, ed. H. J. C. Grierson (London, 1932), 126.
	etc.	To Lady Holland, 10 Jan. 1809: NCS 147.
69	reputation	To Francis Jeffrey, Nov.–Dec. 1808: NCS 143.
	power	To same, Feb. 1804: NCS 89.
	complete	To same, 21 Dec. 1806: NCS 112.
70	none	*Works*, i. 66–7 (from *Edin. Rev.*, 1803).
	congestion	*Works*, i. 65.
71	all	To Francis Jeffrey, Jan. 1808: NCS 124.
	religion	*Works*, i. 185.
72	malice	*Works*, iv. 91, 90.
	conclusion	*Works*, iv. 95–6, 98.
	bishop	*Mem*. 138.
73	lemon	*Mem*. 312.
	acquaintance	From Lord Erskine, 6 Oct. 1806: Reid, 130; MS NCO.
	rectory	*Farington Diary*, iii. 76.
	had it	*Recollections of the Table Talk of Samuel Rogers*, ed. Morchard Bishop (London, 1952), 235.
	society	To Francis Jeffrey, Oct. 1806: NCS 111.
	diocesan	*Mem*. 147.
74	place	*The Correspondence of George Prince of Wales*, *1770–1812*, ed. A. Aspinall (London, 1969), no. 2327.
	them	Lord Eldon to Lady Holland, June 1807: NCS 115.
	safe	To Lady Holland, 13 June 1808: NCS 128.
75	Yorkshire	To William Wilberforce, Feb. 1807: MS Bodleian.
	morning	To Thomas Creevey, May–June 1807: *Creevey Papers*, ed. Sir Herbert Maxwell (London, 1903), i. 166–7.
	consequence	Ibid.

	put it	*Mem.* 148.
	decorous	To Lady Holland, July 1807: *NCS* 117.
	quarter	*Mem.* 151.
76	1807	To Lady Holland, July 1807: *NCS* 117.
	printer	'P. Plymley' to Mr Budd, 26 May 1808: MS Bodleian.
77	goose	*Works*, iii. 279.
	understanding	Ibid. 280.
	freedom	Ibid. 294–5.
	fool	Ibid. 310.
	lawyer	Ibid. 287–8.
78	Kent	Ibid. 297.
	province	Ibid. 343.
	Ireland	Ibid. 369.
	vicinity	Ibid. 329.
	Christians	Ibid. 385.
	not	Ibid. 327.
79	beyond	Ibid. 382.
	mate	Ibid. 323.
	Timothy	Ibid. 281.
	England	Ibid. 302.
	Ireland	Ibid. 363.
80	own	Ibid. 314.
	pen	From Lord Holland, Oct. 1809: *NCS* 162; MS NCO.
	Nebuchadnezzar	To Francis Jeffrey, 18 Nov. 1807: *NCS* 120.
81	absence	To Robert Smith, 4 Feb. 1808: MS Hunt.
	fault	To Lady Holland, 22 Aug. 1808: *NCS* 136.
	September	To same, 29 Sept. 1808: *NCS* 137.
	ever	To Archibald Alison, Sept. 1808: MS W. H. Peal.
82	to be	To Lady Holland, 29 Sept. 1808: *NCS* 137.
	explain	To same, 6 Oct. 1808: *NCS* 138.
	Holland	To same, Oct. 1803: *NCS* 139.
	can	To same, 29 June 1808: *NCS* 134.
	out of it	To same, 24 Oct. 1808: *NCS* 140.
	next	Ibid.
83	York	To Francis Jeffrey, 20 Nov. 1808: *NCS* 142.
	move	To Lady Holland, Christmas 1808: *NCS* 146.
	unhappy	To same, 9 Sept. 1809: *NCS* 158.
84	fool	*Mem.* 154–5.
	dilapidations	To Lord Eldon, 29 July 1820: *NCS* 372.
	not	To Lady Caroline Lamb, 18 June 1809: *NCS* 153.
85	dogs	*Mem.* 205.
	attention	To Lord Valentia, 11 July 1809: MS British Library.
86	Ferry Bridge	To Lady Grey, 29 Nov. 1809: *NCS* 168.
	road	To Lady Holland, 3 Nov. 1810: *NCS* 187.
	yields	To same, 21 Sept. 1809: *NCS* 159.
	morning	To same, 13 Aug. 1810: *NCS* 186.
87	. can	To John Allen, 27 Dec. 1812: *NCS* 226.
	burthen	To same, 1 Jan. 1813: *NCS* 227.
	recede	To Lady Holland, 17 Jan. 1813: *NCS* 228.
	situation	To John Allen, 24 Jan. 1813: *NCS* 229.

	incumbents	See Alan Savidge, *The Parsonage in England* (London, 1964), 166.
88	family	To Lady Holland, 16 Nov. 1816: *NCS* 268.
	1812	York Diocesan Archives R. IV. F18R/3a.
	houses	*Mem.* 206.
	mistake	'Narrative for my Grandchildren': MS D. C. L. Holland.
89	energy	*Mem.* 206–7.
	housemaid	*Mem.* 209–10.
	can	To Lady Holland, 5 Jan. 1814: *NCS* 241.
	appearance	*Mem.* 210.
	succeeded	To John Allen, 2 Apr. 1814: *NCS* 246.
90	pamphlets	*Mem.* 180.
	begin	*Extracts from Journals and Correspondence of Miss Berry, 1783–1852*, ed. Lady Theresa Lewis (2nd edn., London, 1866), iii. 358.
	Yorkshire	To Lady Grey, 30 Dec. 1820: *NCS* 385.
91	trifles	To Francis Jeffrey, 30 Dec. 1814: *NCS* 249.
	corner	*Mem.* 259–60.
92	property	*Mem.* 161.
	bed	*Mem.* 168.
	fork	*Mem.* 236–7.
	county	*Mem.* 207.
93	Sir	*Mem.* 235–6, elaborating Mrs Marcet's notes, now MS NCO.
	earth	*Mem.* 236.
	friend	*Mem.* 211.
	get it	Ibid.
	intoxication	*Mem.* 309.
94	instructive	To Lady Mary Bennet, Aug. 1822: *NCS* 411.
	him	To Lydia White, 29 June 1822: MS Haverford College Library.
	decomposed	To J. A. Murray, 5 Nov. 1817: *NCS* 283.
	welcome	To Lady Grey, 3 Nov. 1819: *NCS* 346.
	parts	To Elizabeth Vernon, Aug. 1817: *Miscellanies of the Philobiblon Society* XV (1877–84), vii. 18–21.
	days	To Lady Mary Bennet, Sept. 1817: *NCS* 281.
	Hostelrie	Catharine Smith to Archibald Constable, 17 June 1824: MS Brotherton Library.
95	jackass	*Mem.* 202.
	preaching	*The Letters of Thomas Babington Macaulay*, ed. Thomas Pinney (i, Cambridge, 1974), 213–14.
	expression	Ibid. 215.
96	reviews	Ibid. 217.
	opened	Lord Houghton, *Academy*, 29 Apr. 1876, reviewing G. O. Trevelyan's *Macaulay*.
	delightful	*Mem.* 415–16.
	groom	*A Sermon preached ... at Malton, at the Visitation, August 1809* (London and York, 1809), 9.
	conversation	*Mem.* 196–7.

	back	*Mem.* 419–20.
97	crows	To Edward Davenport, 10 Feb. 1821: *NCS* 389.
	warmth	Ibid.
	comparison	To Lady Grey, 27 Mar. 1821: *NCS* 392.
	exertion	To Edward Davenport, 1820: *NCS* 355.
	trial	To Lord Grey, 15 Apr. 1820: *NCS* 361.
	meeting	To Lady Holland, 4 Oct. 1823: *NCS* 427.
	six	To same, Oct. 1825: *NCS* 451.
98	quietly	To Lady Carlisle, 28 Aug. 1828: MS Castle Howard.
	de Bras	To Francis Wrangham, 6 Mar. 1824: MS Fondren.
99	expected	To James Tate, 28 Feb. 1825: MS L. P. Wenham.
	abomination	To Lady Holland, 24 June 1809: *NCS* 154.
	porter	To same, 27 Jan. 1810: *NCS* 175.
	destination	To J. G. Lambton, 5 Dec. 1818: *NCS* 315.
	church	To Lady Mary Bennet, Dec. 1818: *NCS* 315.
	towns	To the Lord Chancellor, 23 May 1834: *NCS* 661.
100	husband	Catharine Smith to Francis Jeffrey, Apr. 1810: *NCS* 180.
	South	To Francis Jeffrey, 23 Sept. 1819: *NCS* 334.
	philosophers	To Dean Hall, 7 Feb. 1827: MS Society of Antiquaries of London.
	seen	To same, 25 Jan. 1827: MS A. S. Bell.
101	candles	To Lady Mary Bennet, 20 Dec. 1820: *NCS* 383.
	weeks	To Lady Holland, 4 Oct. 1823: *NCS* 428.
	salads	To Lady Morpeth, 12 Nov. 1823: MS Castle Howard.
102	today	*Mem.* 425–6; *NCS* 778 of spring 1839 replaces the 'oil of Lucca brown' of *Mem.* with the correct 'crown'.
	depends	To Lady Holland, 5 Jan. 1814: *NCS* 241.
	House	To same, 20 Apr. 1819: *NCS* 327.
	ministers	*Sermon preached at Malton* (1809), 10.
	London	*Mem.* 208.
	diner-out	To Lord Holland, 1 June 1820: *NCS* 367.
103	congregation	*Mem.* 317.
	it too	*Mem.* 261–2.
	Malton	To John Allen, 22 Nov. 1809: *NCS* 166.
	cheese	To Lady Grey, Nov. 1809: *NCS* 165.
	best	Charles Smyth, 'The Evangelical Movement in Perspective', *Cambridge Historical Journal*, vii (1943), 171.
	feet	'Narrative': MS D. C. L. Holland.
104	reviews	To William Smith, 14 Feb. and 5 June 1820: MSS Rochester Univ. Lib.
	now	To Charles Wellbeloved, 29 Dec. 1820: *NCS* 384.
	divines	To same, 28 Nov. 1826: *NCS* 490.
105	quake	*Mem.* 195, 196, 399.
	1821	*Mem.* 213–14.
	alive	To Lady Mary Bennet, Oct.–Nov. 1821: *NCS* 398.
	broadmindedness	*J. S. Rowntree, His Life and Work* (London, 1908),

		209. I am grateful to Mr Martin Higham for this reference.
	arose	'Narrative': MS D. C. L. Holland.
106	laudanum	*Mem.* 408.
	feet	*Mem.* 408–9.
	inaudibly	To John Allen, 10 Mar. 1814: NCS 244.
	Doctor	*Mem.* 405.
	seasons	To Francis Horner, Dec. 1816: NCS 272.
107	by it	Catharine Smith to Lady Morpeth, 1817: MS Castle Howard. See also *Mem.* 212–20.
	prevail	*Journals of Miss Berry*, iii. 358.
	village	To Mrs Hicks Beach, 4 Nov. 1798: NCS 26.
	labour	*Mem.* 166.
	orchards	Reid 168.
	lead	To Duke of Devonshire, 20 Mar. 1823: MS Chatsworth.
108	difficulty	To John Allen, 13 Jan. 1814: NCS 242.
	you	To Francis Cholmeley, 1816: MS NYRO.
	case	*Mem.* 250–1.
	frivolous	To Sir Robert Peel, 30 Aug. 1824: MS British Library.
109	Sessions	To Lord Lansdowne, 22 Dec. 1827: Reid, 240–2.
	period	To Sir Robert Peel, 18 Feb. 1828: MS British Library.
	thieves	*Works*, ii. 64 (*Edin. Rev.*, 1821).
110	confinement	To Lord Lansdowne, 25 Mar. 1819: Reid, 189–91, supplementing NCS 325.
	way	To same, 31 May 1819: Reid, 191–2, supplementing NCS 331.
	others	To Sir Robert Peel, 13 Mar. 1826: MS British Library.
	crime	From same, 24 Mar. 1826: ibid.
111	Review	To same, 27 Mar. 1826: ibid.
	joke	Information from Mr Martin Higham.
	Dragon	To Jonathan Gray, 10 Oct. 1829: NCS 544.
112	mediation	Castle Howard MSS 1/142 *passim*.
	dead	To Lady Grey, 1 Dec. 1809: MS Lord Halifax.
	reviewing	To Francis Jeffrey, 22 Sept. 1824: NCS 440.
113	evacuation	To George Lamb, 3 Feb. 1827: MS Kansas Univ. Lab.
	matters	To Edward Davenport, Nov. 1824: NCS 442
	surprise	To Francis Jeffrey, 10 Nov. 1826: MS Nat. Lib. of Scotland.
114	order	To same, 7 Apr. 1823: ibid.
	dull	To Lady Mary Bennet, July–Aug. 1818: NCS 301.
	long	To Francis Jeffrey, 30 Dec. 1821: NCS 403.
115	clergyman	'Narrative': MS D. C. L. Holland.
	carrot	*Mem.* 205.
	does	'Narrative': MS D. C. L. Holland.
	doing	*Mem.* 262.
	presence	To Francis Cholmeley, 11 July 1811: MS NYRO.
	himself	Walter Jerrold, *Bon-Mots of Sydney Smith and R. Brinsley Sheridan* (London, 1893), 54.
116	bless	*Journals of Miss Berry*, iii. 358.

	nonsense	To T. R. Malthus, 19 Feb. 1820: MS Yale Univ. Lib.
	scarcity	To John Allen, 28 Aug. 1818: NCS 304.
	where	To Douglas Smith, summer 1820: NCS 368.
	night	To Lady Grey, 16 Sept. 1821: NCS 395.
117	conversation	Mem. 163.
	London	To Lady Holland, 5 Dec. 1810: NCS 191.
	advantage	To Lord Holland, autumn 1812: NCS 224.
	take it	To same, 26 Oct. 1812: NCS 225.
118	400	To the Farmer's Magazine, Aug. 1819: NCS 338; MS Brotherton Library.
	teats	To William Vernon, 29 Mar. 1818: MS Lord Harcourt.
	there	To Francis Cholmeley, 21 Sept. 1817: MS NYRO.
	Rousseau	To Lady Holland, 24 June 1809: NCS 154.
	both	Mem. 192.
119	gaol	Works, iv. 399 (Reform Bill speech).
	you	To Henry Brougham, 20 Sept. 1826: MS Univ. Coll. London.
	professionally	Mem. 226.
	Dissenters	Mem. 221.
	encourage it	Mem. 222.
	shame	Mem. 207–8, 261.
120	complete	Mem. 402; Reid, 164.
	emancipation	See T. M. Higham, 'Sydney Smith and Catholic Toleration', Ampleforth Journal LXXXI (1971), 46–59.
	pains	To Lady Holland, 17 Jan. 1813: NCS 228.
	motion	Works (2 vols. London, 1859), ii. 196–201; correct date, 1823, confirmed by correspondence.
121	contempt	Works (2 vols., 1859), ii. 201.
	permit	Ibid.
	profession	To Duke of Devonshire, 20 Mar. 1823: MS Chatsworth.
	worth while	To John Allen, Apr. [1823]: NCS 446.
	effective	To Francis Wrangham, 19 and 26 Apr. 1823: MSS Fondren.
122	side	To same, 21 Mar. 1825: MS Fondren.
	way	To same, Apr. 1825: ibid.
	men	Works, iv. 365.
	subject	Ibid. 370.
123	opinions	Ibid. 362.
	Protestant	Ibid. 361n.
	refutations	To Lady Grey, 29 Jan. 1826: NCS 455.
124	like	Works, iii. 214, 229–31.
	bigotry	G. W. E. Russell, Sydney Smith (London, 1905), 121.
125	surveyor	To Lady Carlisle, Jan. 1826: MS Castle Howard.
	the subject	To Lord Carlisle, 19 Jan. 1826: ibid.
	that subject	To Duke of Devonshire, 5 Nov. 1827: MS Chatsworth.
	labourer	To Henry Howard, 2 Aug. 1830: NCS 561. below, p.155

126	Brandsby	To Francis Cholmeley, 8 Oct. 1809: MS NYRO.
	children	To same, 4 Nov. 1809: ibid.
	splendour	To same, 23 Nov. 1810: ibid.
	cake	To same, 27 Nov. 1810: ibid.
	long	Ibid.
	miserably	To same, 22 Oct. 1808: MS NYRO.
	Popery	To same, 4 Nov., 8 Oct. 1809: ibid.
127	fire	To same, 11 July 1811: ibid.
	reclaim it	To same, 26 Nov. 1815: ibid.
	sum	Catharine Smith to Francis Cholmeley, 9 May 1818: ibid.
	Nunnery	Same to same, 12 June 1822: ibid.
	there	To Francis Cholmeley, 15 Oct. 1817: ibid.
	dishes	To Richard York, 9 Oct. 1817: MS York.
128	England	To same, 15 Dec. 1835: ibid.
	mention	To same, 18 Dec. 1829: ibid.
	turn	To same, 15 Dec. 1835: ibid.
	colt	To same, 20 Mar. 1837: ibid.
	sounds	To same, 16 Oct. 1840: ibid.
129	Alas	To same, 7 Feb. 1834: ibid.
	woman	To same, 28 Nov. 1820: ibid.
	conversation	To Lady Mary York, 8 Oct. 1825: ibid.
	coat	To Richard York, 11 Apr. 1834: ibid.
	brush	To same, 15 Dec. 1835: ibid.
	nonsense	To same, 18 Dec. 1829: ibid.
130	whole	See, e.g. the 'Memoir' of her father by Lucy Raikes, nee Wrangham: MS C. E. Wrangham.
	consistent	To Francis Wrangham, 9 May 1829: MS Fondren.
	for me	To same, 18 Dec. 1809: ibid.
	parson	To same, 28 June 1810: ibid.
	sesquipedality	To same, n.d.: ibid.
	from it	To same, 9 June 1816: ibid.
131	Bawtry	To same, June 1814: ibid.
	severity	To same, 30 Apr. 1814: ibid.
	advice	See above, p. 98
	Bishop	To Francis Wrangham, 17 June 1842: MS Fondren.
	them	To same, 23 June 1812: ibid.
	tomb	To same, 6 Sept. 1813: ibid.
	Algiers	*Letters of James Tate*, ed. L. P. Wenham, Yorks. Archaeological Society CXXVIII (1966), 58.
	rapacious	To Lady Carlisle, 28 Aug. 1828: MS Castle Howard.
	prose	To Lady Copley, 26 Dec. 1825: MS Fondren.
132	night	To Francis Wrangham, 26 July 1828: ibid.
	preferment	To same, 8 Aug. 1828: ibid.
	of Castle Howard	To Lady Carlisle, 18 Feb. 1828: MS Castle Howard.
	at Castle Howard	*Mem.* 216.
133	existence	To Lady Holland, 1 Feb. 1815: *NCS* 250.
	apothecary	To Lady Morpeth, 1 Dec. 1821: MS Castle Howard.
	Flinn	To Duke of Somerset, 17 Sept. 1824: MS Bucks RO.

	early	G. S. Hillard, *Life, Letters and Journals of George Ticknor* (1876), ii. 150.
134	employed	To Lord Carlisle, 29 Aug. 1819: MS Castle Howard.
	frankness	To same, 1 Sept. 1819: ibid.
135	repose	From same, Oct. 1824: ibid.
	sinned	To same, 30 Oct. 1824: ibid.
136	right	To same, 10 Jan. 1825: ibid.
	year	To Lord Morpeth, 5 Sept. 1825: ibid.
	obtained	To Lord Carlisle, 21 Sept. 1821: ibid.
	well	To Lord Grey, Sept. 1818, 24 Nov. 1818: NCS 306, 312.
137	away	To Lady Georgiana Morpeth, 17 Feb. 1821: MS Castle Howard.
	Yorkshire	To Lord Grey, Sept. 1818: NCS 306.
	neighbours	To Lady Grey, 14 Oct. 1825: NCS 452.
	umbrella	To Lady Carlisle, ?1826: MS Castle Howard.
	you	To same, 1828: ibid.
	friend	To Lady Georgiana Morpeth, 5 Sept. 1819: NCS 342.
138	Smith	To same, 16 Feb. 1820; NCS 356 amended by MS Castle Howard.
	amusement	To Lord Carlisle, 11 Feb. 1826: ibid.
139	care	Reid, 298–9.
	impression	To Lady Carlisle, 18 Feb. 1828: MS Castle Howard.
	Stoic	To same, 7 July 1829: ibid.
140	end	To same, 5 Sept. 1840: ibid.
	heaven	To J. A. Murray, 29 Nov. 1821: NCS 400.
	tavern	To Lady Morpeth, 31 Oct. 1821: MS Castle Howard.
	meaning	From Lord Carlisle, Oct. 1821: MS NCO.
	moment	Reid, 102.
141	evil	To Lady Holland, 2 Feb. 1816: NCS 255.
	anacreontic	To Francis Jeffrey, 7 Aug. 1821: NCS 393.
	blackguard	Robert Smith to Bobus Smith, 28 Apr. 1824: MS 10L.
	not	Same to same, 16 Apr. 1826: MS IOL.
	£50,000	To Bobus Smith, ?July 1826: MS IOL.
	seventy	Smith papers, IOL, 1826 *passim*.
142	trifling	To Cecil Smith, 30 Aug. 1827: MS NCO.
	commented	To Catharine Smith, 4 May 1826: NCS 477.
	shillings	To same, 7 May 1826: NCS 479.
143	*ecclesiastica*	To William Smith, 14 Feb. 1820: MS Rochester Univ. Lib.
	hypocritical	To Lord Holland, 1 June 1820: NCS 367.
	unfair	Ibid.
	man	To Duke of Somerset, 17 Sept. 1824: MS Bucks RO.
	bestow	To Duke of Devonshire, 10 Mar. 1823: MS Chatsworth.
144	gang	To Lady Carlisle, 7 Jan. 1829: Castle Howard.
	House	To Richard Heber, 20 Aug. 1824: MS Bodleian.
	nothing	To John Headlam, 20 Aug. 1827: MS St. Paul's Cathedral Library.
	Bett	To Cecil Smith, 4 June 1827: MS NCO.

145	come	To Lady Holland, 17 Feb. 1828: NCS 518.
	obliging	Ibid.
	rider	Ibid.
	man	To Lady Carlisle, 18 Feb. 1828: MS Castle Howard.
	away	To same, Oct. 1828: ibid.
	England	To Lady Holland, 5 Nov. 1828: NCS 521.
146	character	Catherine Crowe to Saba Lady Holland, 13 July 1845: MS NCO.
	year	To E. J. Littleton, 7 Nov. 1828: NCS 522 amended by MS Staffordshire RO.
	intolerance	*Works*, iii. 261–75.
147	patronage	To Lady Holland, 5 Nov. 1828: NCS 521.
	done	'Narrative': MS D. C. L. Holland.
	affectionate	To Lord Holland, summer 1828: NCS 519.
	me	To Mrs Meynell, summer 1829: NCS 540.
148	overpowered	To Lady Mary York, Apr. 1829: MS York.
	Florey	To Archbishop of York, 22 Aug. 1829: NCS 538, amended by *Harcourt Papers*.
149	novels	To Lady Grey, 13 July 1829: NCS 533.
	death	To Mrs Beilby Thompson, 6 Aug. 1829: NCS 535.
	absent	To Lady Holland, 19 Sept. 1829: NCS 542.
	points	To Lady Morley, autumn 1829: NCS 543.
	disposition	To Philip Henry Howard, 13 Aug. 1829: NCS 537.
	enchanting	To George Tierney, 23 Nov. 1829: MS Hampshire RO.
150	state	To J. A. Murray, 24 Oct. 1830: NCS 564.
	homicides	To Lady Grey, 22 Sept. 1833: NCS 641.
	nature	To Mrs Meynell, Summer 1829: NCS 540.
	best	To Richard York, 18 Dec. 1829: MS York.
	People	To Lord Bathurst, 15 Dec. 1829: NCS 553a.
	slippers	To Saba Holland, 3 June 1835: NCS 685.
	Versailles	To Sir Roderick Murchison, 26 Dec. 1841: NCS 868.
	appearance	To Richard York, 5 Sept. 1840: MS York.
151	Baronet	To Lady Holland, 15 Oct. 1830: NCS 563.
	clergyman	To same, 19 Sept. 1829: NCS 542.
	opinions	To J. N. Fazakerly, Oct. 1829: NCS 546.
	seventy	To Lady Ashburton, 3 Dec. 1843: NCS 952.
	expected	To William Smith, 19 July 1830: MS Rochester Univ. Lib.
	donkey	To Lady Grey, 6 Sept. 1829: NCS 541.
152	heels	To J. A. Murray, 14 Dec. 1829: NCS 553.
	lady	To Lady Holland, July 1831: NCS 585.
	parson	To Emily Hibbert, 5 Jan. 1832: NCS 604.
	applying &c.	To Lady Grey, 14 Jan. 1834: MS Lord Halifax.
153	1835	To Lord Morpeth, 4 Aug. 1835: MS Castle Howard.
	has	To Lady Holland, 11 Jan. 1834: NCS 651.
	pitch	To Lady Carlisle, 21 Nov. 1835: MS Castle Howard.
	times	To Lady Holland, 6 Apr. 1830: NCS 557.
	Amen	To Catharine Smith, 14 May 1830: NCS 560.
	roast	To J. A. Murray, Aug. 1834: NCS 665.

163	anywhere	Hillard, *George Ticknor*, i. 414.
	1837	To Lord John Russell, 28 June 1837: MS P. R. Glazebrook.
	salvation	*Works*, iii. 179; later editions substitute 'the pious Simeon' for 'the Psalmist' erroneously cited.
164	thereof	To Mrs Villiers, 4 July 1837: NCS 740.
	ever	To Mrs Austin, 9 Nov. 1837: MS D. R. Bentham.
	Victoria	Ibid.
	to it	To R. Wilmot Horton, 3 Nov. 1833: MS Derby Public Library.
	misrepresentation	To Lord Holland, 17 Nov. 1834: NCS 671.
	to me	Ibid.
165	one	To Lady Holland, 25 Nov. 1834: NCS 673.
	disrepute	To Lord Holland, 18 Apr. 1835: NCS 683.
	recollection	Ibid.
	sincere	Ibid.
166	imposed	To R. Wilmot Horton, 6 Dec. 1835: NCS 706, amended by MS Derby Public Library.
	bishop	*Mem.* 283.
	for it	To Lady Holland, 3 Jan. 1841: NCS 823, amended by MS D. R. Bentham.
	prevails	To Charles Babbage, n.d.: MS British Library.
	money	To Mrs Meynell, Oct. 1839: NCS 791; cf. NCS 584.
	intended	To Lady Grey, 12 Oct. 1834: NCS 668.
167	1837	To Christopher Wordsworth, 13 July 1835: NCS 689.
	deficiency	To Lord Melbourne, 25 Mar. 1836: NCS 714.
	else	To Lord Palmerston, 7 Apr. 1836: MS Osborn Collection, Yale.
	Office	To Lord John Russell, 2 May 1836: MS Public Record Office.
	of 63	To same, 3 Apr. 1837: NCS 734.
	receiving it	To William Cowper, 7 June 1837: MS Royal Library, Windsor. (*By gracious permission of HM the Queen.*)
	cleverness	To Lord John Russell, 28 June 1837: MS P. R. Glazebrook.
	misconduct	Endorsed on Sydney's letter to Lord Palmerston, 7 Apr. 1836: MS Osborn Collection, Yale.
168	year	To Lady Grey, 26 Aug. 1842, 21 Dec. 1843: NCS 887, 960.
	soon	*Mem.* 302.
	consideration	To William Hawes, 21 Aug. 1844: MS British Library.
169	Alexandria	To Dean of Ely, n.d.: MS NCO.
	essential	To C. R. Cockerell, June 1832: NCS 615.
	regard	*Mem.* 298–9.
	order	From C. R. Cockerell, 10 July 1832: NCS 618.
170	do so	To same, 11 July 1832: NCS 620.
	advice	To same, 22 Nov. 1838: NCS 766.
	forgotten	To same, 26 Nov. 1838: NCS 767.
	him	To same, 26 Aug. 1832: NCS 621.

	made of	To same, 24 Apr. 1839: NCS 781.
171	him	*Mem.* 299.
	clean	To H. H. Milman, 18 July 1838: MS Osborn Collection, Yale.
	business	*Mem.* 300; G. L. Prestige, *St Paul's in its Glory* (London, 1955), 25–9.
	subjects	To W. H. Hale, 19 Nov. 1843: NCS 1036.
	Clerk	To Christopher Hodgson, 9 Aug. 1841: MS Fondren.
172	Church	To Lady Ashburton, Mar. 1836: NCS 716.
	Smith	*Letters of Tate,* ed. Wenham, 73.
	o'clock	To Lady Morley, Oct. 1831: NCS 591.
	substituted	To the Warden of Minor Canons, 10 Apr. 1839: Prestige, *St Paul's,* 251–2.
	headache	To same, 2 July 1839: ibid. 253–4.
	subjects	Ibid.
	substitute	Ibid.
173	rights	To same, 6 July 1839: Prestige, *St Paul's,* 254–5.
	Sunday	To same, 7 July 1839: ibid. 255–6.
	recipients	Ibid. 12–13.
	Metropolis	To Lord John Russell, 22 Sept. 1837: NCS 1024.
	art	To same, 19 same, 19 Nov. 1837: NCS 1026.
	witness	*Parliamentary Papers,* 1841: VI.
174	year	'Narrative': MS D. C. L. Holland.
	likely	To Lord Grey, Feb. 1840: MS Durham University.
	Barnes	To same, 30 Nov. 1839: ibid.
	connexions	To Lady Grey, 16 Jan. 1840: NCS 799.
	list	To Cecil Smith, 13 Mar. 1842: MS Ray.
	family	To Lady Grey, 25 Sept. 1843: NCS 937.
	others	R. H. D. Barham, *R. H. Barham,* ii. 163.
	good	To Catharine Smith, 23 Oct. 1843: NCS 945.
175	Grey	To Lady Grey, 21 Dec. 1843: NCS 960.
	predecessor	*Mem.* 344–5.
	mother	To Bishop Blomfield, Nov. 1843: NCS 947.
	cruelty	To Mrs Grote, 3 Jan. 1844: NCS 965.
	him	To W. H. Hale, May 1841: NCS 1031.
	adequate	To same, 20 Dec. 1840: NCS 1027.
	alteration	Ibid.
176	meaning	To W. H. Hale, 11 June 1844: NCS 1037.
	me	R. H. D. Barham, *R. H. Barham,* ii. 188–9.
	Layman	*Works,* iii. 93.
177	them	To Lady Carlisle, 4 Nov. 1835: MS Castle Howard.
	instigated it	Own Chadwick, *The Victorian Church* (i, London, 1966), 134.
178	building	*Works,* iii. 39.
	nobleman	Ibid. 41.
179	infamous	ibid. 42–3.
	significance	Ibid. 44.
	head	Ibid. 62
180	*earth*	Ibid. 71.

	manner	Ibid. 75.
	prosperity	Ibid. 79–80.
181	Bishops	Ibid. 68.
	days	*Letters of Tate*, ed. Wenham, 80.
	recompensed	*Works*, iii. 81.
	respect	To Lord John Russell, 10 Feb. 1837: Spencer Walpole, *Life of Lord John Russell* (London, 1899), i. 288n.
182	opinions	To same, 24 Nov. 1835: MS Univ. California, Los Angeles.
183	power	*Works*, iii. 91–2.
	wit	Ibid. 101.
	Dissent	Ibid. 105.
	atoms	Ibid. 113.
184	provocation	To Lady Carlisle, spring 1838: MS Castle Howard.
	measure	*Works*, iii. 117.
	thee	To Lady Grey, 15 Nov. 1838: NCS 765.
	life	*Works*, iii. 135–6.
185	remedy	To Lady Ashburton, 9 Jan. 1837: MS Harvard.
	me	To Bishop Blomfield, Feb. 1837: Prestige, *St Paul's*, 249–51.
	Commission	To Sir George Philips, 30 July 1836: NCS 720.
	letters	To Mr Gore, 26 Jan. 1837: MS Ray.
	1838	To Lady Holland, 6 Sept. 1838: NCS 759.
	tack	*Elizabeth Lady Holland to her Son, 1821–1845*, ed. Earl of Ilchester (London, 1946), 167.
186	impertinence	To Lady Carlisle, 5 Sept. 1840: MS Castle Howard.
	mankind	To Bishop Blomfield, 5 Sept. 1840: NCS 814.
187	knocks	To Christopher Hodgson, 1840: Russell, *Sydney Smith*, 176; MS Ray.
188	before	*Mem.* 312.
	wine	To Richard York, 11 Apr. 1834: MS York.
189	seen	To Georgiana Harcourt, 21 Mar. 1835: NCS 682; MS Univ. California, Los Angeles.
	rout	To Mrs [Austin], 8 Apr. 1840: NCS 802.
	fragrance	To R. M. Milnes, 11 May 1841: NCS 840.
	proof	To Georgiana Harcourt, 10 May 1842: NCS 881.
	come	To Thomas Moore, 12 Mar. 1841: NCS 861, dated Reid, 327.
	Harcourt	To Georgiana Harcourt, 7 July 1842: NCS 883; this passage from MS D. R. Bentham.
190	eat	To Lord John Russell, 26 Apr. 1843: MS P. R. Glazebrook.
	of it	To Mrs Davenport, 7 June 1836: MS Osborn Collection, Yale
	tastes	*Mem.* 306–7.
	at all	Catharine Smith's postscript on Sydney to Georgiana Harcourt, 15 Aug. 1841: MS D. R. Bentham.
191	offers	To Lady Grey, 15 Nov. 1838: NCS 765.
	funeral	To same, 15 Nov. 1841: NCS 863.

	with him	To Edward Everett, 15 May 1843: MS Massachusetts Historical Society.
	talked	Lord Macaulay to Saba Lady Holland, 17 Nov. 1854: MS NCO.
	talk	NCS, p. 763n.
	name	To Paulet Mildmay, 5 Sept. 1837: MS Yale,
	me	To Sir George Philips, Sept. 1838: NCS 761.
	know him	The Letters of Charles Dickens (Pilgrim Edition, i, Oxford, 1965), 546.
192	reaction	Dickens Letters (ii, Oxford, 1969), 261.
	execute	To Charles Dickens, 6 Jan. 1843: NCS 908.
	them	To same, ?May 1843: NCS 908, portion redated by Dickens Letters (iii, Oxford, 1974), 533n.
	it on	To Lady Carlisle, 17 Sept. 1843: MS Lord Halifax; see Dickens Letters, iii. 542n.
	Idolaters	Letter of [1843]: MS Benoliel Collection, Free Library of Philadelphia; see Dickens Letters, iii. 42n.
	poets	To R. M. Milnes, 20 June 1838: NCS 756.
193	evening	See, int.al., R. H. D. Barham, R. H. Barham, ii. 84–6.
	money	To R. M. Milnes, 22 Apr. 1842: NCS 880.
	else	To same, 20 Apr. 1842: MS Trinity College, Cambridge.
	sense	James Pope-Hennessy, Monckton Milnes, The Years of Promise (London, 1949), 131.
194	me	To R. M. Milnes, 22 Apr. 1842: NCS 880.
	Philosophy	Sketches, 319.
	diffidence	To Lady Ashburton, 21 Aug. 1840: MS Ray.
	you	To Georgiana Harcourt, Sept. 1843: NCS 934.
	13th	To Lady Georgiana Grey, 7 Apr. 1840: MS Lord Halifax.
	hard	To Lady Canning, 2 July 1836: MS Pierpont Morgan Library, New York.
	can	To Charles Babbage, 21 Mar. 1842: MS British Library.
195	dramatic	Greville Memoirs, ed. Strachey and Fulford, ii. 152.
	jest	Harriet Edgeworth to Elizabeth Waller, 24 May 1822: MS Mrs Howard Colvin, who kindly sent me this reference.
	ever	Diary of Frances Lady Shelley, ed. Richard Edgcumbe (London, 1912–13), i. 39–40.
	day	Oliver Elton, A Survey of English Literature, 1780–1830 (London, 1920), ii. 279.
196	boot	E. H. Dering, Memoirs of Georgiana Lady Chatterton (2nd edn., London, 1901), 86–7.
	amusing	Charles and Francis Brookfield, Mrs Brookfield and her Circle (London, 1905), i. 122.
	quoting	Henry Crabb Robinson on Books and their Writers, ed. E. J. Morley (London, 1938), 493.
197	dry	Greville Memoirs, ed. Strachey and Fulford, v. 206–7 (entry for 25 Feb. 1845).

	thing	Ibid., iv. 43.
	point	Andrew Lang, *The Life and Letters of John Gibson Lockhart* (London, 1897), ii. 329.
	Church	Haydon, *Diary*, ed. Pope, v. 188.
	sensuality	Lang, *Lockhart*, ii. 330.
198	take it	*Mrs Brookfield and her Circle*, ii. 479; see also A. J. C. Hare, *The Story of My Life* (London, 1900), vi. 325–6.
	teeth	Hesketh Pearson, *The Smith of Smiths* (1934), Harmondsworth, 1948, 206.
	propriety	R. H. D. Barman, *R. H. Barham*, ii. 166–8.
	fury	Stephen Neill, *Anglicanism* (London, 1977), 234.
	guests	R. H. D. Barham, *R. H. Barham*, ii. 168.
	own	Nancy Mitford, *The Ladies of Alderley* (London, 1938), 55.
199	appeared	*Recollections of the Table-Talk of Samuel Rogers*, ed. Alexander Dyce (New Southgate, 1887), 290n.
	look	See above, p. 151.
	dinners	To Lady Davy, 21 Sept. 1842: NCS 894.
	commented	Ian Jack, *English Literature 1815–1832* (Oxford, 1963), 330.
	mistakes	To Mrs Austin, 30 Nov. 1836: MS D. R. Bentham; a phrase transferred in NCS to 747.
	flock	To Georgiana Harcourt, 19 July 1838: NCS 758; MS D. R. Bentham.
200	spot	Ibid.
	intelligible	Edward Everett to Peter Brooks, 17 Apr. 1844: MS Massachusetts Hist. Soc.
	world	*Mem.* 382.
201	flowers	*Mem.* 383–4.
	grave	To Lady Grey, 8 Jan. 1838: NCS 750.
	variety	To same, 1 Feb. 1836: NCS 710.
	life	To Sir George Philips, 28 Feb. 1836: NCS 712.
	myself	To Mrs Paulet Mildmay, 12 Dec. 1840: Reid, 326–7.
202	better	To Paulet Mildmay, 27 Aug. 1836: Reid, 301–2.
	Paris	To Lady Grey, 11 Sept. 1835: NCS 696.
	coming	To R. Wilmot Horton, Dec. 1835: NCS 706.
	wet	To Lady Grey, 3 Oct. 1835: NCS 698.
	Ellice	Ibid.
	go to	To Mrs Austin, 11 Oct. 1835: NCS 700.
	Jove	To Lady Grey, 20 Oct. 1835: NCS 701.
203	character	To Richard York, 27 Oct. 1835: MS York.
	discretion	To Lady Holland, 1 Jan. 1836: NCS 707.
	reptiles	To Lady Carlisle, 9 May 1837: MS Castle Howard.
	me	To Caroline Fox, 28 May 1837: NCS 738.
	more	To Lady Carlisle, 9 May 1837: MS Castle Howard.
	sounding	To Caroline Fox, 28 May 1837: NCS 738.
	contracting	Ibid.
	disappointment	To Lady Holland, 21 Sept. 1836: NCS 722.

204	coast	To Paulet Mildmay, 29 Aug. 1838: MS Yale.
	again	To Lady Grey, Sept. 1838: NCS 762.
	Somersetshire	To Mrs Austin, Dec. 1838: NCS 770.
	poultry	To Lady Grey, Aug. 1840: NCS 812.
	see you	To R. M. Milnes, 23 July 1840: NCS 811a.
	country	To Lady Grey, 4 Aug. 1841: NCS 851.
	tap	To Georgiana Harcourt, Sept. 1843: NCS 934.
	method	To Lady Grey, 18 July 1843: NCS 927.
205	door	To same, 24 Aug. 1841: NCS 853.
	dean	To J. A. Murray, 12 Sept. 1842: NCS 889.
	rules	*Works* (2 vols, 1859), 324, 325.
	perceptible	Miss Fox, June 1842: *Miscellanies of the Philobiblon Society* XV (1877–84), vii. 17–18.
	anxiety	To Sir Robert Peel, 20 June 1842: *Morning Chronicle* and MS British Library.
206	Ireland	To Lady Grey, 27 Aug. 1832: NCS 623.
	digestion	To Mrs Meynell, 16 Dec. 1832: NCS 630.
	beautiful	To R. Wilmot Horton, 15 Jan. 1835: MS Derby Public Library.
	remain	To same, 8 Aug. 1835: ibid.
207	committed	To same, 8 Feb. 1836: ibid.
	memorial	To Paulet Mildmay, 5 Sept. 1837: MS Yale.
	wisely	To Sir George Philips, Sept. 1838: NCS 761.
	came out	To Richard York, 5 Feb. 1839: MS York.
208	river	*Works*, iii. 8–9.
	NO BALLOT	Ibid. 32–4.
	convulsions	To Lord Durham, 3 Mar. 1839: NCS 776.
209	the ballot	To Mrs Crowe, 6 Jan. 1840: NCS 798 and MS Osborn Collection, Yale.
	much	To Charles Sumner, 16 Aug. 1838: MS Harvard.
	London	Edward Everett to Peter Brooks, 17 Apr. 1844: MS Massachusetts Hist. Soc.
	trousers	*Mem.* 317.
210	philoyankeeist	To Francis Jeffrey, 23 Nov. 1818: NCS 311.
	Capitol	*Works*, ii. 16–17, 227; and see Sheldon Halpern, *Sydney Smith* (New York, 1966), 121–2, 123.
	60 per cent	Edward Everett to Peter Brooks, 17 Apr. 1844: MS Massachusetts Hist. Soc.
	world	*Works* (2 vols, 1859), ii. 326.
211	resoundingly	*Mem.* 351–5; Hillard, *Ticknor*, ii. 214.
	Pennsylvania	*Works* (2 vols, 1859), ii. 327, 329.
	tone	Hillard, *Ticknor*, ii. 215.
	earnest	To Lady Grey, 8 Nov. 1843: NCS 950.
212	funds	*Works* (2 vols, 1859), ii. 331, 332.
	told	To J. A. Murray, 17 Dec. 1843: NCS 958.
	world	To Miss Berry, 28 Aug. 1844: *Berry Journals*, ed. Lewis, iii. 488.
	do so	To Captain Morgan, 7 Dec. 1843: NCS 954.
213	coffin	To Lady Grey, 28 Feb. 1843: NCS 911.
	sauciness	Bobus Smith to Robert Smith, 12 Jan. 1818: MS IOL.

	affairs	Lord Hastings to Courtney Smith, 24 May 1817: MS (copy) IOL.
	fast	To Lady Holland, 18 Nov. 1827: *NCS* 513.
	brother	To Cecil Smith, Feb. 1843: MS NCO.
	defunct	To same, Feb. 1843: MS NCO.
	canter	To same, 15 Mar. 1843: MS NCO.
	for her	To same, 5 Apr. 1843: MS NCO.
	unpleasant	To Lady Grey, 31 Mar. 1843: NCS 914.
214	shoe	To Mrs Meynell, July 1834: NCS 664.
	colchicum	To Lady Morgan, 14 Nov. 1842: in her *Memoirs* (London, 1863), ii. 471.
	lyre	To Arthur Kinglake, 30 Sept. 1837: NCS 745.
215	realities	To Richard York, 9 Apr. 1840: MS York.
	clergy	To Lady Holland, 13 Sept. 1842: NCS 891.
	heroically	To Sir George Philips, 28 Dec. 1843: NCS 963.
	improved	To Georgiana Harcourt, July 1844: NCS 996.
	condition	To Lady Holland, 26 Aug. 1844: NCS 1006.
	gone	To Lady Grey, 12 Aug. 1844: NCS 1001.
	holiday	Ibid.
216	1844	To same, July 1844: NCS 993.
	flowers	To Lady Carlisle, 12 Aug. 1844: NCS 1002.
	observations	To Lady Holland, 26 Aug. 1844: NCS 1006.
	man	To Henry Holland, Aug. 1844: NCS 1003.
	Clergy	To Lady Grey, 20 Aug. 1844: NCS 1004.
	wish	To same, 11 Oct. 1844: NCS 1013.
217	of me	To Lady Carlisle, 11 Oct. 1844: NCS 1017, amended by MS (transcript) Lord Halifax.
	puddings	To Sir Robert Peel, 22 Nov. 1844: MS British Library.
	up on it	To Lady Grey, 7 Nov. 1844: NCS 1018.
	suggestion	To Dean and Chapter, 25 Dec. 1844: NCS 1038.
	me in it	To Eugène Robin, 29 July 1844: NCS 990.
218	evil now	*Works*, i. vi–vii.
	pleased	*Letters to 'Ivy' from the First Earl of Dudley*, ed. S. H. Romilly (London, 1905), 131–2 (of April 1811).
	day	Hertfordshire R O, Lytton Add. MSS, L. & P. III.

INDEX

Lockhart, John Gibson 197, 198
Londesborough, Yorkshire 122, 123–4
London Institution 56
Longman, Thomas Norton 153
Longman, William 191
'Lottery, The' (clerical promotion) 178, 182–3
Low Spirits 137–8
Luttrell, Henry 93, 151, 153, 195, 199
Lyndhurst, Sarah *Lady* 131, 145
Lyndhurst, *1st Lord* 144
Lytton, Edward G. E. L. Bulwer, *1st Lord* 218

Macaulay, Thomas Babington, *1st Lord* 92, 95–6, 103, 190–1, 215
Macaulay, Zachary 95
Mackintosh, *Sir* James 19, 35, 36, 44, 47, 48, 53
Mackintosh, R, J, 48
Maltby, Edward 35
Malthus, Thomas Robert 113, 116, 152
Malton, Yorkshire 96, 102, 103, 111–12
Marcet, Alexander 93, 94
Marcet, Jane 54, 92–3, 94, 106, 200, 204
Markham, William, *Archbishop of York* 73, 80
Maylestone ('Milestone'), *curate* 122–3, 143
Medicine 105–7, 138–9, 150, 200
Melbourne 154, 164, 165, 166, 167, 206
Mendelssohn, Felix 189
Methodists 68, 70–71, 104, 198
Meynell, Georgiana 161, 206
Mildmay, Paulet 191, 201, 204, 207
Mills, Molly 93
Milman, Henry Hart 168, 171
Milnes, Richard Monckton, *1st Lord* 96, 189, 192–4, 196, 204
Milton, *Lord* 75
Minor Canons, College of 171, 172–3
Mithoffer, *valet* 17
Monk, James Henry, *Bishop of Gloucester* 184
Montvilliers, Normandy 6
Moore, Thomas 189, 195
Morgan, *Capt.* 212
Morgan, Sydney, *Lady* 214
Morley, Francis, *Countess of* 149, 172
Morning Chronicle 205, 210–11
Morpeth, Lady Georgiana, *Countess of Carlisle* 101, 106, 133, 136–40, 143, 153, 177, 183, 192, 202, 216, 217
Morpeth, *Lord, 6th Earl of Carlisle* 81, 124, 136–40, 183, 202, 214
Murray, John 210

Murray, *Sir* John Archibald, *Lord Murray* 34, 35, 46, 54, 93, 149, 152, 153, 155, 160, 205

Nares, Robert 29, 30, 38–9
Netheravon, Wiltshire 8–10
Neuchatel, Switzerland 12, 13
New College, Oxford 6–7, 8, 10, 12
New Lanark 15–16
New River Company 3, 43
Noel, *Sir* Gerard 43
North, *Baron* 18

O'Connell, Daniel 120, 216
Olier, Mary 51, 65, 140
Oxen 88, 117–18
Oxford University 6–7

Palmerston, *3rd Viscount* 167
'Parallelogram, The' 108
Paris, visits (1826) 142; (1835) 128, 202–3
Parliamentary Reform 155–9, 176
Parr, Samuel 36, 38
'Partington, Mrs' x, 158–9, 179, 206
Pâté de foie 198–9, 203
Peel, *Sir* Robert 108–9, 110–11, 205, 217
Pegge, *Sir* Christopher 105
Pennsylvania, State of 209–12
Perceval, Spencer 77–8, 79, 80
Peter Plymley's Letters 75–80, 120, 122, 125, 154, 181, 184
Philips, *Sir* George 100, 151, 191, 201, 207
Phrenology 113
Playfair, John 67
'Poetical Medicine Chest' 138–9
Pope, Alexander 134
Pope-Hennessy, James 193
Powlett, William 32
Public Schools 5–6, 113, 130
Publius [*later* Publilius] Syrus 4
Pybus, Catharine Amelia, *see* Smith
Pybus, Charles 24–5, 26
Pybus, *Mrs* 22, 24, 25

Quakers 104–5, 113, 154
Quarterly Review 69, 85, 103, 210
Queen Anne's Bounty 87–8

Railways 204–5
Randolph, Francis 145
Read, Charles R. 111–12
Reeve, Henry 56
Reform Bill, *see* Parliamentary Reform
Reid, Thomas 57
Rennel, Thomas 36
Ricardo, David 113